THE
ENGLISH ECCLESIASTICAL
TENANTS-IN-CHIEF AND
KNIGHT SERVICE

BISHOPRICS AND ABBACIES HOLDING IN CHIEF BY KNIGHT SERVICE

THE
ENGLISH ECCLESIASTICAL TENANTS-IN-CHIEF AND KNIGHT SERVICE

ESPECIALLY IN THE THIRTEENTH AND FOURTEENTH CENTURIES

BY

HELENA M. CHEW, M.A., Ph.D.

Lecturer in History in the University
of London

OXFORD UNIVERSITY PRESS
LONDON: HUMPHREY MILFORD
1932

PRINTED IN GREAT BRITAIN

TO
MY MOTHER

PREFACE

THE researches of which the results are embodied in the present monograph (presented and accepted for the London Doctorate of Philosophy in 1926), were suggested by a preliminary study (for the M.A. degree) of the general conditions of military tenure in medieval England.[1] They were undertaken partly with the object of testing, by reference to new sources of information, the conclusions of the earlier constitutional historians as to the relations between the Crown and its immediate tenants *per servicium militare* in the later Middle Ages; but primarily with a view to gaining fresh light upon the obscure problem of the contemporary relation between the Crown-vassals and their under-tenants. The process of the decline of the feudal military organization has frequently been traced, but from the standpoint of the tenants-in-chief rather than from that of the rearvassals; and the current generalizations have seldom had a firmer basis than that afforded by casual entries in the more accessible chronicles and cartularies.

The limitation of the scope of the investigation to the clerical tenants was primarily a dictate of convenience. On the one hand, their small number in comparison with the lay feudatories, and the stability of their tenure as contrasted with that of the temporal lords whose fees were subject to the vicissitudes of alienation, partition and escheat, made possible a comprehensive and detailed study, upon which generalizations could safely be based; on the other, the material, particularly for conditions of the subinfeudated lands, promised to be more abundant in the case of the clergy than of the laity. Besides the monastic chronicles, the cartularies, and the bishops' registers, the ministers' and household accounts appeared to offer an extensive and largely unexplored field for research from which to supplement the data furnished by the central archives.

The extent to which the original purpose of the survey has been fulfilled will be apparent in the following pages. As far as the relations of the Crown and its immediate tenants were concerned, it proved possible to reconstruct in considerable detail the military history of the great ecclesiastical fiefs from

[1] *Scutages and Aids in England particularly in the fourteenth century.*

the middle of the twelfth to the middle of the fourteenth century; and to draw therefrom certain definite conclusions as to the conditions of tenure and the alternations of service and commutation at different periods. Although, however, these conclusions have an important bearing on wider constitutional issues, it would be unsafe, in view of the fact that the position of the clerical tenants was in some respects peculiar, to assign to them a general validity.

As regards the relation of the tenants-in-chief to their sub-tenants, the results yielded were necessarily less definite. Here the wide distribution, and still more the inaccessibility of the material, presented a serious initial problem. The records of the great medieval ecclesiastical corporations have no common repository. The dissolution of the monasteries resulted in the destruction or loss of many of the records, and in the scattering of the remainder. Cartularies, court-rolls, and ministers' accounts exist in considerable quantities, but they are distributed up and down the country in public and private collections to which they have come in the course of their modern wanderings. The episcopal records have, in comparison, suffered few vicissitudes of fortune, but they remain for the most part in the custody of the appropriate diocesan authorities or of the Ecclesiastical Commissioners. The whereabouts of the scattered ecclesiastical records may to some extent be gathered from the bulky volumes of the Historical Manuscripts Commission, or from the concise guide issued by the Editors of the *Victoria County History*; but the contents of local and private collections remain to a large extent unexplored and un-indexed. The recent scheme, sponsored by the Master of the Rolls, for the assembling and preserving of manorial records, promises to facilitate greatly the task of the researcher in certain important directions; but it is too soon as yet to form any general estimate of the nature or the quantity of the extant materials for a study of conditions on the clerical fees.

The proportion which is at present accessible in print is, moreover, small. Within recent years the activities of the Lords of the Treasury and of private societies have resulted in the publication of a number of monastic cartularies; while the printing of the episcopal registers is proceeding apace under the direction, in particular, of the Canterbury and York Society.

The court- and account-rolls remain, however, for the most part unpublished, although it is probable that the growing interest in administrative history will do much in the next few years, to render them more readily accessible to students.

In view of these difficulties, I found it necessary at the outset to mark out for myself a definite area of research; and practical considerations determined the lines to be followed. The fact of my residence and permanent employment in London precluded the possibility of any continuous work on provincial collections, and I therefore determined to limit my purview to such material as was available in print, supplemented by the unprinted records and cartularies in the British Museum, Public Record Office, and other London repositories. Within these limits the amount of evidence bearing directly upon the discharge of knight service, proved to be comparatively small. Of the various sources the monastic cartularies were the most productive, since besides covering a wider area of time than any of the other classes of records dealt with, they are concerned specifically with questions relating to land-tenure and service. The episcopal registers were of less value, for with the exception of the Lincoln rolls, they date only from the latter half of the thirteenth century, when the feudal military organization was already declining. Such entries as relate to military service are, moreover, purely incidental to the main purpose of the record. Indeed, in one case only—that of Hereford, where the exigencies of border warfare kept military matters well to the fore—was any considerable bulk of evidence yielded. As regards the court- and account-rolls, the results of my investigations have been still more disappointing. Not only is the number of thirteenth-century court rolls limited, but of those which remain the majority are concerned with purely manorial business. The records of the Ramsey Court of Broughton appear to have no parallel, at least among the deposits at the Public Record Office and the British Museum. Among the account rolls survivals, particularly of thirteenth-century date, are fortuitous, and I have not had the good fortune to discover any records (other than the Winchester Pipe Rolls) bearing directly on the commutation or the incidence of military service.

In consequence, I cannot claim that my study of the conditions of tenure in the thirteenth and fourteenth centuries on the great ecclesiastical fiefs is in any sense conclusive. At the most I have succeeded in filling in the outlines traced by earlier students of the subject, and in indicating the directions in which research may profitably be continued if and when additional sources of information become accessible.

My study of the conditions of knight service incidentally revealed the need for the further investigation of several allied topics. Apart from the problem of 'barony', with which I have made some attempt (neither the first, nor, it is to be feared, the last!) to deal, the related question of the position of the great churchmen in Parliament obviously requires reconsideration in the light of the feudal military records. The need for deeper research into the meaning of tenure in frankalmoign, of which I was constantly reminded during the preparation of this volume, has since to a large extent been met by Miss Elizabeth Kimball, in her recent articles in the *English Historical Review*. Professor F. M. Stenton's important series of Ford lectures (*English Feudalism 1066–1166*) unfortunately appeared in print too late to be made use of for the purposes of this essay.

I should like to take this opportunity of acknowledging my indebtedness for much detailed help and advice to scholars working in allied fields, and, in particular, to Professor Elizabeth Levett, Miss Evelyn Jamison, Miss Elizabeth Kimball, Miss Helen Cam, Miss E. Swift, Dr. Rachel Reid, Dr. Fowler, Professors W. A. Morris and S. K. Mitchell, and last, but not least, to Professor F. J. C. Hearnshaw, of King's College, for many years my chief and director of studies. From the late Professor T. F. Tout, to whom, as my external examiner for the Doctorate of Philosophy, it fell to pass judgement upon this book in its original form, I received not only invaluable criticism, but also that encouragement of which he was so prodigal to students of the younger generation. To the interest shown in my work by him and by the late Sir Israel Gollancz, its appearance in print is largely due. Finally, I have to record my special thanks to my colleague and former teacher Mr. Hilary Jenkinson, of Kings' College and the Public Record Office, to whom I owe not only my interest in medieval records, but any pretensions I may have to medieval scholarship.

In conclusion, I gratefully acknowledge grants in aid of publication from the Publications Fund of the University of London, and from the British Academy, which in 1929 generously voted me the sum of £50 from the Raleigh Fund for History.

In the preparation of the manuscript for the press, the correction of proofs, and the compilation of the index, I have been greatly helped by my mother and by my friend Miss B. M. Mugridge of the General Post Office.

H. M. C.

November 1931.

CONTENTS

CHAPTER I

THE ECCLESIASTICAL TENANTS-IN-CHIEF AND THEIR *SERVICIA DEBITA*

THE question when and how the medieval system of military tenures came into being is one upon which historians have differed widely. Some have regarded it as an indigenous growth, the result of a slow but uninterrupted process of evolution from Anglo-Saxon institutions; others have regarded it as a Norman innovation, imposed ready-made by the conquerors upon the conquered.

It is clear that there existed in pre-Norman England a condition of things which bore some resemblance to the fully-developed feudal organization of the twelfth century. Domesday Book shows that the service of the fyrd was already largely territorialized in the days of Edward the Confessor. The land, at all events in the south and west, had been plotted out into five-hide units, each of which was bound to produce its *miles* for service in the host; and, further, the great lords, both lay and ecclesiastical, were beginning to be held responsible to the king for the service due from all the lands over which they exercised a *dominium*. The old national militia was assuming some of the features of the feudal levy.[1]

The resemblance was, however, superficial. In spite of changed conditions the obligation of the Anglo-Saxon thegn for service was still essentially the old obligation which rested upon him as a freeman; the feudal theory of contract, whereby the tenant-in-chief brought up his contingent for service under the royal banner in fulfilment of a compact made when he received his lands, was as yet undeveloped.[2] Moreover, to prove that there were certain similarities between pre-Norman and post-Norman conditions, is not to prove that the latter grew out of the former. If the theory of the continuity of Anglo-Saxon institutions is to be vindicated, the connexion of the Norman *feodum militis* with the five-hide unit of the Confessor's day must be established; and the evidence for such a connexion is

---

[1] F. W. Maitland, *Domesday Book and Beyond*, pp. 156 seq.
[2] F. M. Stenton, *William the Conqueror*, p. 445.

wholly inadequate. No fixed number of hides can be shown to have constituted a knight's fee.[1] Hence the theory that the knight-service of the Norman tenant-in-chief developed from the obligations of the Saxon thegn proves on investigation to be untenable, and we are driven to seek the origin of the medieval system of knight-service in the customs of the Frankish empire rather than in those of the English kingdom.

The views advanced by the late Dr. J. H. Round in his paper on 'The Introduction of Knight Service into England'[2] are those now generally accepted. Reverting to the discredited theories of Selden and the antiquarians, Round maintained that military tenure, as it existed in England in the Middle Ages, was introduced by the Normans, and was established by the Conqueror himself as part of the general land-settlement which followed the Conquest. The embryonic feudalism of the Anglo-Saxon state was replaced by the fully-developed feudal organization of the Continent. William distributed the conquered lands among his Norman followers, or restored them to their former owners, on the plan already prevailing in the Duchy, viz. in return for the service of a specified number of fully-armed knights; and he defined the number not in relation to the five-hide rule of his Saxon predecessors, but to the *constabularia* or unit of the Norman feudal host.

The ecclesiastical tenants-in-chief afford an admirable illustration of Round's thesis. The Conquest entailed no such radical redistribution of the lands of the Church as resulted from the forfeiture and re-grant of the bulk of the lay estates. The bishop and the monastery might be shorn of an occasional manor, but William could not venture to dispossess them as he could dispossess the thegn or the earl, and they appear for the most part to have preserved their pre-Conquest endowments virtually intact. Here, then, if anywhere, one would expect to find proof of that evolution of the Norman knight from the Saxon thegn which was so unhesitatingly affirmed by the historians of the older school. The existing data, however, so far from support-ing any theory of institutional continuity, testify to the in-dependent origin of the Norman system of military tenures. The chronicles agree in ascribing to the Conqueror the assess-

[1] J. H. Round, *Feudal England*, pp. 293 seq.   [2] Ibid., pp. 225 seq.

·ment of the Church fiefs for knight-service,[1] and Matthew Paris
enables us to date the transaction with still greater precision.
He assigns the fixing of the ecclesiastical *servicia debita* to the
year 1070, when, he says, William 'episcopatus autem et abbatias omnes que baronias tenebant, et eatenus ab omni servicio
seculari libertatem habuerant, sub servitute statuit militari'.[2]
Matthew, it is true, is far from being a contemporary authority,
but his statement doubtless represents the tradition of his own
house of St. Albans, and it accords well with ascertained facts.
The absorption of the Conqueror in military affairs renders
improbable an earlier date. It was not until 1070 that the work
of internal reorganization was seriously undertaken, and that,
in particular, the first advances were made towards the ecclesiastical resettlement of the conquered kingdom. On the other
hand, the date cannot well have been later, since we learn from
the Ely chronicle that in 1072 the king called upon the abbots
and bishops throughout England to furnish their 'debita militie
obsequia' for the expedition against Malcolm of Scotland.[3] By
a curious chance there has been preserved a writ of summons
to Abbot Æthelwig of Evesham,[4] which Round connects with
this very campaign,[5] and which shows the new military system
in full operation. The abbot is to summon all those beneath
his sway to perform their due service, and is to appear in person
at the place of muster with the five knights representing his own
contingent.

The substantial accuracy of the account given by Matthew
Paris seems, therefore, indisputable.[6] The military service for
which the great churchmen were responsible in the twelfth and
thirteenth centuries was imposed upon them by the Conqueror,

---

[1] *Chronicon Monasterii de Abingdon*, Rolls Series, ii. 3; *Historia Ecclesie
Eliensis* (ed. 1848), p. 276; Matthew Paris, *Historia Anglorum*, R.S., i. 13.
See also Round, *Feudal England*, pp. 298-9. Selden (*Titles of Honour*, p. 579)
notes the entry in a medieval hand, in the margin of the manuscript of Paris
of which he made use, of the comment: 'Hoc anno servicium Baronie
imponitur Ramesie'.

[2] Matthew Paris, loc. cit.   [3] *Historia Eliensis*, p. 276.

[4] Cotton MSS. Vespasian, B. xxiv, f. 15 [18].

[5] Round, *Feudal England*, p. 304.

[6] Further corroboration of Matthew's statement is afforded by the
numerous evidences of early subinfeudation on clerical estates, for which
vide infra, Chap. IV, pp. 115 seq.

who thereby brought the ecclesiastical estates into line with the lay fiefs which had been carved out in the course of the Conquest.

There still remains the possibility that the Normans, in fixing the new conditions of tenure, made use of the existing framework of the Saxon five-hide system. The evidence to the contrary is, however, overwhelmingly strong. Matthew Paris tells us that William assessed the knight-service of the bishops and abbots 'pro voluntate sua'; [1] and he is corroborated by the independent testimony of other chroniclers.[2] Finally, an examination in detail of the liabilities of the various ecclesiastical estates establishes beyond reasonable doubt that the quotas were an expression of the arbitrary will of the king, and bore no necessary relation to either the extent or the value of the land.

It is not until the reign of Henry II—almost a century after the completion of the Conquest—that sources become sufficiently abundant to enable us to form an exact idea of the personnel of the ecclesiastical tenants of the Crown, or of the extent of their obligations. In 1156 begins the continuous series of pipe rolls, on which were enrolled the accounts of scutages, and other feudal payments assessed on the basis of the knight's fee; and ten years later the evidence of these accounts is supplemented by the famous *Carte Baronum*—the returns made by lay and clerical tenants alike to the great inquest of service which was instituted by Henry in 1166. The appended list, compiled by Round from the above-mentioned sources, shows the ecclesiastical tenants *in capite* with their quotas, as they were in the middle of the twelfth century.

Bishops.	*Servicium Debitum.* Knights.	Bishops.	*Servicium Debitum.* Knights.
Canterbury . .	60	London . . .	20
Lincoln . . .	60	Exeter . . .	17½[4]
Winchester . .	60	Coventry and Lichfield	15
Worcester . . .	50 [60][3]	Hereford . . .	15
Ely . . .	40	Durham . . .	10
Norwich . . .	40	York . . .	7
Salisbury . . .	32	Chichester . .	2
Bath and Wells . .	20	[Chapelry of Bosham] .	[7¼[4]]

[1] *Historia Anglorum*, loc. cit.
[2] *Historia Ecclesie Eliensis* (Rerum Anglicarum scriptorum veterum, I),

Religious Houses.	Servicium Debitum. Knights.	Religious Houses.	Servicium Debitum. Knights.
Peterborough	60	Wilton	5
Glastonbury	40	Ramsey	4
St. Edmunds	40	Chertsey	3
Abingdon	30	St. Benet's, Holme	3
Hyde	20	Malmesbury	3
St. Augustine's, Canterbury	15	Cerne	2 [3][4]
Tavistock	15[1]	Pershore	2 [3][5]
Westminster	15 (?)[2]	Middleton	2
Coventry	10	Sherburne	2
Shaftesbury	7 [10][3]	Winchcombe	2
St. Albans	6	Abbotsbury	1
Evesham	5	Michelney	1

p. 275: 'Praecepit illi [i.e. abbati] *ex nutu regis* custodiam .xl. militum habere in insulam.' See Round, loc. cit.

[3] In 1156 the Bishop of Worcester was charged with scutage on 60 fees, but claimed that he owed the service of 50 knights only. Pipe Roll, 2 Henry II, ed. Hunter (Record Commission), p. 63.

[4] It is probable that the original liability of the bishop was for 10 knights, and that the number entered above is explained by the inclusion in his *servicium* of 7½ knights due from the chapelry of Bosham, which had been bestowed by the Conqueror upon Bishop Osbern. Under Henry II the college was temporarily transferred to the Bishop of Lisieux, and was accounted for by him in Sussex. No allowance was, however, made to the Bishop of Exeter, who continued to be held responsible for 17½ fees. In 1177 the chapelry reverted to its original owner, and henceforward the Bishops of Exeter were charged with 7½ fees in Sussex in addition to the 17½ for which they responded in Devonshire. Finally, in 1320, the king granted to Bishop Walter de Stapeldon, for good service rendered and to be rendered, that the chapelry of Bosham should for the future be held in free alms, quit of scutage. *Calendar of Charter Rolls*, iii. 431.

[1] The abbot was charged on 10½ fees for the scutage of 1166; but in 1161 and 1162 he responded for 15, which may therefore be accepted as his correct *servicium*.

[2] The case of Westminster presents considerable difficulties. In 1156 the abbot was charged on 75 fees, but claimed that he owed a service of 15 knights only. The entries for 1161 and 1162 are incomprehensible: but in the later pipe rolls the abbot is regularly assessed for 15 fees, so that the protest made in 1156 was apparently accepted.

[3] The Abbess of St. Edwards was charged on 10 fees in 1156; but her *servicium* appears in 1161 and 1162 as 7 only.

[4] The Abbot of Cerne responded for 3 knights in 1156 and 1161, but his assessment was reduced to 2 in 1162. He received from Henry II, probably about this time, a charter which fixed the service of the abbey at 2 knights 'ad scutagium' and 1 'in expedicione'. *C.Ch.R.* ii. 143.

[5] In 1156 the abbot was charged with scutage on 3 fees, 'sed dicit quod non debet nisi .ij. milites'. *Red Book of the Exchequer*, R.S., i. 14.

Here we have forty ecclesiastical tenants, acknowledging between them a *servicium* of some 741½ knights, or about one-seventh of the total *servicium debitum* of England, as estimated by Round.[1] They include the two archbishops, thirteen suffragan bishops, with the chapelry of Bosham as an appendage of the see of Exeter, and twenty-four religious houses. Among the latter are the two great nunneries of Shaftesbury and Wilton, and the priory of Coventry—the only instance of a cathedral priory charged with military responsibilities towards the Crown. Its inclusion in our list is explained by the fact that at the date of the Conquest it ranked as an independent abbey, and as such was assessed for knight-service in 1070. Subsequently Bishop Robert of Limesey (1085–1117) moved the see of Chester to Coventry and reduced the status of the abbey without, however, relieving it of the military duties with which it was burdened.

A comparison of the *servicia* of the individual tenants as given above with the hidage of the lands for which they were due effectually disposes of the possibility that the Conqueror's assessment was based upon any principle of hidation. To quote only a few examples: the twenty knights with which the abbey of Hyde was charged in the twelfth century represented a little under 300 hides, according to the Domesday computation;[2] Ramsey's service of four knights was rendered for between 300 and 400 hides;[3] Shaftesbury's service of seven for 344½;[4] while, on the other hand, the abbey of Tavistock, which appears in Domesday Book as holding not more than 30 hides,[5] was burdened with a *servicium* of no less than fifteen knights. The case of the bishopric of Worcester is of special interest in view of Maitland's suggestion that here, at least, the medieval liability of the see can be traced back to a Saxon source.[6] Before the Conquest the bishop was responsible to the king for the service due from the three hundred hides of land comprising his triple hundred of Oswaldslaw. On the principle, therefore, of one *miles* for every five hides, he was bound to furnish sixty knights

---

[1] Round estimated the total *servicium debitum*, clerical and lay, at about 5,000 fees. *Feudal England*, p. 292.

[2] Dugdale, *Monasticon Anglicanum*, ii. 429.

[3] *Cartulary of the Abbey of Ramsey*, R.S., iii. 208.

[4] *Monasticon*, ii. 472.   [5] Ibid. 489.

[6] F. W. Maitland, *Domesday Book and Beyond*, pp. 158 seq.

for the royal host—the exact number, as Maitland argued, on which he was charged at the beginning of the reign of Henry II. The argument does not, however, hold good. In the first place, the Exchequer assessment of sixty knights was challenged by the bishop, who acknowledged a *servicium* of fifty knights only. In the second place, as Round pointed out,[1] the service in the twelfth century was rendered for all the episcopal estates and not merely for the hundred of Oswaldslaw. It represented, in fact, not 300 but between 500 and 600 hides.

Obviously the five-hide theory is untenable; and it seems equally clear that no alternative scheme of valuation will account for the variations between the quotas. The late Mr. W. J. Corbett, in his article in the *Cambridge Medieval History* on the Norman Conquest of England, was at some pains to classify the lay and ecclesiastical baronies of the early Norman period on the basis of the valuation given in Domesday Book. The conclusion he reached was that in the assessment of the tenants-in-chief for knight service there was 'much caprice and no uniformity'. While it could be generally asserted that quotas of 40 or more knights were imposed on most baronies of over £200 annual value, and quotas of between 20 and 40 on baronies with an annual income of £100 to £200, it remained true that many poor estates were heavily burdened; and that, especially in the case of the ecclesiastics, some wealthy ones escaped with a disproportionately light assessment.[2] Such violent discrepancies, for instance, as appear between the service due from Peterborough or Glastonbury or St. Edmunds, and that owed by Ramsey or St. Albans or Shaftesbury, are not explained by any proportionate differences in either the value or the extent of the lands. Moreover, some of the great ecclesiastics were exempted altogether from the new responsibilities. Of the bishoprics which were in existence at the time of the Conquest, Rochester alone is missing from our list; and its omission is due not to the fact that it escaped assessment, but to the fact that it stood in a dependent relation to the see of Canterbury, rendering its service to the archbishop instead of to the king.[3]

---

[1] *English Historical Review*, xii. 493.
[2] *Cambridge Medieval History*, v. 505 seq.
[3] Round, *Feudal England*, p. 250.

On the other hand, of the religious houses which are known to have flourished in 1070, such important foundations as the Conqueror's own abbey of Battle, the pre-Conquest houses of Gloucester, Burton, Waltham, and Athelney, the nunneries of Barking and St. Mary's Winchester—all of which are entered in Domesday Book as holding in chief—do not appear.[1] Their exemption cannot be satisfactorily explained save on the hypothesis that the determining factor in the assessment was the royal will. Each tenant-in-chief made what bargain he could with the king, who may on occasion have been induced to respect immunities granted by his Saxon predecessors, but who was doubtless in general influenced solely by immediate political considerations. Thus the exceptionally heavy burden imposed on the abbey of Peterborough is probably accounted for by the strong nationalist tendencies which the house had displayed during and after the Conquest.[2] Chichester's light assessment may be ascribed to the poverty and general insignificance of the see (which was located at Selsey in 1070); Durham's to its 'palatinate' status and to its peculiar responsibilities in regard to the defence of the border; while the explanation of the Archbishop of York's small *servicium* is doubtless to be found in the impoverishment of the see, which resulted from William's ruthless devastation of the north in 1069.

The exact circumstances in which the Conqueror's settlement of the Church lands was effected must necessarily remain a matter of conjecture. It is possible that it was carried out at the great ecclesiastical council which met at Winchester in April 1070, and which was responsible for the deposition of Archbishop Stigand and of various other of the English bishops and abbots; or in the later assembly at Windsor which was chiefly concerned with filling the episcopal and abbatial vacancies. Both Matthew Paris and the Abingdon chronicler imply that some record of the transaction was made at the time by the Crown, for its own convenience;[3] but it does not appear

---

[1] This list is not exhaustive: several smaller houses such as Cranborne, Horton, Romsey, Amesbury, Wherwell, also escaped assessment.

[2] Round, *Feudal England*, p. 163; *Victoria County History, Northampton*, i. 283.

[3] '*inrotulans* episcopatus et abbatias . . . quot milites sibi et successoribus suis hostilitatis tempore voluit a singulis exhiberi.' *Historia Anglorum*, i. 13.

that there was any written agreement as between the king and
the individual tenant. The *servicia debita* of the clerics, as of
the lay baronage, seem in the Norman period to have been a
matter of tradition rather than of record; and that there was
frequent uncertainty and confusion as to the precise extent of
the liability in individual cases is amply attested by the early
pipe rolls of Henry II. Before 1166 we find in dispute the
services of the Bishop of Worcester, the Abbot of Pershore, the
Abbess of Shaftesbury, and the Abbots of Tavistock and Westminster.[1] In a few instances it is clear that tenants secured from
the Crown a definite readjustment of their obligations. Thus
the Abbot of Cerne, who was charged on three fees in 1156
and 1161, received from Henry II a charter reducing the abbey's
service to two knights 'ad scutagium' and one 'in expedicione';[2]
and the Abbot of Evesham who, as has been shown, owed five
knights under William I,[3] secured from Henry I a recognition
that he held his lands for four and a half knights 'in expedicione
me presente'.[4] The well-known charter of Henry I to the
Bishop of Ely, reducing the liability of the see for scutage from
£100 to £60, possibly, though by no means certainly, represents
a proportionate reduction of the bishop's *servicium debitum*.[5]
Probably, therefore, the total of the quotas as originally fixed
in 1070 was slightly higher than is indicated by the earliest
pipe roll accounts.

One other fact emerges from a study of the lists of ecclesiastical tenants, to which attention may be drawn in passing,

'Cum jam regis edicto *in annalibus annotaretur* quot de episcopiis quotve de
abbatiis ad publicam rem tuendam milites . . . exigerentur.' *Chronicon
Monasterii de Abingdon*, R.S. ii. 3.

[1] *Supra*, p. 4, n. 4; p. 5, nn. 1, 2, 3, 5.

[2] *Supra*, p. 5, n. 4.   [3] *Supra*, p. 5.

[4] See the confirmation by Henry III of a charter of Henry I granting to
Evesham all its lands free of all secular service and scutage, 'salvo tamen et
retento servicio quatuor militum et dimidii in expedicione, me presente'.
C.Ch.R. i. 257.

[5] Round, *Feudal England*, p. 268; *Liber Eliensis*, Lib. III, no. xxi. An
entry in the Ramsey cartulary suggests that the original obligation of this
house may have been greater than the four knights recognized in 1166.
See the charter of William Rufus to Ralf, brother of Ilger: 'Mando vobis
me clamasse Aldwinum abbatem Ramesie quietum de servicio decem
militum in festis. Et deinceps tres mihi habeat sicut antecessores sui facie-
bant, in septentrionali parte fluminis Tamesie' (i. 235).

although its implications will be more fully considered else-where.[1] It is clear that the allocation of military responsibilities in 1070 was final. No clerical tenures-in-chief by knight-service were created after that date, although the century following the Norman invasion was one of unprecedented activity in the ecclesiastical sphere. New bishoprics were founded, and a great crop of monastic institutions sprang to life. The conversion of the abbey of Ely into a bishopric in 1109 involved, it is true, no addition to the ranks of the tenants-in-chief, since the bishop merely stepped into the position formerly occupied by the abbot, and assumed those duties in relation to the Crown for which his predecessors had been held responsible; but in 1133 a new tenure-in-chief was created when the see of Carlisle was carved out of the province conquered from the Scots by William Rufus. Simultaneously the monastic revival was attaining its climax. At the date of the Conquest monasticism had been almost extinct in the midlands and the north. The twenty-four monasteries assessed by the Conqueror for knight-service were situated ex-clusively in the south and east of England; so that a line drawn from the Wash to the Bristol Channel marks roughly the limit of their distribution.[2] With the coming of the Normans how-ever, pre-Conquest houses such as Crowland, Bardney, Thorney, and Whitby, which had been destroyed at the time of the Danish incursions, rose once more from their ruins; new Benedictine communities such as St. Mary's York, Selby, Shrewsbury, Colchester, and Faversham were founded through the piety and liberality of kings and barons; while the new orders which had grown up on the Continent—Cluniacs, Cistercians, the various orders of regular canons—were now for the first time repre-sented in England. Yet not one of these foundations, whether monastic or episcopal, of royal or of baronial origin, appears in our list of the military tenants of the Crown in the twelfth century.

It is true that, when at the end of the reign of Henry III the continuous series of military summonses begins, many new names are found among the recipients of individual writs. In the thirteenth and fourteenth centuries the Bishops of Carlisle

[1] *Infra*, Chap. V. See my article in the *E.H.R.* xli, pp. 161 seq.
[2] See the map forming the frontispiece to this volume.

and Rochester, and from the beginning of the reign of Edward I, the four Welsh bishops, were regularly summoned to perform feudal service in the king's armies; while during the same period no less than twenty-six heads of religious houses, over and above the twenty-four who figure as military tenants-in-chief under Henry II, received similar writs. The Abbesses of Barking, Romsey, and Winchester, the Abbots of the Benedictine houses of Bardney, Battle, Burton, Chester, Colchester, Crowland, Eynsham, Gloucester, Reading, Selby, Shrewsbury, Thorney, Whitby, and St. Mary's York; and of the Augustinian foundations of St. Augustine's Bristol, Cirencester, Dunstable, Keynsham, Leicester, Thornton, and Waltham; together with the Prior of the Cluniac house of Bromholm, and the Prior of St. John of Jerusalem, were all individually summoned at different times between 1244 and 1385. These summonses suggest that an increase in the numbers of the clerical tenants-in-chief by knight-service took place during the thirteenth century; and their testimony has hitherto been unhesitatingly accepted. Not only has it been commonly supposed that all who were personally summoned held of the king *per servicium militare*; but, on the hypothesis that the greater vassals alone were entitled to a special summons, it has been further assumed that the number of military tenants was actually larger than the number of recipients of individual writs.[1] In point of fact, such assumptions are wholly unwarranted. The mere fact of the issue of a writ by the Chancery constitutes no proof of the military status of the addressee; it must further be shown that the claim implicit in the writ was admitted and the summons obeyed. There are abundant materials for determining the composition of the feudal armies of the thirteenth and fourteenth centuries, and it is in these records rather than in the unsupported evidence of the writs of summons that the key to the personnel of the clerical tenants must be sought.

By collating the evidence of the scutage accounts in the pipe rolls, which after 1194 record the names of tenants quit for service or a fine as well as of those liable for scutage; of the scutage rolls, on which from 1214 onwards were entered the

[1] See, for instance, Parry, *Parliaments and Councils of England*, pp. 67-8, note *m*.

names of all whom the performance of service or the payment of a fine entitled to collect scutage for their own use from their sub-tenants; [1] of the marshal's rolls which under Edward I and Edward II furnished details of the proffers made at the place of muster; [2] and of the rolls of fines which began to be separately compiled in the thirteenth and fourteenth centuries,[3] it is possible to determine the response made to many of the summonses issued by Henry III and the three Edwards.[4] An analysis of the resultant data shows that only those ecclesiastics responded in money or in men who had recognized military liabilities under Henry II or William I. In spite of the evidence of the writs of summons, there is nothing in the records of feudal service to indicate that any addition was made in the thirteenth century to the ranks of the clerical tenants of the Crown by knight-service.

Nor are we compelled to argue solely from the silence of the military records. There is in many cases positive evidence that service was not due from those ecclesiastics of whose response to the royal summons no record is to be found. Among the bishops, Rochester, as we have seen, rendered his service in the eleventh century not to the king, but to the Archbishop of Canterbury.[5] Later he repudiated this dependence, but claimed to hold his lands in free alms quit of all earthly service.[6] The bishopric of Carlisle, we learn in the thirteenth century, was similarly free from all military obligations to the Crown.[7] The Welsh bishops, although they were regularly summoned after

---

[1] Scutage rolls exist for the armies of 1214, 1221, 1223, 1224, 1228, 1229, 1230, 1231, 1242, 1246, 1257, 1282, 1303, 1306, 1311, 1327. See Scutage Rolls, Nos. 1–8 and 13; and *Calendar of Chancery Rolls, Various*.

[2] Marshal's rolls exist for 1277, 1282, 1303, 1306, 1311, 1323. See Palgrave, *Parliamentary Writs*, i. 195, 228; ii. 401; Chancery Miscellanea, 5/6, 5/7, 5/10.

[3] See especially the roll of estreats of fines, 48 Henry III to 1 Edward III, Exchequer Lord Treasurer's Remembrancer, Miscellaneous Roll, 1/13.

[4] For 1221, 1223, 1224, 1228, 1230, 1232, 1246, 1257, 1277, 1282, 1300, 1303, 1306, 1311, 1314, 1323, 1327.

[5] *Supra*, p. 7.

[6] Round, *Feudal England*, p. 250; *Registrum Roffense*, ed. Thorpe, pp. 70 seq.

[7] Ibid., loc. cit.: 'Nihil enim tenet episcopatus [Roffensis] per baroniam de rege. Set per puram elemosinam, quod non est dicendum de aliquo Episcopatu Anglie nec de Archiepiscopatu, nisi duntaxat Karleolen.'

the accession of Edward I, performed no service. In 1303, indeed, the Bishop of St. David's sent to the muster a representative who declared on his behalf before the Constable and Marshal, 'quod ecclesia sua Meneuensis libera est et libera extitit ab antiquo, ita quod nec regibus nec principibus aliquod servicium hactenus exibuit temporale per quod nullum servicium debet in Scocia vel alibi'.[1]

As to the religious houses, the majority to which summonses were addressed were of Anglo-Saxon or early Norman origin, and all were in existence before the middle of the twelfth century, so that their omission from the early lists of tenants-in-chief by knight-service is in itself fairly conclusive of the non-military character of their tenure. Many of those of later date were, indeed, not of royal foundation and held little, if any, land *in capite*. Positive evidence of their immunity from military duties is, moreover, available. For instance, the Abbess of the pre-Conquest house of Barking, who was summoned fifteen times between 1244 and 1327, was in 1306 attached to answer for failure to respond to the summons of 34 Edward I. She appeared by attorney, and declared that she owed no service, but held all her lands in free, pure, and perpetual alms. Her charters were scrutinized, and since no record of service by the abbesses of the house was to be found on the Marshal's rolls or elsewhere, she was discharged 'ad presens sine die'.[2] The Abbot of Battle, summoned four times, was quit by the Conqueror's grant 'ab omni . . . consuetudine terrene servitutis . . . et de exercitu';[3] Burton and Gloucester, both dating from the pre-Norman period, were summoned eight and fourteen times respectively, but were both returned in the great inquest of service of 1212 as holding their lands in frankalmoign;[4] Chester, summoned on eight occasions, held not of the Crown, but of the Earls of Chester—by whom it had been refounded as a Benedictine community in 1093—in pure and perpetual alms, rendering 'nichil preter preces et oraciones';[5] Cirencester, a

---

[1] Marshal's roll of 1303; Chanc. Misc. 5/6, m. 1.
[2] Exchequer Lord Treasurer's Remembrancer, Memoranda Roll, No. 77; Communia, Recorda, Michaelmas, m. 15.
[3] *C.Ch.R.* iii. 195, 335; *Red Book*, i. 6.
[4] *Book of Fees*, i. 51, 151.
[5] Ancient Petitions, 191/9547; *Cal. of Close Rolls*, 1330–1333, pp. 587–9.

house of Augustinian canons founded by Henry I in 1117, was summoned five times, but was exempt by charter from all aids, scutages, and expeditions;[1] the Abbot of the East Anglian house of Crowland, who received eleven individual summonses, proved in 1321 to the satisfaction of the Exchequer, that he did not hold by barony and had never performed service in the armies of the king or his progenitors;[2] the Abbot of Reading (founded by Henry I in 1121) was quit by charter of all aids and scutages;[3] the Master and brethren of St. John of Jerusalem enjoyed all their possessions by royal grant 'libera et quieta de exercitu et equitatu, et homagiis . . . et de omnibus auxiliis';[4] the abbey of Selby, one of the foundations of the Conqueror, held its lands in all the counties of England in free and perpetual alms and quit of scutage;[5] the Abbot of Shrewsbury was exempt by grant of the Earls of Shrewsbury, by whom the house was founded in 1083, 'ab omni consuetudine et vexatione et exactione vicecomitum . . . et ab omni servicio seculari'.[6]

The list might be indefinitely extended, but time and space forbid the multiplication of examples. Two exceptional cases call, however, for special mention. First, the abbey of St. Mary's York held all its possessions by charter of Richard I in free alms, 'libera et quieta ab omni terreno servicio in perpetuam possessionem', subject only to the obligation, whenever the men of Yorkshire were summoned to the host, of sending the banner of Our Lady with them into action.[7] In the armies of the thirteenth and fourteenth centuries the abbey is accordingly represented by a mounted *serviens* who acts as standard-bearer.[8] Secondly, the Prior of Bromholm in Norfolk received from Henry III in 1245 the grant of a serjeanty, for which he rendered service by a mounted cross-bowman in the armies of Edward I and Edward II.[9] Neither house, it will be noted, owed knight-service in the strict sense of the term; and the general conclusion that, despite the evidence of the writs of summons the

---

[1] *C.Ch.R.* v. 213.
[2] Exchequer King's Remembrancer, Memoranda Roll, No. 94; Communia, Recorda, Easter, m. 114.
[3] *C.Ch.R.* i. 14–15.   [4] Ibid. v. 86.   [5] *Monasticon*, iii. 504.
[6] *C.Ch.R.* v. 49. See also *Red Book*, i. 6.   [7] Ibid. iii. 112.
[8] Chanc. Misc. 5/6, m. 1; 5/7, m.1; *Parl. Writs*, ii. 404; Chanc. Misc. 5/10, m. 4.   [9] *C.Ch.R.* i. 283; *Parl. Writs*, i. 198.

number of clerical tenants-in-chief remained constant from 1070 onwards is, therefore, unaffected.

Before the topic is finally dismissed one further line of investigation remains to be followed. The possibility of a connexion between the increase in the number of military summonses addressed to ecclesiastics and the land legislation of Edward I is too obvious to be ignored. Admittedly the statute *Quia Emptores* (1290), of which the chief provision was that for the future none should grant land in fee simple to be held of himself,[1] affected the conditions of tenure for ecclesiastical no less than for lay persons. Its ostensible result was to render void all subsequent grants in frankalmoign by mesne lords; 'so that', as Lyttleton writes, 'if a man seised of certain tenements which he holdeth of his lord by knights service, and at this day he . . . granteth by licence the same tenements to an abbot . . . in frankalmoign, the abbot shall hold immediately the tenements by knights service of the same lord of whom his grantor held, and shall not hold of his grantor in frankalmoign, by reason of the same statute'.[2] Thus every gift of land to a churchman by a tenant-in-chief holding by knight-service would, after 1290, normally result in the creation of a new clerical tenant 'in capite per servicium militare'. Have we here the explanation of the practice of the Edwardian Chancery in issuing writs of military summons to non-military tenants? That *Quia Emptores* affords at best a very incomplete solution of the problem can be readily demonstrated. Evasion of this, as of most medieval legislation, by agreement or collusion was always possible. Coke, commenting in the seventeenth century on Lyttleton's statement, remarks: 'It is to be understood that a man seised of lands may at this day give the same to a bishop, parson, &c., and their successors in frankalmoign, by the consent of the king and of the lords mediate and immediate of whom the land is holden; for the rule is 'quilibet potest

---

[1] 'De cetero liceat unicuique libero homini terram suam . . . pro voluntate sua vendere. Ita tamen quod feoffatus teneat terram illam . . . de eodem capitali domino et per eadem servicia et consuetudines per que feoffator suus illam prius tenuit. . . . Et sciendum quod istud statutum locum tenet de terris venditis tenendis in feodo simpliciter tantum.' *Statutes of the Realm*, i. 106.

[2] Lyttleton, *Treatise of Tenures*, ed. Tomlins, 1641, i, sect. 140.

renunciare juri pro se introducto'.[1] Any question of the effective-
ness of the law apart, however, it is evident that the Chancery
policy did not originate in or after 1290. Of the thirty-two non-
military bishops and abbots to whom individual writs were
addressed, only six—the Priors of Bromholm and St. John of
Jerusalem, the Abbots of Eynsham, Leicester, and Thornton,
and the Abbess of Romsey—were summoned for the first time
after the date of the statute. The Prior of Bromholm was summoned, as we have already seen, in respect of the serjeanty
granted him by Henry III. Of the remaining five, one or two
can be proved to have received recent accessions of territory
which might account for their inclusion among the recipients
of individual writs. In 1307, for instance, the Abbot of Thornton was granted by royal licence certain lands in Arnold in
Holderness, held by William de Ros of Helmsley as of the
honour of Aumale.[2] The abbot received his first military summons for the Scottish expedition of that same year. In 1313
the lands formerly held by the Templars, whose order had been
recently suppressed, were surrendered to the Hospitallers;[3] and
in 1316 the Prior of St. John of Jerusalem was summoned to
serve in the army of Scotland. In 1315 Simon de Seneville
secured a licence to alienate his manor of Lockington to the
Abbot of Leicester,[4] to whom an individual writ was for the
first time addressed in the following year. In neither case,
however, was the summons obeyed or any military obligation
acknowledged. Indeed, in 1341, the Abbot of Thornton,[5] and
in 1352 the Abbot of Leicester,[6] were released from attendance
at Parliament on the ground that they held nothing of the king
in chief or by barony; while about 1335 the Prior of St. John
of Jerusalem triumphantly vindicated his claim that 'totes les
terres et [tenementz] de mesme Hospital aussi bien ces qe iadys
furent du Temple . . . come ces de Hospital [avaunt dit]

---

[1] Lyttleton, *Treatise of Tenures*, ed. Tomlins, 1641, i, sect. 140.
[2] *Calendar of Patent Rolls*, 1301–1307, p. 254.
[3] Ibid., 1313–1317, p. 52.   [4] Ibid., p. 212.
[5] *C.P.R.*, 1340–1343, p. 248; *Lords' Report on the Dignity of a Peer*,
Appendix IV, p. 529. Cf. Exch. L.T.R. Mem. Roll, No. 77; Brevia Baronibus,
Trinity, m. 53.
[6] *C.P.R.*, 1350–1354, p. 230. Cf. Cole, *Documents Illustrative of English
History*, p. 14.

feussent donez et assignez as ditz hospital et Temple en pure et perpetuel aumoigne'.[1]

It may, therefore, be definitely affirmed that the increase in the number of military summonses issued to ecclesiastics in the thirteenth and fourteenth centuries was not warranted by any corresponding increase in the number of clerical tenures-in-chief 'per servicium militare'.[2] If the intention of the Crown was to exact service where none was due, the attempt was evidently unsuccessful. It failed to extend the range of military responsibilities beyond the tenants who had been assessed for knight service by the Conqueror.

In the meantime, however, efforts had been made to increase the profits from existing military tenures. In 1166 Henry II carried through his great inquest of service and made the returns the basis of a revision in the royal interest of the *servicia debita* as created a century earlier.

William, in fixing the military service due to the Crown, had concerned himself solely with his immediate vassals. The tenants-in-chief were free to furnish their contingents by any means they pleased. In practice most of them found it convenient to parcel out their estates among their dependents on terms similar to those upon which they themselves held of the king; but, since individual requirements or inclinations were the determining factor, there was no approach to uniformity in the process of subinfeudation. Some chose to enfeoff the exact number of knights which constituted their *servicium debitum*; others enfeoffed fewer and maintained the residue on their demesne; but the majority enfeoffed more than the number of *milites* for which they were responsible, so that the total of knights actually enfeoffed was considerably in excess of the total service due to the Crown from its military tenants. It was with the intention of removing this discrepancy and of

---

[1] Ancient Petitions, 10235/205.

[2] The case of Normandy affords an interesting parallel. Here, as Professor Haskins has shown, the ecclesiastics were assessed for knight-service at some early date (perhaps under Robert the Magnificent); and the number so burdened was never subsequently increased. The Norman Inquest of 1172 shows that only nine monastic houses rendered military service to the Duke at that date, and those nine were the oldest foundations in the Duchy. (C. H. Haskins, *Norman Institutions*, ch. i.)

diverting the profits of the extra feoffments from the seignorial
to the royal coffers, that Henry II instituted in 1166 an inquiry
into the conditions of subinfeudation on the estates of his immediate vassals.

The tenants-in-chief, lay and ecclesiastical, were instructed
by general writ addressed to the sheriff to furnish information
under the following heads:

1. How many knights had been enfeoffed before the death
   of Henry I?
2. How many have been enfeoffed since?
3. How many (if any) remain chargeable to the demesne?
4. What are the names of the knights enfeoffed? [1]

The care and scrupulosity which characterize most of the
returns suggest that they were made in ignorance of the king's
intentions. The purpose of the inquiry became clear, however,
when two years later, the aid to marry Henry's daughter Matilda
to Henry the Lion of Saxony was assessed, not upon the traditional basis, but upon a new *servicium* carefully framed for the
profit of the Crown from the particulars furnished in the *Carte
Baronum*. The royal policy is summed up by Round, in the
following passage: 'Instead of either adhering to the old assessment (*servicium debitum*) or uniformly substituting a new one
based on the fees actually created, the Crown selected in every
case whichever of these two systems told in its own favour
and against the tenant of the fief. If he had enfeoffed fewer
knights than his *servicium debitum* required, the Crown retained
that *servicium* as the irreducible minimum of his assessment;
but if he had created an excess of fees, the Crown added that
excess to his pre-existing assessment and increased the service
due from him *pro tanto*.'[2] The lay tenants affected were charged
in the Pipe Roll under the headings 'de veteri feffamento' and
'de novo feffamento'; the ecclesiastics were allowed to register
a mild protest against the innovation by the use of the formulae
'de militibus quos recognoscit' and 'de militibus quos non
recognoscit'.

The way in which individual clerical tenants were affected

---

[1] The tenor of the writ is given in the return of the Archbishop of York
(*Red Book*, i. 412). See also Round, *Feudal England*, pp. 237 seq.

[2] Ibid., p. 242.

by the royal policy of 1166–8 is best explained by reference to the appended tables, which have been compiled from the pipe rolls and from the *Carte* in the Red and Black Books of the Exchequer.

Bishops.	*Fees charged before* 1166.	*Fees returned in the Carte of* 1166. *O.F.*	*N.F.*	*D.*	*Fees charged in* 1168. *Rec.*	*Non-Rec.*
Bath and Wells .	20	$19\frac{3}{4}$	+	—	20	—
Canterbury .	60	No *Carta*; inclusive return of 84, $\frac{1}{2}$, $\frac{1}{4}$.			In hand. $84\frac{3}{4}$	
Chichester .	2	$9\frac{1}{2}$	3	—	4	$5\frac{1}{2}$, $\frac{1}{20}$
Coventry and Lichfield. .	15	$12\frac{1}{4}$	1_{5}, $\frac{5}{8}$, $\frac{1}{7}$	—	15	—
Durham . .	10	64	$4\frac{5}{6}$, $\frac{3}{10}$	—	10	$60\frac{2}{3}$, $\frac{1}{4}$
Ely . . .	40	$56\frac{1}{4}$	$16\frac{1}{2}$	—	40	$16\frac{1}{4}$
Exeter . .	$17\frac{1}{2}$	$33\frac{1}{2}$, $\frac{1}{3}$	$1\frac{1}{3}$, $\frac{1}{2}$	—	$15\frac{1}{2}$	17+
Hereford . .	15	14	—	$4\frac{1}{2}$[1]	15	$3\frac{1}{2}$
Lincoln . .	60	102	2	—	60	42
London . .	20	36	—	—	20	17+
Norwich[2] . .	40	$33\frac{3}{4}$	1	—	40	$8\frac{3}{4}$
Salisbury . .	32	$40\frac{1}{2}$	$2\frac{1}{2}$, $\frac{1}{10}$	—	32	$8\frac{1}{2}$
Winchester .	60	$70\frac{1}{2}$[3]	—	—	60	$14\frac{1}{2}$
Worcester .	50	50	8	—	50	8
York . .	7	43+	$\frac{1}{2}$, $\frac{1}{3}$, $\frac{1}{12}$, $\frac{1}{20}$	—	20	$23\frac{1}{2}$

The principle that the old *servicium* is retained unaltered if it exceeds the total feoffment is illustrated by the cases of the Bishops of Bath and Coventry, although the Abbot of Evesham affords an exception to the rule. The abbey was charged in the pipe roll before 1166 with five knights; but subsequently it was assessed for $4\frac{1}{2}$ only. This was the number returned in the abbot's *Carta* as of the old feoffment; and the explanation of its acceptance by the Exchequer is doubtless the charter of Henry I referred to above.[4] Instances of the application of the principle that where the fees actually created exceed the tradi-

[1] These are said, in the bishop's return, to belong to his demesne, but they should actually be returned as 'de novo feffamento'.

[2] It seems impossible to reconcile in any way the assessment of 1168 with the return of 1166 as given in the Red and Black Books of the Exchequer.

[3] The *Carta* gives a list of both past and present tenants, with variations in the service owed. If the *new* service only be reckoned the total is $70\frac{1}{2}$ fees; if the *highest* service, whether old or new be reckoned, the total is $74\frac{1}{2}$ fees.

[4] *Supra*, p. 9.

Abbots.	Fees charged before 1166.	Fees returned in the Carte of 1166.			Fees charged in 1168.	
		O.F.	N.F.	D.	Rec.	Non-Rec.
Abbotsbury	1	1	½+	—	1	—
Abingdon	30	33	—	—	30	3
Cerne	2	6½	—	3½ [1]	2	8
Chertsey	3	4	—	—	3	1
Coventry	10	7⅚	—	2⅙	10	—
Evesham	5	4½	½	—	4½	—
Glastonbury	40	43½+	—	—	40	4½
Hyde	20	No *Carta*; inclusive return of 20			20	—
Malmesbury	3	No return			3	—
Michelney	1	1	—	—	1	—
Middleton	2	—	—	2	2	—
Pershore	2	2	—	—	2	—
Peterborough	60	63½, ⅓	—	—	60	3¾
Ramsey	4	4 'in communi'			4	—
St. Albans	6	6	—	—	6	—
St. Augustine's	15	No *Carta*; inclusive return of 15			15	—
St. Benet's	3	3¼, ⅖	—	—	3$\frac{9}{10}$	—
St. Edmund's	40	52¾	¼	—	40	12½
Shaftesbury	7	10$\frac{1}{12}$, ⅕	—	—	7	3¼, ⅙
Sherborne	2	2⅕	⅖, ⅔	—	2⅕	—
Tavistock	15	16	1½	—	16 'de veteri'	1½ 'de novo'
Westminster	15	23⅖, ½, ⅓	—	—	15	8+
Wilton	5	5	—	—	5	—
Winchcombe	2	1	—	1	2	—

tional *servicium debitum* the former and not the latter is made the basis of assessment are more frequent,[2] since the majority of the great ecclesiastics created more fees than they required for the discharge of their duties to the Crown. Here, however, a distinction is apparent between the treatment of laymen and clerics. Whereas the lay tenants were charged in 1168 on both old and new feoffment, the ecclesiastics were charged on the old feoffment only. They responded for the fees of the *servicium debitum* under the heading 'de militibus quos recognoscit' and for excess fees created before the death of Henry I or 'in

[1] These are properly 'de novo feoffamento' and not 'de dominico'.
[2] They include all the bishops save the two already mentioned and nine of the heads of religious houses—Abingdon, Cerne, Chertsey, Glastonbury, Peterborough, St. Edmund's, Shaftesbury, Tavistock, Westminster.

demesne', under the heading 'de militibus quos non recognoscit'. No attempt was made to put fees of the new feoffment under contribution, save in a few exceptional cases. The Bishops of Durham and Worcester appear to have included under the formula 'que non recognoscit' fees created 'de novo' as well as 'de veteri'; while the abbey of Tavistock was, by some curious accident, assessed as if it had been a lay fief, responding in 1168 for 16 fees 'de veteri feffamento' and 1½ 'de novo'. In the case of Sherborne and St. Benet's Holme, where the excess of old feoffment over *servicium* was merely fractional, the old feoffment was adopted as the basis of assessment, and no distinction was drawn between fees recognized and not recognized. Two instances also occur of the creation in 1168 of a new and higher 'recognition'. The Bishop of Chichester who, before 1166, acknowledged two knights only, returned in his certificate of that year 9½ fees as of the old feoffment, and 3 as of the new, and was charged for the aid to marry upon 4 fees 'que recognoscit' and 5+ 'que non recognoscit'. The Archbishop of York, who, in the early pipe rolls responded for 7 knights, returned in 1166 43+ fees 'de veteri', together with several fractions 'de novo'. In 1168 he was charged on 20 fees 'que recognoscit' and 23½ 'que non recognoscit'. Both prelates had escaped exceptionally lightly in 1070, and their acquiescence in the drastic revision of their original obligations is proof that the circumstances which had conditioned the Conqueror's low assessment of their lands had disappeared by the middle of the twelfth century. The Bishop of Exeter, on the other hand, furnishes an example of loss to the Crown. He recognized 17½ knights before 1166, and returned in his *Carta* 33 fees as of the old feoffment. In 1168 and subsequently he was charged, probably as a result of a clerical error, with 15½ fees 'que recognoscit', and 17½ 'que non recognoscit'.

The question remains, how far was Henry II's attempt to create a new *servicium debitum* successful? Round, at the time when he wrote his epoch-making essays on *The Introduction of Knight Service into England*, held that the results were lasting. 'The change thus made by the restless king', he wrote, 'was permanent in its effect; and thenceforth the only assessment recognized was that based upon the fees which by 1166 had

been created "de veteri" and "de novo".'[1] A closer examination of the later records shows that, as he himself later realized,[2]
this statement needs modification. The opposition aroused by
the royal policy was so strong as to preclude the possibility of
more than partial success. In the case of the lay tenants a small
increase was effected in the total service due to the Crown.
The sums charged against fees of the new feoffment fell universally and hopelessly into arrears, and by the end of the reign
of Henry II the attempt to secure payment had been virtually
abandoned; but where the number of fees of the old feoffment
exceeded the number of the traditional *servicium debitum*, the
king was successful in substituting the former for the latter
as the permanent basis of assessment. In the case of the ecclesiastical tenants the change was almost negligible. As we have
already seen there was a fractional increase in the assessment
of the abbeys of Sherborne and St. Benet's; while the quota
of the Bishop of Chichester was raised from 2 to 4 knights,
and that of the Archbishop of York from 7 to 20. No other
permanent alteration was effected. There is no record of any
payment upon fees 'que non recognoscit' save when the fief
was in the king's hand, and by 1187 they, like the lay fees 'of
the new feoffment', had ceased even to be entered on the roll.
A curious entry in the fourteenth-century register of Bishop
Swinfield of Hereford suggests, indeed, that the Crown had
formally surrendered its claim to the profits of the extra feoffments. The passage, which relates to the 'unrecognized' fees
of the episcopal barony, expressly states that Henry II, having
assessed the aid to marry on the information supplied by the
baronial *Carte*, issued 'letters patent' to his tenants-in-chief,
promising that in future they should not, by reason of the said
Carte, be burdened beyond their ancient service; and naïvely
adds that the said letters ('sicut solet dici veraciter a fidedignis
antiquis') were afterwards sent to be preserved in the treasury
of St. Paul's in London.[3] In spite of its anachronisms and
absurdities, there is perhaps a substratum of truth in this story.

---

[1] Round, *Feudal England*, p. 286.
[2] Introduction to the Pipe Roll of 33 Henry II, pp. xxv seq.
[3] *Register of Bishop Swinfield of Hereford*, 1283–1317 (Canterbury and
York Society), pp. 414 seq.

The wholesale omission in 1187 of the fees 'que non recognoscit' and 'de novo feffamento' points to a definite change of policy about that date, while a possible motive is supplied by the need for conciliating important interests after the disastrous conclusion of the Becket controversy, and the subsequent disorders.

The policy of 1168 was not, however, permanently abandoned. John seems to have renewed the attempt to bring all fees under contribution; and the temporary realization of his project was facilitated, as far as the ecclesiastical tenants-in-chief were concerned, by his quarrel with the Papacy, and the seizure of Church lands following upon the promulgation of the interdict in 1208. For the administration of the estates of the dispossessed clergy it was necessary that the Crown and its officials should be furnished with full lists of the persons holding land under them; and many such seem to have been compiled by inquisition or otherwise during the years 1208 to 1213. There have survived in the Red Book and the Book of Fees returns of this date for the archbishoprics of York and Canterbury, the bishoprics of Rochester, Norwich, Hereford, Lincoln, Ely, London, Exeter, and Worcester, and the abbacies of Holme, St. Albans, Chertsey, Malmesbury, Peterborough, and Hyde.[1] The information thus obtained was apparently utilized by the Exchequer in the assessment of the scutages of Scotland (1209) and Wales (1211) which appear in the pipe roll of 13 John. The accounts were drawn up with unusual elaboration; the number of fees being generally entered on the roll, whether the tenant concerned was charged or quit. Most of the clerical estates, including even the bishoprics of Norwich and Winchester, which were in the hands of the king's confidants, John de Gray and Peter des Roches, were assessed for all feoffments, although the method of entry varied. Sometimes the grand total only was given; sometimes the traditional categories of 'recognized' and 'unrecognized' fees were employed; while occasionally the basis of assessment was the old and new feoffment as given in the returns of 1166.[2] The figures seldom differ by more than

---

[1] *Book of Fees*, i. 34–48; *Red Book*, ii. 469, 473, 476, 491, 495, 508, 514, 524, 541, 551, 556.

[2] e.g. the Archbishopric of Canterbury was charged on $84\frac{3}{4}$ fees (Pipe Roll, No. 57, Kent). The Abbot of Westminster paid on 15 fees 'que recognoscit' and $7\frac{1}{3}$, $\frac{2}{5}$ 'que non recognoscit' (ibid., Lond. and Middlesex).

a mere fraction from those of the *Carte* of Henry II : but the bishopric of Exeter had charged against it 22+ 'unrecognized' fees as opposed to the traditional 17½ ;[1] the bishopric of Bath (*servicium debitum* 20) was assessed upon a total of about 24 fees, of which 4 would appear to have been created since 1166, when the bishop returned 19+ as of the old feoffment and none as of the new ;[2] and the abbey of Shaftesbury (*servicium debitum* 7) upon a total of 11+ as against the 10+ acknowledged in 1166.[3] In all, over 200 surplus ecclesiastical fees seem to have been brought under contribution in 1211.[4] In the next year the royal policy culminated in the great inquest of service, authorized by writ of 10 June, in which the sheriffs were directed to make returns to the Exchequer, hundred by hundred, of all tenures-in-chief by knight-service or by serjeanty within their respective bailiwicks, so that the location of the fees of the king's tenants might be ascertained as well as the amount of their service.[5]

So much activity might have been expected to produce pro-portionately important results; but, in point of fact, we find that John effected no permanent increase in the number of fees for which the ecclesiastical tenants responded at the Exchequer. In the collection of the early scutages of Henry III the tradi-tional assessment was gradually resumed; and the only trace remaining of the attempt to tax the surplus feoffments is the reappearance on the roll, in certain cases, of the old charge upon 'unrecognized' fees.[6] The Bishops of Ely, Hereford, Exeter, and Winchester, and the Abbot of Chertsey, for example, were henceforward regularly assessed for the fees 'que non recog-noscit' as well as for those 'que recognoscit', although there is no evidence of payment save on the acknowledged *servicium*. The Abbess of Shaftesbury and the Abbot of Cerne were similarly charged, until formally acquitted by royal charter in

---

The bishopric of Salisbury was assessed on 40½ fees 'de veteri feffamento' and 2½ 'de novo' (Pipe Roll, No. 57, Wilts.).

[1] Ibid., Devon. Compare the list of fees given in the *Red Book*, ii. 556, 557.

[2] Ibid., Somers. and Dors.; *supra*, p. 19.

[3] Ibid., loc. cit.; *supra*, p. 20.

[4] S. K. Mitchell, *Studies in Taxation under John and Henry III*, p. 102, n. 43.

[5] *Book of Fees*, i. 52–5.

[6] See the accounts of the scutages of Biham, Montgomery, Bedford, and Kerry (Pipe Rolls, Nos. 65, 68, 73).

17 Henry III and 34 Henry III respectively.[1] It is significant, however, that in all these cases the figures which appear in the thirteenth century are those of the Henry II Pipe Rolls, and not of the scutage accounts of 1211.[2]

Notwithstanding the failure of John's policy, Henry III made definite attempts in 1235 and 1242 to revert to the principle of a general assessment. In the former year the aid to marry the king's sister Isabella was ordered to be levied not merely upon the number of fees for which the tenants-in-chief were accustomed to respond at the Exchequer, but upon all land held by military tenure, or, as the official phrase ran, 'tam de novo feoffamento quam de veteri'.[3] To ensure that no fees should escape taxation, the sheriffs were directed in May 1236 to report to the Exchequer the number of fees held in each vill by the lesser tenants by knight-service or by serjeanty, while the prelates and greater lay-vassals were to make similar returns of all their feoffments, with the vills in which they lay and the names of those who held them.[4] In spite of these precautions the sum realized did not meet the expectations of the Crown.[5] Many of the prelates holding by knight-service evaded the issue raised by the form of the grant by 'fining' for the aid in the same way as the non-military abbots.[6] Even in those cases where payment was made upon a feudal basis the 'unrecognized' fees were seldom included. The Abbot of Peterborough, though charged with 127 marks for 63½ fees paid only 120 for the 60 knights of his traditional *servicium*, declaring that the remaining

---

[1] *C.Ch.R.* i. 177; Pipe Roll, No. 78, Somers. and Dors.; *C.Ch.R.* ii. 143.

[2] The Bishop of Bath is assessed on 20 fees only (Pipe Roll, No. 65, Somers. and Dors.); the Bishop of Exeter on 15½+17½ (Pipe Roll, No. 68, Devon); the Abbess of Shaftesbury on 7+3¼, ⅙ (Pipe Roll, No. 65, Somers. and Dors.).

[3] Patent Rolls, 1234–1237, p. 189. The ecclesiastics were said to grant the aid 'de omnibus feodis suis, tam de illis de quibus nobis respondent quando scutagium detur, quam de illis que retinent ad opus suum' (Madox, *History and Antiquities of the Exchequer*, i. 607).   [4] *Book of Fees*, i. 574.

[5] That these were large is indicated by the statement of the Burton *Annales* (p. 364) that Stephen de Segrave estimated the old feoffment at 32,000 fees, 'et ad tantumdem plene et plane potuit novum scutagium de novis terris assumari et inrotulari' (Mitchell, *Taxation*, p. 211).

[6] See the 'Roll of the Aid of the Prelates', printed in the *Book of Fees*, i. 558 seq. About 17 bishops and abbots (military) paid fines. The accounts of the aid were not entered on the pipe roll. The surviving fragments of original accounts are printed in the *Book of Fees*, i. 417 seq.

7 were 'superdemanda'.[1] The attempt of the Crown to obtain detailed information as to the location of all fees, whensoever and howsoever created, was similarly frustrated by the passive resistance of the tenants-in-chief. The returns of only four prelates—the Prior of Coventry, the Abbots of Pershore and St. Edmund's, and the Bishop of Worcester—have survived; but they suffice to illustrate the opposition which the royal policy encountered. The bishop returned 49½ fees of the old feoffment, adding 'de novis enim respondere nescimus quia nulla habemus'. The Abbot of St. Edmund's duly returned 40 as of old and 12 as of new creation, but emphatically denied his obligation to respond for the latter, and disclaimed all knowledge of their whereabouts, declaring nonchalantly, 'In what vills they lie, or what and how many in each place, God knows; we do not!'[2]

Limited as was the success of the levy of 1235, a further attempt to tax all feoffments was made seven years later in connexion with Henry's great expedition to Gascony. On this occasion there seems little doubt but that the original intention of the Crown was to exact from all its tenants-in-chief either personal service or its pecuniary equivalent in the shape of a fine; while converting the scutage into a general tax payable as the composition for the service owed by their rear-vassals, and leviable directly by the sheriffs without the customary mediation of the mesne lords.[3] This distinctly revolutionary policy proved, however, impossible of execution. Tenants-in-chief who had served claimed the scutage of their under-tenants according to precedent;[4] while even those who had compounded for their service usually succeeded in obtaining writs authorizing them to collect and respond at the Exchequer for the scutage of their own fees, if not to retain it for their own use.[5] Although so far defeated, the Crown maintained its attempt to control the levy,

---

[1] *Book of Fees*, i, Aid of the Prelates, p. 565.   [2] Ibid. i. 584–5.

[3] This is suggested by the heading in the pipe roll: 'Fines militum ne transfretent cum rege in Wasconiam preter scutagia sua que regi sponte concesserunt ad istam transfretationem' (Pipe Roll, No. 86); and by the occasional application to the levy of the name 'auxilium' (ibid., No. 87; *Book of Fees*, ii. 639). For the method of collection see the writ to the sheriffs, 19 May 1242 (Close Rolls 1237–1242, p. 486).

[4] Scutage Roll, No. 6; *C.R.*, 1237–1242, pp. 488–93, 507, 508, 521–3.

[5] This is evident from numerous entries on the Close and Memoranda Rolls. See Mitchell, *Taxation*, p. 231, n. 37.

and to obtain information as to all feoffments. On 19 May 1242 the sheriffs were directed to return to the Exchequer particulars of all fees, whether of old or of new creation, held of the king's tenants-in-chief within their repective bailiwicks;[1] and in October they were further ordered to furnish details of the location of such fees ('in quibus villis et de cuius honore').[2] The results were evidently unsatisfactory, for in December fresh instructions were issued authorizing them to empanel juries, and with their assistance to ascertain and report the tenant, overlord and locality of every fee, and the honour of which it formed a part.[3] The opposition offered was still, however, so strong, that the Crown was eventually compelled to exempt from the inquiry the lands of all tenants who had secured a writ 'de scutagio habendo'.[4] The accounts of the proceeds of the scutage, which, as in 1235, were not entered upon the pipe roll, have not survived, so that it is difficult to form any exact estimate of the final results of the levy. As to the relation to it of the ecclesiastical tenants some general conclusions can, however, be drawn. The bishops evaded the issue by offering instead of scutage an aid at the rate of three marks upon the traditional *servicium* only.[5] Of the religious, many as in 1235 joined with the non-military abbots in offering *dona*; but it is not clear that on this occasion such payments were invariably accepted as covering their scutage. The Abbot of Hyde paid a fine of 50 marks, and in consideration thereof was pardoned the scutage upon his five non-infeudated fees, but was charged on the remaining fifteen.[6] Further, the episcopal and abbatial lands were not completely excluded from the scope of the vice-comital inquests; for the *Book of Fees* contains at least partial returns for some twelve bishops and twenty-one religions.[7] That the

---

[1] *C.R.*, 1237–1242, p. 486.

[2] Exch. L.T.R. Mem. Roll, No. 14, m. 3.

[3] Madox, *Exchequer*, i. 681; *Book of Fees*, ii. 638.

[4] Exch. L.T.R. Mem. Roll, No. 14, m. 5; Mitchell, *Taxation*, p. 234.

[5] Madox, *Exchequer*, i. 609, n. *c*; *C.R.*, 1237–1242, p. 487; Mitchell, *Taxation*, p. 236.

[6] *P.R.*, 1232–1247, p. 284; Madox, *Exchequer*, i. 609, n. d.

[7] *Book of Fees*, ii *passim*; e.g. the Archbishops of Canterbury and York; the Bishops of Durham, Lincoln, Chester, Worcester, Hereford, London, Salisbury, Winchester, Bath, and Exeter; the Abbots of Peterborough, Evesham, Pershore, Abingdon, Ramsey, St. Edmunds, St. Benet's, Hyde,

Crown was not permanently successful in changing the basis of assessment is, however, abundantly clear. When in 1245 the king demanded an aid for the marriage of his eldest daughter, the magnates were determined to safeguard themselves against a repetition of the policy of 1235 and 1242, and the grant was eventually made on the express condition that the tenants-in-chief should respond 'for those fees only which they held of the Crown, and from which they owed knight-service'.[1]

This was the end of the controversy under Henry III. For the rest of the reign payment was made upon the traditional number of fees. The Crown had failed once more to effect a permanent increase in the service recognized by its immediate vassals. Even the slight gain which it had obtained under Henry II from the increased recognitions of Chichester, York, St. Benet's, and Sherborne was later partially counterbalanced by losses in other directions. Attention has already been directed to the faulty assessment in 1168 of the Bishop of Exeter, and to the loss which this involved must be added the subsequent reduction of the Bishop of Worcester's *servicium* from 50 to $49\frac{1}{2}$ fees, and the complete disappearance from the later records of the abbey of Middleton, which responded under Henry II for two fees, but is entered in the inquest of 1212 as holding in free alms.[2] When, therefore, in the thirteenth century, the scutage accounts on the pipe roll become stereotyped, we find that the fees recognized by ecclesiastical tenants total only $751\frac{1}{2}$, $\frac{4}{5}$, as against the $741\frac{1}{2}$ recognized before 1166. The net result of the policy of Henry II had been to increase the clerical *servicia debita* by $10\frac{4}{5}$ fees.

The success of the Crown was, moreover, in practice still further limited. At the very time when the entries in the pipe roll were becoming fixed, they were ceasing to represent the actual military obligations of the tenants. In the course of the thirteenth century a distinction was gradually drawn between the number of fees recognized for financial purposes and the number recognized for military purposes. While the former

Glastonbury, Westminster, Tavistock, Michelney, Cerne, Abbotsbury, Sherborne, Shaftesbury, Malmesbury, Wilton, Chertsey, St. Augustine's, Canterbury; and the Prior of Coventry.

[1] Exch. L.T.R. Mem. Roll, 31 Henry III, cited by Madox, *Exchequer*, i. 593-4.   [2] *Book of Fees*, i. 90.

remained, as we have seen, roughly the same as at the end of the reign of Henry II, the latter dwindled to a mere fraction of its original strength. The insignificant increase in the total of fees upon which the feudal payments were assessed, was more than counterbalanced by a sweeping reduction in the amount of corporal service to which the Crown was entitled from its immediate tenants.

Various factors combined to produce this important modification of the conditions governing military tenure. The first was undoubtedly the increasing inability of the tenants-in-chief to exact personal service from their dependants. This was in part a consequence of the ruralization of the lesser tenants which followed rapidly upon the completion of the Conquest; in part an effect of subinfeudation and of the subdivision of knights' fees into minute aliquot parts, and of the simultaneous development of the practice of commutation. Already by the end of the twelfth century the sub-tenants, especially on the great ecclesiastical fiefs, were beginning to deny their liability to serve in person. Jocelin de Brakelond tells us that in 1198 the knights of St. Edmund's declared that they were not bound to perform corporal service outside England,[1] and the twelfth-century Evesham cartulary records a similar reluctance on the part of that abbey's tenants to discharge their obligations.[2] At the same time that this spirit of defiance was becoming apparent among the sub-tenants, the power of the seignorial courts was declining, so that it became increasingly difficult for the lords to compel obedience without recourse to the assistance of the Crown. An additional and most important factor contributing to the reduction of the quotas of the feudal tenants was the character of the campaigns in which they were expected to take part. After the accession of the Angevins the connexion of England with the Continent became even closer than before, and armies had constantly to be raised for service beyond the Channel. These continental campaigns not only involved a wearisome and expensive voyage, but were frequently of longer duration than was customary in feudal warfare. The forty days

[1] *Chronicon Jocelini de Brakelond* (Camden Society), p. 63.
[2] Evesham Cartulary, quoted by Wrottesley in his edition of the Burton Cartulary, Wm. Salt Collections, ii. 2.

rule which was common in the Edwardian period may not have
been universally applied in the twelfth and thirteenth centuries;
but it was certainly understood that the term of service exacted
should be reasonable. Hence the obvious expedient for the
king, when embarking on an unusually lengthy campaign, would
be to drive a bargain with his tenants whereby he accepted a
reduced contingent in return for prolonged service. Finally,
the enhanced cost in the thirteenth century of equipping and
maintaining a knight must be taken into account. The nature
of the change is indicated by the increase in the rate of pay
from the eightpence which appears to have been usual under
Henry II,[1] to two, three, or even four shillings *per diem* under
his immediate successors,[2] an increase which was probably due
in the main to the growing elaboration and costliness of equipment. Not only were the knights themselves much more
heavily armoured and armed, but the horses which they rode
were of a correspondingly massive and expensive type.[3]

In view of these various considerations it became impossible
for the Crown to insist on all occasions upon the production
by the tenant-in-chief of the full contingent which he had
recognized in the eleventh and early twelfth centuries. The
earliest concession to changing conditions seems to have been
the adoption of the principle of joint equipment. In 1157,
Henry II is said to have summoned one-third of the total
servicia debita of the country for a campaign against the Welsh,
'ita ut duo milites de tota Anglia tertium pararent'.[4] In 1191
William Longchamp appears to have acted on a similar plan,[5]
while three years later the same expedient was adopted by
Hubert Walter to provide an army for the war in Normandy.[6]
In 1195 each baron was instructed to cross to France with a few
picked men only, and in 1198 the whole body of tenants-in-
chief was invited to combine to furnish a contingent of three

---

[1] Round, *Feudal England*, pp. 271–2.

[2] In 1198 Abbot Samson of St. Edmunds hired knights for service in
Normandy at three shillings *per diem* (*Chronicon Jocelini de Brakelond*, p. 63).

[3] J. E. Morris, *Welsh Wars of Edward I*, p. 49.

[4] *Chronicon Roberti de Torigny*, R.S.; *Chronicles of the reigns of Stephen,
Henry II, and Richard I*, iv. 193.

[5] Round, *Feudal England* (citing Richard of Devizes), p. 409.

[6] *Chronicon Magistri Rogeri de Hovedene*, R.S., iii. 242: 'Deinde precepit
quod unusquisque faceret sibi tertiam partem servicii militaris.'

hundred knights. This latter project having failed, a tenth of
the entire feudal levy was later summoned for service in France [1]
—a precedent which was closely followed by John in 1205.[2]
During the succeeding century, what had been merely an occasional expedient, gradually became a regular practice. The so-
called 'Unknown Charter of Liberties' (discovered by Mr.
Round in 1893, and generally ascribed to the period immediately preceding the granting of the Great Charter) suggests
that there was already at the end of John's reign a definite
understanding that reduced service should be accepted from
the greater tenants-in-chief, at least for foreign campaigns.[3] In
clause VII of this interesting but enigmatic document the king
pledges himself to grant relief, by the advice of his barons, to
all owing a service of more than ten knights. Whether or not
the charter had any independent validity, the spirit of this
provision seems to have been respected, for there is ample
evidence that under Henry III the immediate vassals of the
Crown normally served with quotas which represented a mere
fraction of their nominal contingents, such service apparently
being accepted in full discharge of their obligations. Among the
ecclesiastics, we find the Bishop of London (nominal *servicium
debitum* 20) represented in 1218 by 7 knights, and in 1223 and
1265 by 6;[4] the Bishop of Salisbury (32) by 9 in 1210, and 5
in 1218, 1246, and 1265;[5] the Abbot of Abingdon (30) by 5 in
1218 and 1223, and 3 in 1265;[6] the Abbot of Peterborough (60)
by 30 in 1218, 6 in 1223, and 5 in 1246;[7] and the Abbot of

---

[1] *Chronicon Jocelini de Brakelond*, p. 63: 'Precepit rex Ricardus omnibus
episcopis et abbatibus Anglie, ut de suis baroniis novem milites fecerunt
decimum.'

[2] Stubbs, *Select Charters*, p. 281; Rotuli Litterarum Patentium, f. 55 a.

[3] *E.H.R.* viii. 288; ix. 119, 326; xx. 719; McKechnie, *Magna Carta*,
1913, p. 486, Clause VII: 'Adhuc hominibus meis concedo ne eant in exercitu extra Angliam nisi in Normanniam et in Britanniam et hoc decenter;
quod si aliquis debet inde servicium decem militum consilio baronum
meorum alleviabitur.' See, on the whole question of the *quota* under
Richard I and John, the *Cambridge Medieval History*, vi. 216 seq.

[4] Scutage Roll, No. 2, m. 22; No. 3, m. 1; Exch. L.T.R. Misc. Roll,
1/13, m. 13.

[5] Praestita Roll; Rotuli de Liberate, 172 seq.; Scutage Roll, No. 2, m. 22;
Chanc. Misc. 5/1; Exch. L.T.R. Misc. Roll, 1/13, m. 13.

[6] Scutage Roll, No. 2, m. 22; No. 3, m. 1; Exch. L.T.R. Misc. Roll,
1/13, m. 13.

[7] Scutage Roll, No. 2, m. 22; No. 3, m. 1; Chanc. Misc. 5/1.

Hyde (20) by 3 in 1218 and 1223.[1] There is no evidence that any formal reassessment was effected. Acceptance of a reduced contingent was at first, it would seem, an act of royal grace, and the size of the quota was determined by the royal will. Gradually, however, the Crown lost its option in the matter; and when, in the latter half of the thirteenth century, the series of Marshals' rolls begins, we find that the procedure has crystallized. The quotas have, in most cases, become fixed; and the reduced service has come to be all that is 'recognized' as due from their holdings by the greater tenants-in-chief.[2]

The appended tables, showing the fees recognized by the clerical tenants in the thirteenth and fourteenth centuries for (a) financial purposes and (b) military purposes, illustrate the way in which the interests of the Crown were affected by the changing conditions of service.

Bishops.	Fees recognized for financial purposes.	Fees recognized for military purposes.
Bath and Wells . . .	20	2
Canterbury[3] . . .	—	—
Chichester . . .	4	$2\frac{1}{2}$
Coventry and Lichfield .	15	2
Durham	10	10–9
Ely	40	6[4]
Exeter	$15\frac{1}{2}$	2
Hereford	15	5
Lincoln	60	5
London	20	5
Norwich	40	5
Salisbury	32	5[5]
Winchester . . .	60	5
Worcester . . .	$49\frac{1}{2}$	3
York	20	5

[1] Scutage Roll, No. 2, m. 22; No. 3, m. 1.

[2] See in particular the roll of service performed in Wales in 1246 (Chanc. Misc. 5/1), where the Bishop of Bath (20) provides 2 knights and 'recognizes' 2; the Bishop of Salisbury (32) furnishes 2 knights and 6 serjeants and 'recognizes' 5. The Abbots of Abingdon and Peterborough, however, though proffering only 4 and 5 knights respectively, still 'recognize' their old *servicium*. The list of fines paid in 49 Henry III (Exch. L.T.R. Misc. Roll, 1/13) shows the reduction a stage further advanced.

[3] No record of service or commutation for Canterbury exists after 1232, and the last occasion upon which the archbishop is notified as quit for service is in 1223.

[4] In 34 Edw. I the bishop served for 3 fees only, and in 16 Edw. II for 5.

[5] In 34 Edw. I Salisbury served for 3 fees; in 31 Edw. I for $4\frac{1}{2}$.

Abbots.	Fees recognized for financial purposes.	Fees recognized for military purposes.
Abbotsbury . . .	1	1
Abingdon	30	3
Cerne	2	1
Chertsey	3	3
Coventry	10	2
Evesham	4½	4½
Glastonbury . . .	40	3
Hyde	20	3
Malmesbury . . .	3	3
Michelney . . .	1	1
Pershore	2	2
Peterborough . . .	60	5
Ramsey	4	4
St. Albans	6	6
St. Augustine's . . .	15	1
St. Benet's . . .	3½, ⅗	2½
St. Edmunds . . .	40	6
Shaftesbury . . .	7	3
Sherborne	2⅗	2[1]
Tavistock	15	1
Westminster . . .	15	?[2]
Wilton	5	1
Winchcombe . . .	2	2

It is evident that the reduction in service was not based upon any uniform principle, although the greater tenants, on the whole, profited more than those whose obligations had from the first been small. The Bishop of Durham, and the Abbots of Abbotsbury, Chertsey, Evesham, Malmesbury, Michelney, Pershore, Ramsey, St. Albans, and Winchcombe, who all acknowledged originally a *servicium* of less than the minimum of ten specified in the 'unknown' charter, obtained no relief whatever. On the other hand, the quota of the Bishop of Worcester was reduced from 49½ knights to 3, that of the Abbot of Glastonbury from 40 knights to 3, that of the Bishop of Norwich from 40 to 5, and of the Abbot of Abingdon from 30 to 3. The Bishops of Lincoln and Winchester and the Abbot of Peterborough secured the reduction of their respective contingents from 60 to 5; the Bishop of Ely and the Abbot of St. Edmunds from 40 to 6. The

[1] In 4 Edw. II and 16 Edw. II Sherborne served with 1 knight only.
[2] There is no record of the performance of service by the Abbot of Westminster under Edward I or later.

F

loss sustained in consequence by the Crown becomes strikingly apparent when the total of fees recognized for military purposes in the fourteenth century is compared with the total recognized in the twelfth. The ecclesiastical tenants who, under Henry II, had furnished some 750 knights for the royal armies, now furnished a maximum of 121½, or less than one-sixth of their old *servicium*.

To sum up: we have seen that the military obligations of the great churchmen were, in the first instance, arbitrarily fixed by the Conqueror in or about 1070. In 1168 Henry II endeavoured, with very limited success, to increase them, by placing under contribution all fees created in excess of the old *servicium debitum*; and his policy was ineffectually revived by John and Henry III. Simultaneously, however, a distinction was being gradually drawn between the fees recognized for financial purposes and those recognized for military purposes. Although the number charged on the pipe roll with scutage or aid remained unchanged, the Crown was compelled to acquiesce in a drastic reduction of the number for which service was rendered in the feudal host; and by the end of the reign of Henry III, the tenants-in-chief had come to regard this new *servicium* as all that could properly be demanded from them. Since their obligations towards the king were now normally discharged by the proffer of either the accepted quota of corporal service, or its money equivalent in the shape of a fine, scutage was relegated to a purely secondary position as the commutation of the service of the under-tenants. The result was to provoke the Crown to a renewed effort to establish its claim to the profits of all feoff-ments. In 1242 Henry III had obtained a special grant of the scutage of the under-tenants in addition to the service or fine exacted from their lords. His failure to make the grant effective did not, as we shall see, deter Edward I from reviving the ex-periment, on his own initiative, in 1279. Rejecting the con-tention of the tenants-in-chief that service with a reduced con-tingent covered all their liabilities, he demanded from them, further, payment of scutage upon all the remaining fees of their traditional *servicia debita*. The policy thus initiated was main-tained by him and his two successors, in the teeth of the baronial opposition, for more than half a century, and culminated in an attempt to circumvent the resistance of the tenants-in-chief by collecting from the under-tenants direct.[1]

Beneath the many variations of the royal policy between 1168 and 1340 it is possible, therefore, to distinguish a single unifying principle. Throughout the period the constant preoccupation of the Crown was to enforce the doctrine inherent in Anglo-Norman feudalism that all *servicium militare* is *servicium regale*, and to insist, as the Conqueror had done at the famous gathering on Salisbury Plain, upon the reality of the bond between itself and the occupants of the lower rungs of the feudal ladder. The motive underlying its endeavour varied from time to time, becoming, as the military importance of feudalism declined, more and more frankly mercenary, but the justificative theory remained the same. The uncompromising opposition of the feudal tenantry, however, reinforced by the disintegrating effects of continual subinfeudation and the subdivision of fees, made the ultimate defeat of the Crown inevitable. In the twelfth and thirteenth centuries the tenants-in-chief successfully upheld their claim to act as intermediaries between their under-tenants and the king, and to enjoy the profits of the surplus feoffments on their lands. Later, their triumph was to be carried still further. At the very time when the Crown was strenuously asserting its right to scutage on the old *servicium* as well as to fine or service on the new, the opposing principle was making irresistible headway. The end of the thirteenth and the beginning of the fourteenth century, saw the old service superseded in many cases by the new for fiscal as well as for military purposes. In 1284–5 'Kirkby's Quest' was held 'ut sciatur ubi distringendum sit pro servicio Regis si a retro fuerit',[2] and several of the greater tenants, both lay and ecclesiastical, secured the return of the reduced *servicium* as all that was due from their fiefs. The Bishop of Coventry and Lichfield,[3] and the Bishop of Bath and Wells,[4] for instance, claimed to hold their entire baronies by the service of two knights only; the Bishop of Salisbury by five;[5] the Abbot of Glastonbury by three;[6] and

---

[1] *Infra*, Chap. II.
[2] *Inquisitions and Assessments relating to Feudal Aids*, vol. i, pp. viii seq.
[3] Ibid. v, Stafford, p. 7.   [4] Ibid. iv, Somerset, p. 276.
[5] Ibid. ii, Dorset, p. 4.   [6] Ibid. iv, Somerset, pp. 290, 295, &c.

the Abbess of Shaftesbury by $2\frac{1}{2}$:[1] and in 1303, when the aid
to marry the king's daughter Eleanor was assessed, they paid
upon this basis. The Abbot of Glastonbury responded in
Somerset for three 'pro se et tenentibus ubique';[2] the Abbess
of Shaftesbury in Dorset for the same number, 'quia tenet pro
iij feodis totum quod tenet';[3] while the Bishops of Norwich,[4]
London,[5] and Winchester[6] were charged respectively on five
fees 'pro tota baronia'. Forty-three years later, on the occasion
of the aid to knight the Black Prince, the Bishop of Hereford
successfully claimed to hold all the lands belonging to his
barony by the service of five knights only,[7] and a similar plea
was advanced by the Abbot of Peterborough,[8] in spite of the fact
that the levy was nominally upon fees held 'as well of us as of
others'. By the beginning of the fifteenth century the process
of the reduction of the *servicia debita* had reached completion;
and its consequences are fully apparent in the various levies
upon knights' fees which were imposed during the Lancastrian
period. The aid raised by Henry IV in 1401 for the marriage
of his daughter Blanche was assessed, under the statute of
25 Edward III,[9] upon the socage as well as the military tenants
of the Crown; yet it has been estimated that the yield from
about thirty English counties was rather less than £1,100.[10] A
comparison of this total with the £6,000 odd which, according
to Dr. Mitchell's calculation, had been charged upon the fees
of the old *servicium* for the aid to marry Henry III's eldest
daughter in 1245[11] affords some measure of the loss sustained
by the Crown in the course of the preceding century and a half.

[1] *Feudal Aids*, ii, Dorset, p. 1.   [2] Ibid. ii, Dorset, p. 30.
[3] Ibid. ii, Dorset, p. 30.   [4] Ibid. iii, Norfolk, p. 417.
[5] Ibid. ii, Essex, pp. 133 seq.   [6] Ibid. iv, Somerset, p. 298 n.
[7] *Register of John de Trellek*, pp. 232, 331 (Cant. and York Soc.).
[8] MSS. of the Society of Antiquaries, MS. xxxviii, ff. 148 seq.
[9] *Statutes of the Realm*, i. 322, 25 Edw. III, Stat. 5, c. 11.
[10] J. Ramsey, *Lancaster and York*, i. 152.
[11] Mitchell, *Taxation*, p. 243.

CHAPTER II

THE CLERICAL TENANTS-IN-CHIEF BY KNIGHT-SERVICE, AND THE PRINCIPLE OF COMMUTATION

FROM our examination of the military obligations of the ecclesiastical tenants *in capite* we must pass to consider the methods whereby those obligations were discharged.

According to the strict letter of the feudal law, the king was entitled to the corporal service of all his immediate vassals, and probably during the early Norman period at least, such service was on the whole regularly and willingly performed. It is, however, impossible to doubt that the practice of commutation early invaded the feudal military sphere, and that payment of scutage became, at the option of the Crown, an alternative to personal attendance with the host.

That same passion for continuity which inspired the attempts to trace the origin of knight-service to the Anglo-Saxon five-hide system, led historians such as Stubbs to connect the scutage with the *fyrdwite* as exemplified in Domesday Book. The Worcestershire custom whereby the man who neglected the summons to the fyrd must pay to his lord forty shillings, which the lord must either employ in hiring a substitute or must render to the king,[1] bears, it is true, certain superficial resemblances to the later levy; but the underlying principle is, as Baldwin points out, essentially different. The *fyrdwite* was in the nature of a fine for default of service, while the scutage was merely the agreed commutation of service, assessed as a general levy under royal supervision and at a uniform rate per knight. Its origin is to be sought not in any pre-existing institution, but in the general tendency of the times to express services of all kinds in terms of money; and more particularly in the growing reluctance of the tenants, mediate and immediate, to perform the corporal service for which they were liable.[2]

No detailed evidence with regard to the scutage is available

[1] Maitland, *Domesday Book and Beyond*, p. 159.
[2] J. F. Baldwin, *The Scutage and Knight Service in England*, pp. 4 seq.

before the reign of Henry II, when the continuous series of pipe rolls begins; but the scattered references which occur in the single extant pipe roll of Henry I, and in letters and charters of the Norman period, suffice to demonstrate beyond reasonable doubt, the antiquity of the institution. Not only is mention of payments 'pro militibus', or 'de auxilio militum', which seem to be synonymous with scutage, fairly common under Henry I and Stephen; [1] but scutage appears *eo nomine* in a number of contemporary documents.[2] The most convincing proof is, however, afforded by a charter of Henry I (A.D. 1127?) to the church of Ely, relieving it of £40 of the £100 'quas predicta ecclesia solebat dare de scutagio quando scutagium currebat per terram meam Anglie'; [3] and a confirmation by Gilbert, Earl of Pembroke (d. 1149), of land at Parndon, Essex, to the church of St. Mary of Southwark 'liberam ab omni servicio excepto scutagio quod quando evenerit unum militem dare xx solidos tunc illa det ii solidos. Si miles unus j marcam illa xvi denarios'.[4] Here we see the method of assessment by knights' fees already in full operation.

It is an interesting fact that scutage, when it first appears, seems to be restricted in its application to the lands of the Church. Henry I certainly exacted it from his ecclesiastical tenants-in-chief, for, in addition to the evidence given above, there is extant a letter of Bishop Herbert Losinga of Norwich (d. 1119) to the Justiciar Roger of Salisbury, in which he alludes to the sum of £60 charged upon him 'pro militibus'.[5] The first scutage of which a detailed account has survived—that imposed by Henry II in 1165 for the campaign against his brother Geoffrey in Anjou—was also assessed exclusively upon clerical fees.[6] This coincidence Round was inclined to ascribe to the existence of a peculiar clerical privilege. He hazarded the suggestion that the clergy were bound to serve only for defence, not defiance; and that herein was to be found 'the perfect

---

[1] Round, *Feudal England*, pp. 268 seq.; *Studies on the Red Book of the Exchequer*, pp. 5 seq.

[2] Round, loc. cit.; A. W. Morris, *E.H.R.* xxxvi, pp. 45 seq. A Mention of Scutage in the Year 1100.

[3] *Liber Eliensis*, III, No. XXI, quoted by Round, loc. cit.

[4] Cottonian MSS. Nero, C. iii, p. 228, quoted by Round, *Red Book*, pp. 8–9.   [5] Round, *Feudal England*, p. 270.   [6] *Red Book*, i. 13 seq.

explanation of the fact that scutage, as commutation for service, is an institution, when it first appears, peculiar to church fiefs'.[1]

He based his argument mainly upon the famous Oxford debate on foreign service. In April 1196 Richard I directed the Justiciar, Hubert Walter, to muster a force for the approaching war with Philip Augustus of France. The lay barons were to cross the Channel attended by not more than seven knights each, so that they might serve for a proportionately long period; the ecclesiastics were merely to furnish such aid 'in militibus' as should earn them the royal commendation and gratitude.[2] No immediate action appears to have been taken on these instructions, but in the great council held in December of the following year, the archbishop submitted to the baronage a modification of the original scheme. He proposed that they should combine to provide the king with either a body of three hundred knights to serve in Normandy for a year, or the money equivalent. The demand was vehemently opposed by Bishop Hugh of Lincoln, who, taking his stand upon the prescriptive rights of his church, denied his obligation to serve the king 'extra metas anglie'. His lead was followed by Herbert of Salisbury, and according to St. Hugh's biographer, the project had to be abandoned.[3] A subsequent attempt to raise the necessary force on the principle of joint equipment, met with opposition on similar grounds. In 1198 the knights of St. Edmund's, when called upon to furnish a tenth of their *servicium debitum* for the war in Normandy, declared that they owed no personal service overseas, although they acknowledged their liability for scutage.[4]

The fact that exemption from foreign service was thus simultaneously alleged by three of the great clerical tenants lends a certain plausibility to Round's theory; but it cannot of itself be accepted as conclusive evidence, especially when it is remembered that in 1213 similar allegations were made by the lay baronage without a shadow of historical justification.[5] To any

---

[1] *Feudal England*, pp. 528 seq.

[2] Stubbs, Preface to the *Opera Historica of Ralph de Diceto*, vol. ii, pp. lxxx, lxxxi; quoted by F. M. Powicke, *Loss of Normandy*, p. 315.

[3] *Magna Vita Sancti Hugonis*, R.S., pp. 249–50.

[4] *Chronicon Jocelini de Brakelond*, p. 63.

[5] Ralph of Coggeshall, *Chronicon Anglicanum*, R.S., p. 167; *Historical Collections of Walter of Coventry*, R.S., ii. 217–18.

adequate treatment of the problem an examination of the following questions is essential:

(i) How far are the claims put forward in 1197–8 substantiated by earlier evidence?

(ii) How far were they recognized by Richard I, and in subsequent practice?

The first question is the more important, since in regard to the second it might be argued that Richard effected an innovation in procedure. If Round's inference is correct as regards the twelfth century, one would expect, in the first place, a levy of scutage, at least upon the church fiefs, in connexion with every foreign campaign, and, in the second place, a general contribution by all the clerical tenants on every such occasion. Unfortunately the information available on these points is, at this date, extremely scanty. No record remains either of the feudal summonses, or of the composition of the feudal host. The scutage accounts, which from 1156 onwards are regularly enrolled on the pipe roll, supply the only documentary evidence. They furnish details of levies for French expeditions in 1156, 1159, 1161, and 1162 under Henry II, and in 1196 and 1197 under Richard I, for the war in Ireland in 1172, and for an army of Scotland in 1187; as well as for Welsh campaigns in 1165 and 1189.

An analysis of the accounts in these years gives the following results:

Date.	BISHOPS *contributing* (*out of a total of fifteen*).	RELIGIOUS *contributing* (*out of a total of twenty-four*).
1156	12	21
1159	11	18
1161	10	22
1162	11	18
1165[1]	11	14
1172	15	21
1187	13	23
1189	13	15
1196	13	23
1197	13	22

[1] In this campaign many tenants paid, instead of scutage, a sum 'de exercitu' or 'de servientibus' for the provision of an arbitrarily fixed contingent of *servientes* for service in Wales (Round, *Feudal England*, pp. 282–3). I have included these payments in the totals entered above.

These statistics, while definitely establishing the liability of the clerical tenants for scutage in connexion with foreign campaigns, are inconclusive as regards their liability to corporal service. On the one hand, it is not clear that a scutage was levied for every expedition; on the other, the absence of complementary records makes it unsafe to assume either that payment of scutage necessarily entailed, at this period, exemption from service; or alternatively, that exemption from scutage was invariably a result of the performance of service. The omissions which occur in the scutage lists may be due to vacancies,[1] to royal pardons, to special privileges such as exempted the Exchequer officials from contribution,[2] or even to scribal errors or defective accounting.[3] All that the evidence of the pipe rolls entitles us to say is that, under Henry II and Richard I, it was usual for the ecclesiastics to compound for their foreign service when given the opportunity to do so. It does not justify the assumption that no such service was owed. In two instances, indeed, there is independent evidence showing that the reverse was the case. In the cartulary of Ramsey Abbey is preserved a charter of enfeoffment of Abbot Aldwin (?) (1091–1100), granting land in Dillington and Stow to Ranulph, brother of Ilger the king's *dapifer*, in return for the service of one knight 'in Anglia et extra Angliam';[4] while the Abingdon History records a grant by Abbot Faritius (1100–35) of land in Weston to Robert Mauduit for the service of half a knight 'in expedicione ultra et citra mare'.[5]

As far as Wales and Scotland were concerned, there was obviously no remission of military obligations, nor does any attempt seem to have been made to claim it. The number of clerical tenants contributing to the Welsh scutages of 1165 and 1189 was conspicuously small, and there is direct proof that in the former year the Abbot of Abingdon rendered at least partial

[1] e.g. Canterbury was in hand 1161–2; Coventry and Lichfield 1159–61; Ely 1191–7, in the absence of William Longchamp.

[2] In 1156–65, for example, Ely paid no scutage during the treasurership of Bishop Nigel. See *Dialogus de Scaccario*, II, viii and xi.

[3] No scutage account appears for Norfolk and Suffolk in 1156; for Worcester in 1165; for Dorset and Somerset in 1189.

[4] *Ramsey Cartulary*, ii. 259.

[5] *Historia Monasterii de Abingdon*, R.S., ii. 135.

service. In the Norman period the clergy were frequently summoned to serve in Welsh and Scottish campaigns. In 1072, as
we have already seen,[1] the Conqueror called upon all the bishops
and abbots to send their due quotas for service against Malcolm
of Scotland, and later he called them out against the Welsh;[2]
while we know that under Rufus, Archbishop Anselm had his
knights with the king in the Welsh war of 1097.[3]

An examination of the existing data for the twelfth century
does not, therefore, establish the validity of the claims advanced
in the great council of 1197. It remains to see how they were
received by the Crown, and to what extent they were recognized
in subsequent practice.

It has been argued that the phraseology of Richard's letter
in 1195 implies that a distinction was admitted between the
obligations of the lay and the ecclesiastical tenants.[4] Be that
as it may, the opposition to the proposals of 1197–8 called forth
the immediate vengeance of the king; and it is significant that
the penalties imposed were the recognized penalties for default
of service. Richard ordered the seizure of the temporalities of
the recalcitrant bishops of Lincoln and Salisbury. In the latter
instance the royal commands were fully executed. Bishop
Herbert had to cross to Normandy in person to sue for pardon;
and was only restored to his estates 'post injurias, damna, atque
vexationes, et plurimas contumelias', and upon payment of a
heavy fine. St. Hugh, if we are to believe his biographer, was
more fortunate. Such was the reverence for his name and the
dread of his anathema, that the royal officers dared not enter
his lands. Eventually, however, he too found it expedient to
seek a reconciliation with the king, who was only induced to
swallow his wrath and bestow the kiss of peace after the administration of a vigorous shaking by the intrepid bishop![5]

In the case of the Abbot of St. Edmunds in 1198, the victory
of the Crown was complete. Faced by the refusal of his tenants
to serve, and fearful of losing his lands, Abbot Samson sought

---

[1] *Historia Monasterii de Abingdon*, R.S., ii. 9; *supra*, p. 3.
[2] Ibid., loc. cit.: 'Iterum ad Walos exercitus dirigitur. Quo etiam milites
hujus paene omnes ecclesiae proficisci jubentur, abbate domi remanente.'
[3] Eadmer, *Historia Novorum in Anglia*, R.S., p. 37.
[4] Powicke, *Loss of Normandy*, p. 315.
[5] *Magna Vita Sancti Hugonis*, pp. 250 seq.

out Richard in person, and offered to compound for the four knights due from his barony. The king insisted that he wanted men, not money, and the abbot was finally compelled to hire knights and give them enough to cover their expenses during the customary forty days' service. Subsequently, being warned by certain of the king's familiars that the campaign was likely to be of long duration, he paid £100 to be released from all further responsibility in the matter. In return he received a royal writ of aid for the distraint of his tenants, who, however, voluntarily contributed at the rate of two marks the fee to the expenses of the campaign.[1]

Clearly, therefore, the claim of the clergy to immunity from service outside England was not established in 1197. In the foreign campaigns of John's reign no distinction seems to have been made between lay and clerical fees. In 1199 the Abbot of Ramsey, and the Bishops of Winchester and London had knights with the king in Normandy, although the two former were also charged with scutage.[2] In 1194 the practice had been adopted of adding to the scutage account in the pipe roll a list of tenants quit 'per breve regis'. Under John the Archbishop of Canterbury was so enrolled (presumably for service rendered) for the Norman campaigns of 1201, 1202, 1203, and 1204; the Bishop of Durham for 1201, 1202, 1203, 1204, and 1206, and the Bishop of Ely for 1199, 1201, 1202, 1203, 1204, and 1206, and for the Poitevin or Gascon expedition of 1205. William Ste. Mère Eglise of London was quit in 1201, 1202, 1203, 1204, 1205, and 1206, and John de Gray of Norwich in 1202, 1203, 1204, 1205, and 1206. Even for the army of Poitou of 1214, which occasioned so much opposition and controversy, two bishops—Winchester [3] and Worcester—had writs of quittance.

True, the fact that the 'unknown' charter contains a clause releasing the king's tenants from the duty of serving overseas except in Normandy or Brittany,[4] suggests that a desire to limit if not to abolish the obligation to foreign service was general at

---

[1] *Chronicon Jocelini de Brakelond*, p. 63.

[2] *Rotuli Curiae Regis*, ed. Palgrave, ii. 122, 67, 7.

[3] Peter des Roches had knights in the army of 1209 also. It cost the manor of Harwell 11s. 9d. to entertain them on their return from Scotland. H. Hall, *Pipe Roll of the Bishopric of Winchester, 1208–1209*, p. 15, l. 44.

[4] *Supra*, p. 31, n. 3.

the end of John's reign; while under Henry III there are signs of a concerted attempt on the part of the clergy to revive the claims advanced in 1197–8. Expeditions were made to France in 1229, 1230, and 1242, and the relation of the ecclesiastical tenants to all three was peculiar. For the first—the army of Brittany—a scutage was put in charge in a council of the lay baronage held at Northampton in July 1229, before the expedition sailed. All the religious compounded for their service; but the bishops, who had not been present at Northampton, assembled separately at London in October, and granted the king an aid at the rate of three marks the fee, with the proviso that the grant should not be understood to be made in respect of the summons of their contingents for service in France.[1] Letters patent were subsequently issued by the king, acknowledging the aid and providing that by reason thereof neither his own right nor that of the bishops should be increased or diminished.[2] In the following year a further scutage was voted by the lay magnates present with the host in Poitou, and on this occasion the clergy as a whole refused to contribute, declaring by the mouth of the Archbishop of Canterbury at the council held at Westminster in January 1231, 'quod non tenentur viri ecclesiastici judicio subjici laicorum'.[3] Eventually, adopting the precedent of 1229, they granted the king, 'of their mere liberality and for no other reason', an aid at the rate of 40 shillings upon the fees for which they were bound to render military service. As before, the king issued letters patent, declaring that the grant should not constitute a precedent, nor prejudice in any way the liberties of the Church or his own right.[4] In 1242, for the great army of Gascony, the bishops again made a separate agreement with the Crown. Instead of paying scutage they undertook to make the king an aid on lines similar to those followed in 1231.[5] In this agreement the religious apparently did not participate. As in 1229 they were grouped with the lay tenants and were called upon to serve in money or in men. The Abbot of Ramsey proposed to send his due quota to France, and four knights were elected for the purpose

---

[1] Madox, *History of the Exchequer*, i. 607.   [2] Ibid., loc. cit.
[3] *Chronica Rogeri de Wendover*, R.S., iv. 218, 219.
[4] *P.R.*, 1225–1232, p. 429.   [5] Madox, i. 609.

in the court of Broughton, although three of them denied their liability, and had subsequently to be impleaded in the king's court.[1]

The action of the bishops on these three occasions in substituting an aid for the scutage properly due, seems to involve a denial of the right of the Crown to their military service, at all events in France. Such was not, however, necessarily its motive. The fact that, contrary to the principle generally recognized since 1215, the clergy had not participated in the actual grant, would afford an equally valid explanation of their refusal of scutage in 1229 and 1230; while in 1242 they may have been actuated merely by the desire to avoid the reopening of the old controversy as to the right of the king to the profits of their surplus feoffments. In any case, it is clear that they did not succeed in inducing the Crown definitely to abandon any of its claims upon them. Henry III, as already noted, was careful to safeguard the royal rights; and when in 1294 and 1297 Edward I summoned the host for service in Gascony, there was apparently no opposition from the clergy. In 1294 both bishops and abbots compounded for their service;[2] and the Abbot of Ramsey, faced by the renewed refusal of his tenants to serve, sent to the muster six serjeants and one knight at his own expense.[3] Under Edward II the payments made in connexion with this campaign were remitted, but on the technical ground of the king's absence from the host, and not of any clerical privilege.[4] The same principle of feudal law was later alleged by the Earls of Hereford and Norfolk to justify their refusal to perform service in Gascony in 1297.[5]

Summing up, therefore, we find that there is no evidence which compels us to believe that the clergy were at any time exempt from the duty of furnishing corporal service overseas. Claims to that effect were, it is true, periodically advanced, but they seem to have had no basis in fact, and were never admitted by the Crown. Foreign campaigns, by reason of the long and

---

[1] *Ramsey Cartulary*, iii. 50.

[2] *Parl. Writs*, i. 391; Exch. L.T.R. Mem. Roll, Brevia Retornabilia Easter, m. 79 d.

[3] *Select Pleas in Manorial Courts*, ed. F. W. Maitland, pp. 76 seq.

[4] Exch. L.T.R. Mem. Roll, No. 82, Brevia Baronibus Mich., m. 1, *et passim*.   [5] *Infra*, pp. 100–101.

perilous journey, and the heavy expense involved, were unpopular alike with lay and clerical tenants, and all were ready
to avail themselves of any pretext to be rid of the unwelcome
burden. In practice commutation was usually allowed, and was
very generally adopted by the ecclesiastics; but that the obligation to provide corporal service remained unimpaired thereby
is proved by the case of the Abbot of Ramsey, and of the bishops
in the reign of John. It seems clear, therefore, that the limitation
of the incidence of the early scutages to the church fees was
due, not, as Round suggested, to any peculiar clerical privilege,
but merely to the difficulty experienced by the Crown, from an
early date, in securing from its ecclesiastical tenants the corporal
service to which it was entitled.

A further problem of incidence, upon which a study of the
ecclesiastical tenures-in-chief throws some light, is that of the
relation of the scutage to the fines *pro servicio* which began to
be levied towards the end of the twelfth century, and continued
with some gaps and occasional modifications of form until the
final decay of the feudal military organization. These payments,
which consisted usually of lump sums larger than and inclusive
of the scutage, but sometimes of smaller amounts paid in
addition to the scutage, first appear in the pipe rolls of the reign
of Richard I. It seems probable, however, that similar exactions
had already been made in connexion with some of the later
campaigns of Henry II, and, in particular, with the army of
Ireland of 1172.[1] This new method of commutation did not
supersede the old, but was maintained side by side with it.
Every year some tenants fined while others paid scutage; the
same tenant might fine in one year and pay scutage in the next.
For instance, in 1197—the first year in which the clergy are
found compounding for their service on the new principle—two
bishops and seven abbots paid fines while the rest paid scutage;
in 1201 one bishop and thirteen religious fined, and in 1203 one
bishop and seventeen religious.[2] The alternations of the two

[1] See the heading in the pipe roll for this year: 'De scutagio militum
[or baronum] qui nec abierunt in Hyberniam nec milites nec denarios
miserunt.'

[2] The Bishops of Coventry and Lichfield and of Hereford; the Abbots of
Abingdon, Chertsey, Evesham, Hyde, Pershore, Westminster; the Prior of
Coventry, 1197 (Pipe Roll, No. 48). The Bishop of Winchester; the Abbots

forms of composition in the case of individuals is illustrated by the Abbot of Westminster, who fined in 1197 and 1201, and paid scutage in 1202, 1203, 1204, and 1205; and the Abbot of St. Albans, who fined in 1199, 1201, 1203, and 1204, and paid scutage on the remaining occasions.[1]

The fact that the fine and the scutage have thus a parallel history has given rise to the idea that there was from the first a difference of principle between them. Maitland was of opinion that scutage represented the commutation of the service of the under-tenants only, and that a fine was necessary to absolve the tenants-in-chief from the duty of personal attendance with the host.[2] This theory is obviously inapplicable in the case of the clergy, from whom personal participation in warfare could not properly be demanded at all. An alternative suggestion, which is not open to the same objection, is that only by a fine could exemption for the whole tenement be purchased, the payment of scutage being necessarily accompanied by the proffer of at least partial service. The evidence in support of this view is, however, quite inadequate. It is true that there are isolated instances, particularly in the reign of John, of the exaction of scutage from tenants who can be proved to have had knights in the field;[3] but they are merely the exceptions that prove the rule. The thirteenth century, it must be remembered, saw the accomplishment of that sweeping reduction of the *servicia debita* of the greater tenants-in-chief to which reference has already been made; and, as a result, a mere fraction of the nominal contingent of any immediate vassal of the Crown was normally accepted as covering the obligations of both tenant and tenement. Such fractional service purchased for the lord

---

of Abbotsbury, Cerne, Chertsey, Hyde, Malmesbury, Peterborough, St.Albans, St.Augustine's, Shaftesbury, Sherborne, Tavistock, Westminster, Winchcombe, 1201 (Pipe Roll, No. 47). The Bishop of Worcester; the Abbots of Abbotsbury, Abingdon, Cerne, Chertsey, Evesham, Hyde, Malmesbury, Michelney, Pershore, Ramsey, St. Albans, St. Benet's, St. Edmunds, Shaftesbury, Sherborne, Tavistock, Winchcombe, 1203 (Pipe Roll, No. 49).

[1] The Abbot of Westminster (Pipe Rolls, Nos. 43, 47, 48, 49, 50, 51, Worcester). The Abbot of St. Albans (Pipe Rolls, Nos. 45, 47, 49, 50, Essex and Hertford).

[2] Maitland, in Pollock and Maitland, *History of English Law*, i. 269.

[3] e.g. the Abbot of Ramsey and the Bishop of Winchester in 1199 (*supra*, p. 43, n. 2).

not only exemption from payment of scutage into the royal
Exchequer but a writ *de scutagio habendo*, entitling him to
collect for his own use from his under-tenants. In 1224, for
example, the Bishop of Exeter (traditional service 15½ fees)
proffered 5½ knights, and the Abbot of Malmesbury (3 fees)
proffered 1; both were entered on the pipe roll as quit, and each
received a writ of scutage.[1] In 1246 the Bishop of Bath (20
knights) served by 2, the Bishop of Salisbury (32) and the
Abbot of Peterborough (60) by 5, and the Abbot of Abingdon
(30) by 4. All were acquitted as regards the Crown, and had
their writs *de scutagio habendo*.[2]

There remains the thesis, sponsored by Professor Powicke,[3]
that the fine was in fact the special composition exacted for
this same fractional service. On this hypothesis, the burden
of foreign campaigning having been lightened for the baronage
by the adoption of the principle of joint equipment or of the
quota, any tenant who still sought exemption from corporal
service was required to purchase it on the king's own terms,
and not by the traditional method of scutage. The fact that the
appearance of the fines *pro servicio* synchronized with the
institution of the *quota* system, and that they were later so
intimately associated with the new reduced service, lends at
first sight some colour to Mr. Powicke's argument. The
difficulty of reconciling the facts with the theory becomes
immediately apparent, however, when the documentary evidence is examined. If the fine represented the fractional and
the scutage the traditional *servicium*, how are we to account for
the alternations of the two forms of payment which, as we have
seen, occur not only on the same fiefs in different years, but on
different fiefs in the same year? How is it that the Abbots of
Ramsey or St. Albans, who obtained no remission of service,
are often found paying fines in the thirteenth century, while
the Abbot of Peterborough, or the Bishops of London or Hereford, as often escaped on payment of scutage only? Mr. Powicke
contends that, whatever confusion may have arisen in later
reigns, the fine and scutage were clearly distinguished under

[1] Mitchell, *Taxation*, pp. 149 seq.
[2] Ibid., pp. 246 seq.; Chanc. Misc. 5/1; Scutage Roll, No. 7.
[3] In his review of Dr. Mitchell's book, *E.H.R.* xxx, pp. 530 seq.

Richard I; but his contention seems hardly to be supported by the evidence of the pipe rolls, which show us, as early as 1197, both forms of commutation being indiscriminately exacted from the clerical tenants-in-chief.[1] A close study of the records drives us, in fact, to conclude with Mr. Mitchell that the difference between the fine and the scutage was originally one of form rather than of principle.[2] The institution of the fine meant, in practice if not in theory, simply the addition of a further alternative to those already open to the tenant-in-chief. Hitherto he had, at the option of the Crown, discharged his obligations by either (1) the performance of his due service, or (2) the payment of scutage. Henceforward he might be required to do so in any one of three ways: by the proffer of either (1) service, or (2) scutage, assessed according to tradition upon the fees of his *servicium debitum*, or by (3) a fine, arrived at by direct bargaining with the king or his officials. Whether, if he compounded for his service, he obtained acquittance on payment of scutage or of a fine, would depend, presumably, on the understanding he succeeded in reaching with the Crown. The king was clearly entitled to the corporal service of his tenants-*in-capite* according to the conditions of their tenure, and his right to fix the terms upon which remission of that service should be granted was equally indisputable. The increase in the cost of equipping and maintaining a knight from eightpence a day under Henry II to one, two, or three shillings under Richard I,[3] justified him, moreover, in obtaining when he could a more exact equivalent for the loss of the men due to him than was afforded by a scutage at two marks or forty shillings the fee. That fining was never popular with the feudal tenantry is suggested by the fact that towards the end of John's reign, when the constitutional struggle was approaching its crisis, and again during the minority of Henry III when the barons themselves controlled the government, the practice was largely, if not entirely, discontinued. Nevertheless, even from the baronial

---

[1] Ibid., loc. cit.; *supra*, p. 46, n. 2.

[2] Mitchell, loc. cit., pp. 323, 326, *et passim.*

[3] In 1199 knights serving in Devonshire castles received one shilling *per diem* (Pipe Roll, No. 45, m. 17 d). In 1198 Abbot Samson of St. Edmund's paid his knights at the rate of three shillings the day (*Chron. Jocelini de Brakelond*, p. 63).

standpoint, the system had its advantages. The fine—which was usually assessed at the opening of the campaign, whereas scutage was seldom put in charge before its close—absolved the tenant completely from his obligations to his overlord in respect of the army concerned. It enabled him to remain at home without fear of molestation in the form of distraint for service or disseisin for default, and, further, relieved him of all the inconveniences attendant upon the assessment and collection of scutage for the use of the Crown. It must be remembered that the expedient of fining was by no means confined at this date to the military sphere. Liabilities incurred in respect of royal aids and many other forms of exaction, were frequently covered by payments of a similar nature, to the profit of both the parties to the transaction.[1]

On the whole, the persistence of the fine seems less difficult to account for than the survival side by side with it of the scutage. The considerations which induced the occasional acceptance by the king of the traditional form of composition must, in the absence of documentary evidence, remain a matter for speculation rather than for research. The suggestion may be hazarded, however, that as time went on the element of chance became increasingly important. One suspects that the purpose served, in the thirteenth century, by a levy of scutage, as between the king and his immediate vassals, was often simply to bring under contribution tenants who had neglected to answer the royal summons, and who, having omitted to offer either service or a fine at the opening of the campaign, were unable to produce a writ of quittance at its conclusion.

We may say, therefore, that the reign of Richard I ushers in a new phase in the history of knight-service. Before that date

---

[1] e.g. in 1199 the Bishop of Durham paid 1200 marks for the confirmation of his charters 'et ut sit quietus de auxilio domini regis' (Pipe Roll, No. 45; cited by Madox, *Exchequer*, i. 400). In the following year the Abbot of St. Albans paid 310 marks 'pro habenda quietancia carucagii' and for various other concessions (Pipe Roll, No. 46; Madox, i. 401). In 1207 the Abbot of Abingdon fined with the king in 600 marks 'pro habenda quietancia de dominicis feodis, hominibus et omnibus tenentibus suis . . . de auxilio nobis proviso per consilium nostrum Oxon' ', and the assessors of the aid were accordingly ordered to release him from payment and from assessment (*Rot. Lit. Claus.* i. 84 b; Mitchell, op. cit., p. 89).

we have roughly a century in which the tenant-in-chief might discharge his military duties either by (1) service, or (2) scutage; after it we have approximately another century (1189–1277) in which he might do so by either (1) service, (2) scutage, or (3) a fine.

A study of the alternations of these various methods yields some interesting results. As we have already seen, commutation in the case of the ecclesiastics was, under Henry II, usual if not universal; and in one form or another it continued to be generally practised under Richard I. In the early years of John's reign the great majority of the religious still compounded for their service, although after 1201 it became increasingly unusual for them to obtain exemption by payment of scutage only. The bishops, on the other hand, if the evidence of the writs of quittance is to be relied upon, availed themselves less frequently than before of the opportunity for composition, and rarely paid anything more than scutage. During the latter half of the reign conditions on the clerical fees were abnormal as a result of John's quarrel with Stephen Langton and the Papacy. After the fulmination of the interdict in 1208 most of the bishops sought refuge on the Continent, only John de Gray of Norwich and Peter des Roches of Winchester ultimately remaining at their posts.[1] The lands of the absentees were seised into the king's hand, together with many of the great monastic estates; and they remained for the most part in royal custody until after the reconciliation with Innocent III in 1213.[2] The pipe roll accounts of the compositions exacted for the armies of Scotland (1209), Ireland (1210), and Wales (1211) summoned during this period are incomplete; but they suffice to show that the king's hand was heavy on the sub-tenants of the clerical fiefs. In 1209 corporal service seems to have been very generally exacted from them; while in 1210, in defiance of feudal custom, heavy fines were imposed, the knights of Durham alone accounting for £1,519 10s. 0d. for the single campaign.[3] For the Welsh expedition of 1211, as also for the army of Poitou three years later, commutation seems to have

---

[1] J. Ramsay, *The Angevin Empire*, p. 416.
[2] Ibid., pp. 436 seq.
[3] Pipe Roll, No. 57. *Compotus* of the bishopric of Durham.

been general, but it is significant of the declining power of the king that, with few exceptions, he was content with scutage only.[1]

With the accession of Henry III in 1216 normal conditions were resumed. New sources of information become available in this period and enable us to check and supplement the evidence of the scutage accounts in the pipe rolls. The series of scutage rolls begins in 1214, while an embryo marshal's roll has been preserved for the army of Gannoch (1246).[2] An examination of these various sources reveals a striking change in the relations between the clerical tenants and the Crown. An increasing number of abbots as well as of bishops is seen to have rendered corporal service in the armies of Henry III. Whereas under the early Angevins the proffer of service by an ecclesiastic was the exception rather than the rule, it may almost he said that the reverse was now the case. In the army of Biham of 1221 thirteen abbots and ten bishops were quit, presumably for service;[3] in the Welsh expedition of 1223 ten abbots and thirteen bishops had their knights with the king;[4] in that of Bedford in 1224 sixteen abbots and fourteen bishops were represented.[5] Later in the reign, fifteen abbots and nine bishops proffered service for the army of Gannoch of 1246,[6]

[1] Ramsey fined in 1211 in 100 marks for 4 fees (Pipe Roll, No. 57, Cant. and Hunt.).

[2] Chanc. Misc. 5/1: 'Servicium factum domino H. regi Anglie in Wallia anno regni suo vicesimo nono.'

[3] viz. the Archbishop of York; the Bishops of Bath, Coventry, Ely, Exeter, Lincoln, Norwich, Salisbury, Winchester, and Worcester; and the Abbots of Abbotsbury, Abingdon, Cerne, Evesham, Glastonbury, Hyde, Malmesbury, Peterborough, Ramsey, St. Edmunds, Tavistock, Wilton, Winchcombe (Pipe Roll, No. 65; Rot. Litt. Claus., p. 474).

[4] viz. the Archbishop of Canterbury; the Bishops of Bath, Chichester, Coventry, Durham, Ely, Hereford, Lincoln, London, Norwich, Salisbury, Winchester, Worcester; and the Abbots of Abingdon, Cerne, Evesham, Glastonbury, Malmesbury, Peterborough, Ramsey, St. Augustine's, St. Edmunds, Wilton (Coventry, Tavistock, and perhaps also Hyde rendered part service, part scutage) (Pipe Roll, No. 68; Scutage Roll, No. 3).

[5] The Archbishop of York; the Bishops of Bath, Chichester, Coventry, Durham, Ely, Exeter, Hereford, Lincoln, London, Norwich, Salisbury, Winchester, Worcester; and the Abbots of Abingdon, Cerne, Chertsey, Coventry, Evesham, Glastonbury, Hyde, Peterborough, Ramsey, St. Albans, St. Augustine's, St. Edmunds, Shaftesbury, Sherborne, Wilton, Winchcombe (Malmesbury offered service and scutage) (Pipe Roll, No. 68; Scutage Roll, No. 4).

[6] The archbishopric of York; the Bishops of Bath, Ely, Exeter, Lincoln,

and ten abbots and six bishops sent quotas to the Welsh war of 1257.[1] Thus we pass from a condition in which, under Henry II, both bishops and abbots habitually compounded for their service, to one, under John, in which, while the religious continued to offer fines or scutage, the bishops began to serve to an increasing extent; finally reaching under Henry III a stage at which service was commonly rendered by bishops and religious alike.

This is a curious inversion of the process as envisaged by most constitutional historians, who, like Maitland, postulate a gradual but uninterrupted transition from service to commutation.[2] The explanation is probably to be found in the widespread adoption in the thirteenth century of the principle of the *quota*. Doubtless in many cases it was simpler and more profitable for the tenant-in-chief to provide a sufficient number of knights to satisfy the Crown, than to compound for his service by scutage, for which he had to reimburse himself by a levy on his sub-tenants, or by a fine in the assessment of which the determining factor was the arbitrary will of the king.[3]

London, Norwich, Salisbury, Worcester; and the Abbots of Abbotsbury, Abingdon, Cerne, Coventry, Evesham, Glastonbury, Malmesbury, Michelney, Ramsey, St. Albans, St. Augustine's, St. Benet's, Shaftesbury, Sherborne, Winchcombe (Peterborough offered part service, part scutage) (Pipe Roll, No. 90; Chanc. Misc. 5/1; Scutage Roll, No. 7).

[1] The Archbishop of York; the Bishops of Exeter, Lincoln, London, Salisbury, Worcester; and the Abbots of Abbotsbury, Cerne, Hyde, Malmesbury, Michelney, Ramsey, St. Albans, St. Augustine's (fine and service), Shaftesbury, Sherborne (Pipe Rolls, Nos. 102 and 103; Scutage Roll, No. 8).

[2] Pollock and Maitland, *History of English Law*, i. 252–3. 'Speaking roughly we may say that there is one century (1066–1166) in which the military tenures are really military, though as yet there is little law about them; that there is another century (1166–1266) during which these tenures still supply an army, though chiefly by supplying its pay; and that when Edward I is on the throne the military organization . . . will no longer supply either soldiers or money. . . .'

[3] Thus the St. Albans chronicler writes jubilantly in 1277 of the good fortune which attended the house: 'Sane cum quamplures episcopi, abbates, et alii prelati pro majori parte Anglie, pro servitio militare, prece et pretio, finem procurarunt, scilicet pro quolibet milite quinquaginta marcas argenti, ecce! cassatis mutuis contractibus nocivis, sine quibus adeo tempestive pecunia tanta solvi non poterat, ad quinquaginta marcas summam omnium Abbati, salvis sibi equis et toto apparatu, portionem contingentium vix surgebat expensarum' (*Gesta Abbatum; Chronica Monasterii Sancti Albani*, R.S., i. 435).

The facts suggest, in any case, the need for a revision of the commonly accepted theory that the intention of the Crown in permitting the commutation of service for money was to destroy the military power of the baronage and to replace the feudal by a mercenary army. Henry II's frequent use of scutage may, indeed, have been partly due to the imperfect confidence he felt in the loyalty of his barons, but that neither he nor his successors had any intention of allowing their right to the corporal service of their tenants to fall into abeyance is abundantly evident. If the introduction of the fine is to be regarded as an assertion of the determination of the Crown to grant exemption from service only on its own terms, the acceptance of a *quota* in place of the full *servicium debitum* is evidence of its determination to prevent the relation between the king and his immediate tenants from being reduced to a purely cash nexus.[1] The military history of the clerical fiefs proves that the latter expedient was successful to a far larger degree than has hitherto been realized.

Even at this date, however, the performance of service by the ecclesiastical tenants, though a general, was not an invariable rule. For the armies of Kerry and Elveyn in 1228 and 1232 respectively, commutation was universal on the fees of the Church, with the exception of the bishopric of Coventry and Lichfield in the former instance, and of the bishopric of Winchester in the latter, and on both occasions scutage only was taken. Again in 1230, for the expedition to Brittany in connexion with which the bishops granted an aid, all the religious compounded for their service, the majority paying fines.

A careful study of the military and financial records of the reign of Henry III reveals two further developments of the highest importance and significance. The first was the gradual supersession of the scutage by the fine as a means of commutation for the tenants-in-chief; and the second, the increasingly close association of the fine with the new *servicium debitum*

---

[1] As late as the fourteenth century the Crown was able on occasion to insist on the render of corporal service, e.g. in 1311 only those holding less than half a fee were allowed to fine; while in 1327 the privilege of compounding was not extended to the bishops (*infra*, p. 80).

which was being simultaneously evolved. Not only did fining
become the normal procedure for the tenants-in-chief even
when scutage was imposed, but from time to time fines were
levied when no scutage was taken. From 1232 onwards, indeed,
scutages were rare, only four being imposed in twenty-five
years. The feudal host was, however, frequently summoned
in the interval,[1] and fines were taken from the clerical tenants
on at least two occasions, viz. for the campaign against Richard
Marshal in 1233, and for the Scottish expedition of 1244.[2]
There was in both cases some idea of a subsequent levy of
scutage and the fines were assessed with this possibility in
view. Some tenants proffered small sums with a promise to
pay scutage in addition, should it be given; others offered
larger compositions, on condition that, if a levy were made,
they should have the scutage of their tenants for their own use;
if not, that they should be granted a reasonable aid by their
tenants towards payment of the fine, or should be pardoned
a proportionate amount by the Crown.[3] In the later years of
the reign scutage fell definitely into abeyance, and the fine
became the sole alternative to service. Occasional references
to such payments occur during the period of the Barons' Wars;[4]
and, in particular, lists have been preserved of the compositions made by the clerical tenants-in-chief for expeditions in
1264 and 1265.[5] Of these the latter is particularly interesting
as illustrating the tendency to identify the fine, now completely
dissociated from the scutage, with the reduced service which
had become customary in the last half-century. In 1265 the
fines were specifically paid on the new *servicium debitum*,

---

[1] e.g. in 1233 for the campaign against Richard Marshal; in 1241, 1245,
1253 for Wales; in 1244 for Scotland.

[2] Fine Roll, No. 41, pt. 1, m. 4; Pipe Roll, No. 78.

[3] e.g. in 1244 the Abbots of Winchcombe and Holme fined in 10 m.
and 20 m. respectively besides scutage if it were given (Fine Roll, No. 41,
pt. 1, m. 4).

In 1233 the Bishop of London offered 60 m. for failure to perform service
and to have his scutage; the Bishop of Lincoln offered £110, 'ut sit quietus
de militibus mittendis ad exercitum regis', 'et si scutagium inde non currat
idem episcopus habebit literas vic' directas de habendo rationabili auxilio
de predictis feodis ad finem illum adquietandum'. The Bishop of Bath
offered £90. £45 was paid and the rest pardoned (Pipe Roll, No. 78).

[4] See, for example, Sparke, *Historiae Coenobii Burgi*, p. 135.

[5] Exch. L.T.R. Misc. Roll, 1/13.

although they were not, as yet, assessed at a fixed rate *per feodum*.[1]

The result of these changes was that by the close of the reign of Henry III the conditions of feudal service had come to approximate very closely to Maitland's conception of them. The alternatives open to the tenant-in-chief had been reduced to two. He was now expected to respond to the royal summons by the proffer of either (1) service with his recognized contingent (in most cases a mere fraction of his nominal obligation), or (2) its pecuniary equivalent in the shape of a fine. Scutage had ceased to play a part as between the Crown and its immediate vassals and had come to represent simply the commutation of the service of the tenants of mesne lords, or of escheats, wardships, and honours in hand. Maitland perceived that the probable corollary of such a development would be the conversion of scutage into a general tax levied in the royal interest upon the under-tenants, without regard to the service or fine exacted from their lords; but his misconception as to the original relation of the fine and the scutage led him to antedate the process by half a century.[2] The scutage of Gascony of 1242, which he adduces as evidence, was merely an isolated and unsuccessful experiment. It was not until the reign of Edward I that a serious and sustained attempt was made to revolutionize the incidence of the levy.[3] By that date the scutage had lost almost entirely its former significance, and was regarded by a perpetually needy monarchy simply as a potential source of revenue.

In November 1276 Edward summoned the feudal host for service against Llewelyn of Wales;[4] the tenants responding in money or men at the muster held in July 1277 before the constable and marshal at Worcester.[5] On the successful

---

[1] Exch. L.T.R. Misc. Roll, 1/13, m. 12. The entries run:
   De Abbate de Abbodesbyr' pro servicio j militis .x. mar.
   De Abbate de Abindon' pro servicio iij militum .iiij. mar.
   De Abbate de Cerne pro servicio j militis .xx. mar.
   De Abbate de Certes' pro servicio ij militum .xl. mar.

[2] Pollock and Maitland, *History of English Law*, i. 269 seq.

[3] For the detailed history of this attempt see my articles on 'Scutage under Edward I' and 'Scutage in the Fourteenth Century' (*E.H.R.* xxxvii. 321 seq.; xxxviii. 19 seq.).

[4] *Parl. Writs*, i. 193.   [5] Ibid., pp. 197 seq.

termination of the expedition it was decided to levy a scutage—
the first since 1257—and writs for the collection were accordingly issued in February 1279.[1] Now, since the Crown tenants
had already, with few exceptions, discharged their obligations
by the proffer of service or a fine, a scutage under the conditions
which had prevailed in the early thirteenth century would, as
we have seen, have amounted to little more than the fixing of
the rate at which the mesne lords were to collect from their
dependants and the king from the tenants of escheats, wardships, and honours in hand. In order to obviate this contin-
gency, and to maintain the interest of the Crown in the levy,
the Exchequer followed the precedent of 1242 and assessed the
impost, as if it had been an aid, upon all fees, irrespective of the
performance of service or the payment of a fine.[2] This arbitrary
procedure was naturally resented by the tenants-in-chief, the
majority of whom refused to contribute to the scutage, on the
ground that their responsibilities in relation to the campaign
were at an end. To their protests the Crown returned that the
revolution in the incidence of the scutage was fully justified by
the disparity between the number of fees recognized for
military, and the number recognized for fiscal purposes. It
assumed the attitude that acceptance of a reduced contingent
by no means impaired its claim to service or its equivalent from
the remaining fees of its immediate vassals. Thus, while every
tenant-in-chief was expected to respond to the summons by
tendering either service or a fine upon the fees which he
'recognized' (i.e. upon the new *servicium debitum*),[3] he was
required, secondly, to pay scutage at the close of the campaign
as the commutation of the service due from those of his fees
which were not covered by the original proffer. Against these
claims the magnates stood for the view that a completely new
servicium debitum had been created, which was all that could
properly be demanded from their entire holding; and the discharge of which entitled them to collect scutage for their own
use from the fees of their sub-tenants.

---

[1] Exch. L.T.R. Mem. Roll, No. 52, Comm. Easter, m. 4; *C.C.R.*, 1272–
1279, p. 522.　　　　　　　　　　[2] Pipe Roll, No. 123, *passim*.

[3] In 10 Edward I and later the fines were assessed at a fixed rate on the
fee. See Exch. L.T.R. Misc. Roll, 1/13.

The dispute thus initiated in 1279 continued with unabated vigour well into the reign of Edward III. Scutages were imposed in connexion with six subsequent campaigns, viz. the Welsh army of 1282, the Scottish expeditions of 1300, 1303, and 1306 under Edward I, of 1311 under Edward II, and of 1327 under Edward III,[1] and each levy was productive of fresh controversy. The Crown was indefatigable in the prosecution of its claims. In 1314 it instituted a new method of collection, and when its efforts to enforce payment by the tenants-in-chief proved fruitless, it essayed to levy the debts upon the subtenants direct.[2] The opposition showed itself, however, to be no less determined than the Crown. Formal representations were made to Edward I in the parliaments of 1292, 1297, and 1305, and to Edward II in 1315, 1318, and 1320;[3] and the points at issue were argued at length before the Exchequer by the baronial leaders in 1315.[4] It is probable, however, that the passive—sometimes, indeed, the active—resistance of the feudal tenantry ultimately did more to convince the Crown of the impossibility of the task than the arguments of the magnates. By the end of the reign of Edward II it was found that little or no progress had been made with the collection,[5] and under Edward III the Exchequer gradually relaxed its efforts. In 1334 it tacitly abandoned the attempt to enforce payment of scutage by tenants who considered their obligations already discharged, and concentrated its attention upon the collection of those sums about which there was no dispute.[6] Six years later Edward III, hard pressed for funds for the prosecution of the war in France, pardoned by statute all outstanding

---

[1] That for 1282 was levied in 1285; that for 1300 and 1303 in 1305; that for 1306 in 1314; that for 1311 in 1319; that for 1327 in 1337.

[2] Cf. the commissions of 3 November 1314 (*Calendar of Fine Rolls*, ii. 216).

[3] *Rotuli Parliamentorum*, i. 80; Exch. L.T.R. Mem. Roll, No. 68, Comm. Trin., m. 51 d; *Rot. Parl.* i. 166, No. 73; *Memoranda de Parliamento*, 1305, ed. F. W. Maitland, R.S., pp. 123, 126, Introd., p. liv; Exch. K.R. Mem. Roll, No. 88, m. 145; Exch. L.T.R. Mem. Roll, No. 85, Rec. Hil., m. 7; *Rot. Parl.* i. 292, No. 17; H. Cole, *Documents illustrative of English History in the Thirteenth and Fourteenth Centuries*, p. 7; *Rot. Parl.* i. 383.

[4] Exch. L.T.R. Mem. Roll, No. 85, Rec. Hil., m. 7.

[5] *Red Book*, iii. 961–3; Ordinance of the Exchequer, 1326, ch. xxiv.

[6] Exch. L.T.R. Mem. Roll, No. 107, Brev. Ret. Trin., mm. 148, 148 d, 149, 149 d, 150, 150 d.

scutage debts and accounts, as the necessary condition of a parliamentary grant.[1]

Thus ended the attempt to levy the Edwardian scutages. In 1385 Richard II summoned the feudal host to Newcastle to avert a threatened Franco-Scottish invasion.[2] Parliament, however, was careful to guard against the possible revival of the royal claims in this connexion; and in the next year secured assent to a petition couched in the following terms: 'Item si nule escuage soit chalangeable pur cest vostre gracious primer viage fait par vous en Escoce, soit de vostre tres gracious et benigne grace pardone.'[3]

The greater clerical tenants-in-chief afford an admirable illustration of the course and issue of this controversy. All the bishops, with the single exception of Durham, and twelve of the twenty-three religious, had, in the course of the thirteenth century, effected reductions in their *servicia debita*;[4] all, save Westminster and Canterbury, who appear consistently to have evaded their feudal obligations at this period,[5] responded to the Edwardian summonses according to the precedent of Henry III's later years, by the offer of service or a fine. On the whole, the proportion of those who fined was higher in the fourteenth than in the preceding century; but service was still not infrequently rendered. In some years, indeed, it was general. In the army of 4 Edward II eighteen of the religious and eight of the bishops had their due *quota* with the king, fining being permitted only in exceptional circumstances, and again in the Scottish expedition of 16 Edward II corporal service was rendered by eighteen abbots and seven bishops. Between 1277 and 1327 nine Welsh and Scottish summonses were issued (viz. in 1277, 1282, 1300, 1303, 1306, 1311, 1314, 1323, and 1327), the response to which can be determined with some degree of accuracy and completeness.[6] One only of the

---

[1] *Statutes of the Realm*, i. 283; 14 Edw. III, Stat. I, c. 2, c. 3.

[2] Rymer, *Feodera*, vii. 473–4.

[3] *Rot. Parl.* iii. 213.   [4] See table, pp. 32–3.

[5] There is no record of service by the Archbishops of Canterbury after 1232; or by the Abbots of Westminster after 1246. I am unable to account for their apparent exemption.

[6] For 1277 there are available a marshal's roll, roll of fines, and scutage account (*Parl. Writs*, i. 197 seq.; *Fine Rolls*, i. 85–7; Pipe Roll, No. 123);

ecclesiastics—the Bishop of Hereford—served in as many as six of the nine campaigns; two—the Abbots of Abbotsbury and St. Albans—served in five; while ten—the Bishop of Salisbury and the Archbishop of York, the Abbots of Abingdon, Cerne, Malmesbury, Michelney, Pershore, Sherborne, Winchcombe, and the Abbess of Wilton, can be proved to have offered service at least four times. The Abbot of Peterborough was the only prelate who compounded on every occasion.[1]

How far—if at all—did the Crown succeed in exacting scutage from the clerical tenants in addition to the service or fine thus proffered in response to the summons? A comprehensive answer to this question is impossible, since after 15 Edward I no scutage accounts were entered on the pipe roll, and only the most fragmentary records of the later levies have survived.[2] The only scutages of this period of which full details are available are those for the Welsh wars of 1277 and 1282, where accounting followed the traditional lines; and it is upon their evidence primarily that any conclusion as to the results of the new Exchequer policy must be based.

When in 1279 the first Welsh scutage of Edward I was imposed, the clerical as well as the lay tenants were charged in

for 1282 a marshal's roll, roll of fines, scutage account, and list of writs *de scutagio habendo* (*Parl. Writs*, i. 228; Exch. L.T.R. Misc. Roll, 1/13; Pipe Roll, No. 132; Scutage Roll, No. 9); for 1300 a roll of fines and of writs *de supersedendo* (Exch. L.T.R. Misc. Roll, 1/13; Supplementary Close Roll, No. 9); for 1303 a marshal's roll, roll of fines, scutage roll, and list of writs *de supersedendo* (Chanc. Misc. 5/6; Exch. L.T.R. Misc. Roll, 1/13; Scutage Roll, No. 10; Suppl. Close Roll, No. 9); for 1306 a marshal's roll, a roll of fines, a scutage roll, and list of writs *de supersedendo* (Chanc. Misc. 5/19; Exch. L.T.R. Misc. Roll, 1/13; Scutage Roll, No. 11; Suppl. Close Roll, No. 9); for 1311 a marshal's roll, roll of fines, scutage roll, list of writs *de supersedendo* (*Parl. Writs*, ii. 401 seq.; Exch. L.T.R. Misc. 1/13; Scutage Roll, No. 12; Suppl. Close Roll, No. 90); for 1314 a list of fines (Exch. L.T.R. Mem. Roll, No. 84, Brev. Ret. Trin.); for 1323 a marshal's roll and list of fines (Chanc. Misc. 5/10; Exch. L.T.R. Misc. Roll, 1/13); for 1327 a list of fines and scutage roll (Exch. L.T.R. Misc. Roll, 1/13; Scutage Roll, No. 13).

[1] He offered service in 1311, but his contingent failed to pass muster and he was obliged to fine instead (*infra*, p. 88).

[2] Two original inquisitions for the Scottish scutages of Edward I have been preserved (*Calendar of Miscellaneous Inquisitions*, ii, No. 405, pp. 101 seq.; *Feudal Aids*, v. 213 seq.). Fragments of accounts for Edward I, II, and III also exist. Subsidy Rolls, 196/4, 242/62, 242/65, 161/5, 242/70, 242/44, 141/1, 113/1, 87/1, 239/247, 242/67, 240/283, 239/172, 242/69, 173/1, 242/31, 91/3, 91/4, 242/43, 184/2, 242/67.

the pipe roll with scutage on the customary number of fees, without regard to the response made to the summons of two years earlier. The only ecclesiastics who did not figure on the scutage lists were the Archbishop of Canterbury, the Bishop of Bath and Wells, and the Abbot of Glastonbury. The former, as already noted, was from the middle of Henry III's reign exempt in practice if not in principle from military duties.[1] The exclusion of the two latter is probably accounted for by the long controversy over the relation of the abbey to the bishopric which was engendered by Richard I's grant of Glastonbury to Bishop Savaric of Bath. The loss of their independence was keenly resented by the monks, who spared no effort to regain their freedom, but throughout the early thirteenth century the bishops habitually responded for the abbey's service in addition to their own.[2] In 1275 the issue was at length decided by Edward I in favour of the abbot,[3] but difficulties seem to have arisen over the adjustment of the service, and, in consequence, neither Bath nor Glastonbury were assessed for the scutage of Wales. Both, however, had fined for their service in 1277. The only clerical tenants who had not offered either service or a fine in response to the original summons, and who therefore were properly liable for scutage were the Abbots of Chertsey, Tavistock, and Westminster. Of these the Abbot of Tavistock paid immediately and was quit in the pipe roll of 7 Edward I.[4] According to precedent this should have been accepted in full discharge of his liabilities; but in pursuance of the new policy of the Crown he was called upon in 1292 to answer at the Exchequer for his failure to offer men or money in 1277, and was fined five marks for neglect of the royal summons.[5] The

[1] *Supra*, p. 32, n. 3.

[2] *Victoria County History, Somerset*, ii. 72; Johannes Glastoniensis, *Historia de rebus Glastoniensibus*, ed. Hearne, p. 226; Henry III Pipe Rolls, *passim*. The bishop answers for 60 fees in Somerset and Dorset: cf. Pipe Roll, No. 70, m. 15 d; No. 91, m. 15 d; No. 102, m. 12 d. In 48 Hen. III, apropos of the fines paid in that year, the following entry occurs: 'Abbas de Glaston' servicium illud vel finem illum facere deberet Episcopo, et sic idem Episcopus de eodem servicio et servicio proprio respondere deberet domino regi immediate' (Exch. L.T.R. Misc. Roll, 1/13, m. 12).

[3] *V.C.H., Somerset*, loc. cit.

[4] Pipe Roll, No. 123, Devon: 'Idem vicecomes r.c. de xxxij. li. de abbate de Tavistok' de xvj feodis.'

[5] Exch. L.T.R. Mem. Roll, No. 63, Comm. Easter, m. 13 and m. 35 d:

Abbot of Chertsey, more fortunate, escaped with payment of scutage only on the three fees of his traditional *servicium debitum*,[1] while the Abbot of Westminster evaded even this obligation, his scutage debt passing still unpaid on to the exannual roll in 15 Edward II.[2] The remainder, both bishops and abbots, having all either served or fined in the first instance, made haste, when they found themselves charged with scutage, to procure writs of quittance from the Chancery.[3] These the Exchequer, in view of the disparity between the new and the old *servicium debitum*, was reluctant to accept. It was prepared to release the tenants-in-chief from payment of scutage upon that number of fees for which service had been rendered or fine paid,[4] but it required them to show cause why they should be quit on all their fees for service or fine upon a mere fraction.[5] They retorted by an appeal to precedent, declaring both individually and collectively that 'a tempore quo non exstat memoria' service with a reduced contingent had been held to

'Et quia idem abbas non fecit servicium suum in exercitu regis ibidem anno quinto set tantum solvit .xxxij. li. pro scutagio suo xvj feodorum que de rege tenet in capite nullo servicio faciendo, ideo idem abbas in misericordia; pro qua finem fecit per quinque marcas.'

[1] Pipe Roll, No. 136, Surrey and Sussex. The sheriff responds for the scutage of the Abbot of Chertsey.

[2] Pipe Roll, No. 167, London and Middlesex; Exannual Roll, No. 1, London and Middlesex.

[3] These writs occur with increasing frequency in the close and memoranda rolls from 1280 onwards. The formula runs as follows: 'Quia A.B. habuit servicium suum [or finem fecit cum rege] in exercitu suo Wallie anno regni sui quinto, pro servicio x feodorum militum quod tunc Regi recognovit, sicut per inspeccionem rotulorum marescalcie regi de eodem exercitu constat: Rex mandat Baronibus quod ipsum A.B. de demanda quam ei fieri faciant per summonitionem scaccarii de scutagio ad opus Regis levando de predictis x feodis pacem habere permittant, et ipsum inde quietum esse faciant. Teste Rege, etc.'

[4] In 1315 the Council replied to the magnates that 'notificato curie qui fecerunt servicia sua, etc., et pro quibus feodis, supersedebitur levacioni scutagium et facientes servicia illa quieti erunt versus regem de eisdem scutagiis pro tempore servicii de tot feodis pro quot servicium factum fuit' (Exch. L.T.R. Mem. Roll, No. 85, Comm. Rec. Hil. m. 7; cf. petition of 12 Edw. II; Cole, *Documents illustrative of English History*, p. 7).

[5] e.g. in 15 Edw. II the Abbot of St. Augustine's, Canterbury, was summoned before the Exchequer 'ad ostendendum si quid penes se habeat quod per servicium unius feodi quietus esse debeat de servicio xv feodorum predictorum' (Exch. L.T.R. Mem. Roll, No. 92, Rec. Trin.; cf. Abbess of Shaftesbury, Exch. L.T.R. Mem. Roll, No. 93, Rec. Easter, m. 23 d).

cover the obligations of the entire fief.[1] Several of the ecclesiastics, including the Abbots of St. Benet's,[2] St. Augustine's,[3] and Hyde[4] appeared in person or by attorney at the Exchequer at different times to prosecute their claim to acquittance of scutage on the usual grounds. In no case, however, were they able to obtain more than a temporary respite from distraint pending the further deliberation of the court upon the points at issue. In the register of Bishop Swinfield of Hereford, under the date January 1308, a memorandum of the scutage charged upon him in the pipe roll was entered, with the note: 'Let a convenient remedy be sought in the king's court against this demand', and the addition: 'Et sciendum est quod nullus unquam Episcopus Herefordensis fecit servicium militare in exercitu regis nisi per v milites licet scutagium solvere consueverit pro quindecim quando scutagium sive guerra fuit assisum ad pecuniam.'[5]

There is no reason to doubt the sincerity of the protestations of the tenants-in-chief. They were themselves obviously puzzled to account for the discrepancy between the new and the old *servicium debitum*. It seems evident that they retained no memory of the circumstances in which the reduction had been effected—a fact which may in itself be accepted as proof

[1] This is the argument employed by the baronial leaders in 1315: 'Dicunt iidem Comites quod sunt nonulli ex prelatis, comitibus, baronibus, etc. qui omnia tenementa sua que tenent de rege in capite per servicium militare ut de Corona Anglie, etc. tenent per servicium faciendum tantummodo per quatuor, quinque vel sex milites vel alterum certum numerum militum, licet teneant quadraginta vel quinquaginta feoda militaria vel alterum certum numerum feodorum multo maiorem numero militum, per quod videlicet servicium fieri debet, et tam prelati qui nunc sunt et eorum predecessores, quam comites et barones qui nunc sunt et eorum antecessores, omnia tenementa sua que tenent de rege, etc. ut de Corona defendere solent et debent per servicium faciendum in exercitu, etc. per huiusmodi certum numerum militum, etc. et hoc a tempore quo non exstat memoria' (Exch. L.T.R. Mem. Roll, No. 85, Comm. Rec. Hil., m. 7).

[2] Exch. L.T.R. Mem. Roll, No. 75, Rec. Mich., m. 12: 'Et licet summa scutagii superius annotata ad plura feoda se extendat quam servicium predictum, tamen quia predictus abbas clamat habere acquietanciam de scutagio omnium feodorum que tenet de rege per servicium duorum feodorum et dimidii concessum est quod habeat respectum de scutagio predicto donec aliud, etc.'

[3] Exch. L.T.R. Mem. Roll, No. 93, Rec. Mich., m. 12.

[4] Exch. L.T.R. Mem. Roll, No. 94, Rec. Mich., m. 4 d.

[5] *Register of Bishop Richard de Swinfield*, p. 416.

that the new 'recognition' was the result rather of a slow process of evolution than of a definite bargain between the king and his vassals, such as is postulated by Dr. J. E. Morris.[1] Any deliberate revision of the *servicia debita* must have been a matter of record, and would have furnished the tenants-in-chief with an overwhelmingly strong case against the new Exchequer policy. As it was, they were hampered by the lack of evidence, due in part to the long period which had elapsed since the last levy of scutage; in part to the absence (with the exception of the embryo marshal's roll of 1246) of any formal record of service prior to 1277. The Abbess of Shaftesbury, confronted in 1323 with an early charter of Henry III in which she acknowledged a service of seven knights as against the three recognized in the fourteenth century, was obviously at a total loss to justify her position. She fell back upon the expedient of repeated adjournments on the plea that 'her attorney was not yet fully informed on the matter'; or that her steward, who should have produced the charter and muniments of the house for the inspection of the barons of the Exchequer, was engaged in preparing for the approaching visit of the king to Somerset, and could not be spared![2] The Abbot of Abingdon, more enterprising than most of his fellows, ascribed the discrepancy between the three fees on which he served or fined and the thirty on which he was charged with scutage to the fact that his knights rendered castle-guard or its money equivalent to the constable of Windsor, and were not, therefore, liable for knight-service.[3] This same plea was afterwards advanced by the whole body of tenants-in-chief in the parliament of 1315.[4]

---

[1] *Welsh Wars*, p. 42.

[2] Exch. L.T.R. Mem. Roll, No. 92, Brev. Ret. Trin., m. 88; No. 93, Rec. Easter, m. 23 d; No. 94, Comm. Trin. Dies Dati.

[3] Exch. L.T.R. Mem. Roll, No. 74, Comm. Mich. Brev. Bar., m. 8. The abbot declares that he holds 'triginta feoda militum pro .xxx. li. Regi per manus constabularii castri de Wyndesore qui pro tempore fuerit ad wardam eiusdem castri annuatim reddendis et tria feoda militum pro servicio regi debito in exercitibus faciendo'; but 'Barones asserentes servicium regi deberi in exercitibus Regis tam de triginta quam de tribus feodis supradictis ipsum Abbatem de scutagio regis pro eisdem xxx feodis in exercitibus Regis reddendo distringunt minus iuste ac si ipse abbas servicium Regis in exercitibus Wallie pro eisdem xxx feodis facere teneretur'.

[4] *Rot. Parl.* i. 292: 'Les uns des feez as grantz seignurs sont assignez a faire gard de chasteux, come de Dovre, Wyndesoure, Norht et autres

The outcome of the contest over the scutage of 5 Edward I was, as far as the clerical tenants were concerned, that eight bishops (Chichester, Coventry and Lichfield, Ely, Exeter, Lincoln, Norwich, Salisbury, and Winchester),[1] and eleven religious (the Abbots of Abbotsbury, Abingdon, Malmesbury, Michelney, Pershore, Peterborough, Ramsey, St. Augustine's, Canterbury, and Winchcombe, and the Abbesses of Shaftesbury and Wilton)[2] secured eventual acceptance of their writs of quittance and had their scutage debts written off under Edward I or Edward II. The Abbot of Sherborne was quit on the two fees for which he had served in 1277, but was charged with scutage on the extra one-fifth of his traditional *servicium debitum*.[3] Five bishops (Durham, Hereford, London, Worcester, and York) and three abbots (Coventry, Hyde, St. Benet's, Holme) were unsuccessful in securing acquittance, but they seem to have paid nothing, for their scutage debts were transferred entire to the exannual roll in 15 and 16 Edward II.[4]

Chasteux, et tut soit il issi qe les ditz grantz seignurs eint fait lour service au Roi pur tant come il devient faire et come leurs predecessours et leurs aunscestres unt fait ent tut temps pur meyns des feez qe il ne teignent; jatardeis lescuage pur toutz leurs feez entierement est demande de eaux par somonce de l'Escheker aussi bien des fees assignez a la gard des chasteux comes d'autres feez.'

[1] The Bishop of Chichester in 11 Edw. I, Pipe Roll, No. 127, Sussex; Coventry and Lichfield in 12 Edw. I, P.R., No. 128, Stafford; Ely in 9 Edw. I, P.R., No. 125, Cant. and Hunt.; Exeter in 10 Edw. I, P.R., No. 126, Devon, m. 3; Lincoln in 12 Edw. I, P.R., No. 128, Linc., m. 11 d; Norwich in 12 Edw. I, P.R., No. 128, Norf. and Suff.; Salisbury in 31 Edw. I, P.R., No. 148, Wilts.; Winchester in 9 Edw. I, P.R., No. 125, Southants.

[2] The Abbot of Abbotsbury in 11 Edw. I, P.R., No. 127, Somers. and Dors.; Abingdon in 11 Edw. I, P.R., No. 127, Berks., m. 14 d; Michelney in 13 Edw. I, P.R., No. 130, Somers. and Dors.; Malmesbury in 25 Edw. I, P.R., No. 142, Wilts.; Pershore in 19 Edw. II, P.R., No. 171, Worc., m. 21 d; Peterborough in 8 Edw. I, P.R., No. 124, Northants.; Ramsey in 9 Edw. I, P.R., No. 125, Cant. and Hunt.; St. Augustine's in 14 Edw. I, P.R., No. 131, Kent, m. 25; Winchcombe in 10 Edw. I, P.R., No. 126, m. 10 d, Glouc.; Shaftesbury in 12 Edw. I, P.R., No. 128, Somers. and Dors., m. 19; Wilton in 16 Edw. II, P.R., No. 168, Wilts.

[3] The Abbot was quit on his two fees in 11 Edw. I, P.R., No. 127, Somers. and Dors.

[4] The Bishop of Durham in 15 Edw. II, P.R., No. 167, Exannual Roll, No. I, Lincoln; Hereford in 15 Edw. II, P.R., No. 167, Exannual Roll, No. I, Hereford; London in 15 Edw. II, P.R., No. 167, Exannual Roll, No. 1, Essex and Herts.; Worcester in 15 Edw. II, P.R., No. 167, Exannual Roll, No. I, Worc.; York in 15 Edw. II, P.R., No. 167, Exannual Roll, No. I, Yorks; the Prior of Coventry in 15 Edw. II, P.R., No. 167, Exannual Roll,

The Abbots of St. Albans and St. Edmunds were pardoned their scutage among other debts, the latter prelate in consideration of the remission to the king of 1,000 marks which he had borrowed[1] from the moneys for the clerical tenth in the abbot's custody. The case of the Abbot of Evesham presents a difficulty, for his debt disappears from the pipe roll without explanation towards the end of Edward I's reign. The fact that in the interval he had secured several writs of quittance[2] makes it more probable, however, that he was acquitted than that he paid. Finally, we are left with the Abbot of Cerne—the only ecclesiastic who can be proved to have paid scutage in spite of having responded to the summons in 1277. The abbot, who had fined for his service of one fee at the date of the muster, subsequently paid scutage upon two fees according to the terms of his charter,[3] the sheriff responding for the debt in 14 Edward I.[4] Thus, from the evidence of the pipe rolls it is clear that the attempt to collect the scutage of 5 Edward I was, in the case of the clerical tenants, almost entirely unsuccessful. The total yield from the ecclesiastical fees was £42 8s. 0d,[5] as against the £900 odd which should have been produced by a levy on the lines originally contemplated by the Exchequer; and even this sum was paid in slowly and reluctantly.

The situation in regard to the second Welsh scutage was slightly more favourable to the Crown. In 1282 there was, as before, no response to the summons from the Archbishop of Canterbury, while the bishopric of Winchester, which was void

No. I, Warw. and Leic.; the Abbot of Hyde in 16 Edw. II, P.R., No. 168, Exannual Roll, No. I, Southants; St. Benet's, Holme, in 15 Edw. II, P.R., No. 167, Exannual Roll, No. I, Norf. and Suff.

[1] P.R., No. 147, Essex and Herts.; P.R., No. 149, Residuum Norf.

[2] e.g. in 9 Edw. I, Exch. L.T.R. Mem. Roll, No. 54, Comm. Easter, m. 7 d; in 16 Edw. I, *C.C.R.*, 1296–1302, p. 147.

[3] *Supra*, p. 5, n. 4.

[4] The sheriff accounts for the debt in P.R., No. 130, Somers. and Dors.

			£	s.	d.	
[5]	The Abbot of Tavistock	. . .	32	0	0	(16 fees)
	,, ,, Chertsey	. . .	6	0	0	(3 ,,)
	,, ,, Cerne .	. . .	4	0	0	(2 ,,)
	,, ,, Sherborne	. . .		8	0	($\frac{1}{5}$ fee)
			£42	8	0	

and in the king's hand, offered no service. Of the abbots, Cerne and Westminster received special pardons,[1] and Chertsey did not respond, while the abbacy of Evesham was vacant. The rest of the clerical tenants, however, served or fined as in the first Welsh expedition. When in 1285 the scutage was put in charge all were assessed with the exception, as before, of the Archbishop of Canterbury, the Bishop of Bath, and the Abbot of Glastonbury. Of those who had not responded to the summons, the Abbots of Cerne and Chertsey ultimately paid their scutage through the sheriff;[2] but the Abbot of Westminster, as in 1279, evaded payment, his debt being transferred to the exannual roll in 15 Edward II.[3] Five abbots (Malmesbury, Michelney, Pershore, Peterborough, and Ramsey) and three bishops (Coventry and Lichfield, London, and Salisbury) were eventually successful in securing acquittance[4] for service or fine; the Abbot of Sherborne was again quit on the fees of his new *servicium*, paying scutage on the surplus $\frac{1}{5}$ fee;[5] while six abbots (Abingdon, Coventry, Evesham, Hyde, St. Benet's Holme, and Tavistock) and eight bishops (Chichester, Durham, Ely, Exeter, Hereford, Winchester, Worcester, and York) failed to make good their plea and continued to be charged in the pipe roll with scutage until 1322 or 1323, when the debts were transferred to the exannual roll as 'desperate'.[6] The Abbots of St.

[1] Exch. L.T.R. Mem. Roll, No. 66, Comm. Mich., m. 6: 'Rex de gratia sua speciali perdonavit Abbati de Cerne servicium quod Regi debuerat fecisse in exercitu Wallie anno x°', Sept. 13, 22 Edw. I, Exch. L.T.R. Mem. Roll, No. 58, Comm. Trin., m. 13 d. Pardon to Abbot Walter Wenlock 'pro bono et laudabili servicio quod frater Ricardus nuper abbas Westmonasterii et Thesaurarius Regis domino regi impendit' of the service due for the army of 10 Edw. I.

[2] P.R., No. 132, Somers. and Dors.; P.R., No. 136, Surrey and Sussex.

[3] P.R., No. 167, Exannual Roll, No. I, London and Middlesex.

[4] The Abbot of Malmesbury in 25 Edw. I, P.R., No. 142, Wilts.; Michelney in 16 Edw. I, P.R., No. 135, Somers. and Dors.; Pershore in 19 Edw. II, P.R., No. 171, Worc., m. 21 d; Peterborough in 16 Edw. I, P.R., No. 133, Northants.; Ramsey in 21 Edw. I, P.R., No. 138, Cant. and Hunt.; the Bishop of Coventry in 17 Edw. I, P.R., No. 134, Item Staff.; London in 15 Edw. I, P.R., No. 132, Essex; Salisbury in 31 Edw. I, P.R., No. 148, Wilts.

[5] P.R., No. 134, Somers. and Dors. Abbas de Schireburne r.c. de iiij. li. viij. s. de scutagio Wallie de anno x . . . In thesauro viij. s. Et debet iiij. li. li. P.R., No. 136, Somers. and Dors. The abbot is acquitted of the £4 in consideration of the fine proffered in 1282.

[6] The Abbot of Abingdon in 15 Edw. II, P.R., No. 167, Oxon. and Berks.,

Albans and St. Edmunds were pardoned their scutage on the
same terms as before;[1] while the Abbot of St. Augustine's,
Canterbury, had his debt allowed by a writ of 14 Edward III.[2]
Of those who had proffered men or money at the date of the
summons as many as four seem on this occasion to have paid
scutage also. The Abbots of Abbotsbury and Winchcombe and
the Abbesses of Wilton and Shaftesbury all responded through
the sheriff either under Edward I or early in the reign of
Edward II.[3] If, therefore, the number of those who paid scutage
or failed to secure acquittance is considered, the Exchequer
may be said to have achieved a slightly larger measure of success
than in 1279. In point of fact, however, the actual proceeds of
the levy were even smaller than on the previous occasion. The
seven ecclesiastical fiefs which responded directly for the scutage
of 10 Edward I yielded only £40 8s. od.,[4] as against the £42 8s. od.
contributed by the clergy to the scutage of 5 Edward I.

We may conclude, therefore, that the Crown derived but

[1] Exannual Roll, No. I; Coventry in 15 Edw. II, P.R., No. 167, Wor. and
Leic.; Evesham in 16 Edw. II, P.R., No. 168, Exannual Roll, No. I, Worc.;
Hyde in 16 Edw. II, P.R., No. 168, Exannual Roll, No. I, Southants.;
St. Benet's in 15 Edw. II, P.R., No. 167, Norf. and Suff.; Tavistock in
17 Edw. II, P.R., No. 169, Exannual Roll, No. I, Devon. The Bishop of
Chichester in 16 Edw. II, P.R., No. 168, Exannual Roll, No. I, Sussex;
Durham in 15 Edw. II, P.R., No. 167, Lincoln; Ely in 16 Edw. II, P.R.,
No. 168, Exannual Roll, No. I, Cant. and Hunt.; Exeter in 16 Edw. II,
P.R., No. 168, Exannual Roll, No. I, Devon.; Hereford in 15 Edw. II,
P.R., No. 167, Hereford; Winchester in 16 Edw. II, P.R., No. 168, Ex-
annual Roll, No. I, Southants.; Worcester in 15 Edw. II, P.R., No. 167,
Worc.; York in 15 Edw. II, P.R., No. 167, Yorks.

[1] Supra, p. 66, n. 1.

[2] Exannual Roll, No. I, Kent. The abbot is charged with £30 scutage,
but in another hand is added the note: 'Set non debet inde summoneri per
breve regis quod est inter communia de anno xiij° termino Pasche de
hujusmodi debitis allocandis. Et quietus est.'

[3] P.R., No. 134, Somers. and Dors.; No. 136, Glouc., m. 13; No. 142,
Item Wilts.; No. 156, Somers. and Dors.

		£	s.	d.	
[4] The Abbess of	Shaftesbury	14	0	0	(for 7 fees)
,, ,,	Wilton	10	0	0	(,, 5 ,,)
The Abbot of	Chertsey	6	0	0	(,, 3 ,,)
,, ,,	Cerne	4	0	0	(,, 2 ,,)
,, ,,	Winchcombe	4	0	0	(,, 2 ,,)
,, ,,	Abbotsbury	2	0	0	(,, 1 fee)
,, ,,	Sherborne	0	8	0	(,, $\frac{1}{5}$,,)
		£40	8	0	

small profit from its attempt to revolutionize the incidence of the scutage. The failure of the early levies did not prevent the Exchequer from making a strenuous effort to collect the scutages imposed in connexion with the later expeditions to Scotland; but the tenants-in-chief maintained the attitude they had adopted in 1279 and 1285, and the Crown was powerless to enforce its policy in face of their consistent hostility. The receipt rolls, some few fragmentary lists of fees, and the collectors' views of account preserved among the subsidy rolls or on the memoranda rolls, supplemented by the records of petitions in Parliament and by the writs of respite issued from the Chancery, constitute at this period almost our only sources of information. No exact estimate of the yield from the Scottish scutages can be formed from the data they furnish; but some generalizations at least are possible. The records show clearly that, although small sums might from time to time be levied by the collectors from the fees of wardships, escheats, and honours in hand, nothing could as a rule be exacted from the main body of tenants-in-chief who had discharged their liabilities by service or a fine. By their protests in Parliament and before the Exchequer the magnates were able to compel the king, if not to withdraw his claims, at least to suspend them.[1] Both laymen and clerics who had served or compounded for their service were allowed writs *de supersedendo* entitling them to respite until the questions at issue should have been decided;[2] and the collectors in their view of account were similarly respited 'usque super compotum'.[3] As we have seen, no settlement was

---

[1] In 1315 respite for a year was granted (Exch. L.T.R. Mem. Roll, No. 85, Rec. Hil., m. 7; K.R., No. 88, m. 145; *Rot. Parl.* i. 292, No. 17). A further year's respite was granted in 1320 (*Rot. Parl.* i. 383).

[2] *Cal. of Chancery Rolls Various*, pp. 105 seq. Among the ecclesiastics who obtained such writs were the Bishops of Salisbury, Lincoln, London, Bath and Wells, Chichester, Exeter, and Winchester; the Abbots of Peterborough, Cerne, Sherborne, Abbotsbury, Ramsey, St. Albans, Glastonbury, Winchcombe, Hyde, Michelney; and the Abbess of Shaftesbury.

[3] The views of account fall into two clear divisions: (i) containing the sums not in dispute, viz., those arising from wardships, escheats, etc.; (ii) containing the sums for which exemption was claimed on the ground of service or fine. The formula employed runs: 'Et respectuantur usque super compotum suum x li. de quibus [collectores] onerantur de diversis pro quibus habuerunt brevia de supersedendo' (Memoranda Rolls, Edw. II, *passim*).

in fact ever reached between the Crown and its military tenants, and accounting never proceeded beyond the view stage.[1] Hence we may safely conclude that, when in 1340 all outstanding scutage debts and accounts were pardoned by statute, there were included among them most of the sums which had been charged against the great ecclesiastics for the Scottish Wars of Edward I and II.

The question remains—was the king justified in attempting to convert the scutage into a general tax payable without regard to the performance of service or the payment of a fine? Undoubtedly the great disparity that existed in many cases between the old and new *servicium debitum* supplied a prima facie justification. In point of fact, however, the loss sustained by the Crown as a result of the triumph of the principle of the *quota* was far more apparent than real. The value of a knight's service had, as we have seen, enormously increased since the days of Henry II; while, in the fourteenth century, the fines were paid at a proportionately high rate. In 10 Edward I they were assessed at 50 marks the fee [2] in 28 Edward I[3] and 4 and 16 Edward II[4] at £40 (60 m.); in 31 Edward I [5] and 1 Edward III [6] at £20 (30 m.). In 34 Edward I [7] as a special concession, the rate was reduced to 20 m. the fee, to which it fell once more in 7 Edward II.[8] For the Gascon expedition of 1295 fines at the unprecedented rate of 100 m. the fee were exacted,[9] but they were subsequently pardoned because the king was not present in person with the army, and the service was not rendered 'communiter'.[10] When it is remembered that—to cite only one example—the fines of nineteen clerical tenants amounted in 10 Edward I to over £3,000,[11] the claim of the Crown to scutage

---

[1] *Supra*, p. 58; *E.H.R.* xxxviii. 19 seq.
[2] Exch. L.T.R. Misc. Roll, 1/13, m. 11.
[3] Ibid., m. 1.   [4] Ibid., m. 6 and m. 14.
[5] Ibid., m. 2.   [6] Ibid., m. 13.
[7] Ibid., m. 2: 'habita . . . tractatu inter eosdem Thesaurarios et Barones justiciarios et alios de consilio regis ei assidentes ipsis quidem considerantibus quod Rex servicium suum habuit in dictis partibus infra modicum tempus elapsum duobus vicibus, annis videlicit xxviij et xxxj, concordarunt quod hoc vice finis pro feodo sit ad viginti marcas . . .'
[8] Exch. L.T.R. Misc. Roll, 1/13, m. 8 d.
[9] Exch. L.T.R. Mem. Roll, No. 82, Brev. Bar., *passim*.
[10] Exch. L.T.R. Mem. Roll, No. 82, Brev. Bar. Mich., m. 11 d, and *passim*.
[11] Exch. L.T.R. Misc. Roll, 1/13, m. 11. £2,959 2s. 2d. was actually

in addition appears as an unwarranted attempt to enforce payment for the same thing twice over. It is, in fact, impossible
to doubt that the later Plantagenets looked upon the scutage
less as the commutation of service than as an expedient for
raising revenue. Our text-books teach us to regard Edward I
as the enemy and destroyer of feudalism, but an open-minded
examination of his attitude to feudal questions proves that the
traditional view embodies at best but a partial truth. That the
result of his policy, and especially of his land legislation, was
ultimately to hasten the decay of the feudal organization is un-
questioned, but the extent to which this result was intended
or foreseen is problematical. It is certain that no monarch could
have been more tenacious of his rights as feudal lord than was
Edward, especially when they tended directly to his profit. The
importance of his foundation of a paid national force has been
often and rightly emphasized, but the fact that the feudal levy
formed the nucleus of every army he led into Wales or Scotland
is less frequently acknowledged. Similarly, his exploitation of
the new methods of taxation is remembered, if only because
of its association with the development of the idea of representation; but his jealous attempt to preserve the old feudal sources
of revenue—the scutages, and 'incidents' such as the aids, wardship, and marriage, and escheat—is forgotten or ignored. It is
undeniable that in the thirteenth century the needs of the
government finally outgrew the old feudal machinery, and new
devices had to be invented to meet the new requirements. The
first impulse of the Crown, when the breakdown became
evident, however, was to repair and not to replace the existing
machine—the more so because grotesquely exaggerated notions
of the potential yield of the traditional levies were still current.[1]
Hence its preoccupation with the collection of the Edwardian
scutages of Wales and Scotland, and its continual endeavour to
keep itself informed of the allocation and distribution of fees.
Its concern was the greater since the feudal revenues belonged
to it as of right, and did not involve that principle of consent
which complicated the levy of the newer forms of taxation.[2]

paid in 10 and 11 Edw. I. See *Johannes de Oxenedes, Chronica*, R.S., Appendix,
pp. 326 seq. Compotus Magistri Willelmi de Luda custodis de Garderoba.
  [1] *Supra*, p. 25, n. 5. As late as 1315 we find reference made to the 'copiosa

The very statutes which are traditionally regarded as expressing the 'anti-feudal' policy of Edward I are susceptible of quite a different interpretation. Viewed in the light of the struggle of Exchequer and baronage over the incidence of the scutage, they appear rather as part of an attempt—sustained until the middle of the fourteenth century—to infuse new vigour into the moribund feudal institutions, and to restore their original productivity. That this was the purpose of *de Religiosis* is evident from the wording of the 'statute' itself. Its intention is specifically stated to be the prevention of any further loss of the services—'que ad defensionem regni ab inicio fuerunt'— through the passing of land so burdened into the 'dead hand' of the Church.[1] The preamble of *Quia Emptores*, it is true, stresses mainly the loss of incidental profits resulting from over-subinfeudation, but the actual provisions are concerned with *servicia* rather than *consuetudines*.[2] If Edward aimed in 1290 at the elimination of mesne tenure, it was primarily because he hoped by that means to facilitate the collection of the feudal dues, which had been hampered through the excessive lengthening of the tenurial ladder. The statute which, in the sequel, was so greatly to accelerate the disintegration of the feudal superstructure, was, in fact, originally designed to arrest it.[3]

Summarizing, therefore, our conclusions regarding the history of the commutation of knight-service as between the Crown and its immediate tenants, we see that three phases can be distinguished. (i) Until, roughly speaking, the end of the reign of Henry II, scutage was the only alternative to corporal service. (ii) Under Richard I the fine made its appear-

pecunia', which a levy of scutage should produce (Exch. L.T.R. Mem. Roll, No. 85, Brev. Ret. Easter, m. 4).

[1] *Statutes of the Realm*, i. 51.   [2] Ibid., p. 106.

[3] M. Pasquet, in his interesting and suggestive essay on 'The Origins of the House of Commons' (*Trans. R.G.D. Laffan*), discusses the principle and effect of the statute *Quia Emptores*. His conclusions are, however, vitiated by his incomplete comprehension of English feudal institutions. He does not correctly grasp the points at issue between Crown and baronage in the dispute over the incidence of scutage, and he gives a false emphasis to Edward's disregard of what he describes as 'the fundamental feudal principle' of the distinction between tenants-in-chief and subtenants. As we have seen, Edward's policy was in reality no more than the culmination of a tendency inherent in English feudalism from the days of the Salisbury Oath.

ance as a supplementary form of composition; and continued side by side with the scutage until the latter half of the thirteenth century, when it eventually supplanted it. (iii) With the accession of Edward I an attempt was made to revive the interest of the Crown in the scutage by treating it as the commutation of the service of the surplus fees of the tenants-in-chief, which were not covered by the new *servicium*. The relation of the ecclesiastical tenants to the principle of commutation in these various phases was briefly as follows: (i) During the reigns of the first two Angevin kings, bishops and abbots alike seem in general to have compounded by either scutage or a fine, whenever opportunity offered, although there is nothing to prove that they were in any sense specially privileged to do so. (ii) In the thirteenth century we find that, contrary to the generally accepted view, there was a perceptible increase in the amount of corporal service rendered. First the bishops began, under John, to proffer service with greater frequency, and then under Henry III their example was followed by the religious. (iii) After the accession of Edward I commutation became once more the usual, although by no means the invariable practice; but it now took the form of a fine paid at a fixed rate upon the fees of the reduced *servicium*. The Crown attempted to exact scutage in addition, but its demands were strenuously combatted by the clerical tenants, and only in exceptional cases was payment successfully enforced.

As to Maitland's familiar dictum that 'when Edward I came to the throne the feudal military organization has already broken down, and will no longer provide either soldiers or money, save in very inadequate amounts',[1] it is clearly only partially applicable to the fees of the Church. Admittedly the number of knights produced was small in comparison with the numbers of the original *servicium debitum*; but the actual value represented by the late thirteenth- or fourteenth-century *quota* was certainly not less than that of the full contingent of Norman or Angevin days. In the twelfth century, when the rate of pay for a fully-armed knight was eightpence a day, it would have cost the Archbishop of York about 40 marks to maintain his twenty knights in the field for forty days: in 1282 the sum

---

[1] Pollock and Maitland, *History of English Law*, i. 233.

assigned by him for the expenses of the five knights of his reduced *servicium* was £100.[1] Again, while it is true that scutage in the Edwardian period was almost entirely unproductive, it must be remembered that there was simultaneously operative a system of fines yielding perhaps twice the amount which would have been produced by a levy of scutage on the traditional lines. The twenty-seven ecclesiastics who in 1282 paid between them some 3,000 marks in fines,[2] would have been liable for only about half that sum in scutage at the forty-shilling rate on the fees of the old 'recognition'. Finally, the fact that the Crown was able, as late as 1327, to exact a response to its summons for service, shows that half a century after the accession of Edward I the bond between the king and his immediate tenants, though weak, still held; and proves that the determined effort of the later Plantagenets to preserve their feudal privileges was not wholly ineffective.

[1] *Register of Archbishop William Wickwane, 1279–1285* (Surtees Society), p. 325.   [2] *C.F.R.* i. 85 seq.

CHAPTER III

THE ECCLESIASTICAL TENANTS-IN-CHIEF AND THE MACHINERY FOR THE EXACTION OF FEUDAL SERVICE

Now that the position of the clerical tenants in relation both to corporal service and its money equivalent has been defined, it remains to examine, with special reference to the fees of the Church, the machinery employed by the Crown for exacting, under the one form or the other, the service due from its immediate vassals.

I. THE WRITS OF MILITARY SUMMONS

The first stage in the mustering of the feudal host was the issue of the formal summons. In England all knight-service, to whomsoever due, was *regale servicium*, and could only be exacted at the instance of the Crown, which was the pivot of the entire feudal military system.[1] The earliest extant example of a military summons is the writ addressed to Abbot Ethelwig of Evesham which, as already noted, was discovered some years ago by Round and assigned by him with much probability to the year 1072.[2] This is, however, a purely fortuitous survival. There is no continuous record of the summonses available before the reign of John, when the series of Chancery rolls begins; and they did not assume a definite shape until the latter half of the thirteenth century. Under Henry III they began to issue under the traditional triple form of:

(i) writs addressed individually to the greater lay tenants-in-chief;

(ii) writs addressed individually to the ecclesiastical tenants-in-chief; and

(iii) writs addressed to the sheriffs on behalf of the lesser tenants-in-chief both lay and ecclesiastical.

From 1244 onwards it was further usual to enter on the close roll the names of all the recipients of an individual summons.

In spite of slight variations of phraseology the general out-

---

[1] Pollock and Maitland, *History of English Law*, i. 263 seq.
[2] *Supra*, p. 3.

line of the writ was fixed by the thirteenth century. After the
salutation, the statement of the occasion of the summons, and
the appointment of the date and place of muster, there followed
the mandatory clause enjoining upon the addressee, on his faith
and homage, attendance 'cum equis et armis et cum toto servicio
nobis debito'. This formula was employed for lay and clerical
tenants alike, no such clear-cut distinction between the two
classes appearing as in the case of the parliamentary writs.

Setting aside summonses in which irregularities appear—as,
for instance, that of 25 Edward I (Gascony), where writs exist
for the lay tenants-in-chief and for the bishops, but not for the
religious;[1] that of 34 Edward I (Scotland), where no individual
writs addressed to ecclesiastics are discoverable at all;[2] and
that of 26 Edward I (Scotland), where the customary formula
of command is replaced by a polite request 'quatinus . . . ita
decenter et potenter personaliter accedatis . . . quod fidelitatem
et probitatem vestram in hac parte . . . debeamus merito com-
mendare etc.'[3]—we find that between 28 Henry III and the
last muster of the feudal host in 8 Richard II there are records
of twenty full and regular summonses. An examination of these
shows that there were specially summoned at different times
the two archbishops, nineteen bishops (the four Welsh bishops
being included from the accession of Edward I onwards), and
fifty heads of religious houses, including forty-one abbots, four
priors, and five abbesses.[4] The full number of archbishops and
bishops was summoned on one occasion only, viz. in 1327, and
the largest number of heads of religious houses summoned
simultaneously was forty-five—a total reached in 9 Edward II
and again in 12 Edward II. No logical principle can be dis-
cerned in the selection of names. As in the case of the par-

---

[1] *Parl. Writs*, i. 283.   [2] Ibid., p. 376.   [3] Ibid., p. 302.
[4] The Abbots of Abbotsbury, Abingdon, Bardney, Battle, Bristol (St.
Augustine's), Burton, Canterbury (St. Augustine's),Cerne, Chertsey, Chester,
Cirencester, Colchester, Crowland, Evesham, Eynsham, Glastonbury,
Gloucester, Keynsham, Leicester, Malmesbury, Michelney, Middleton,
Pershore, Peterborough, Ramsey, Reading, St. Albans, St. Benet's, St.
Edmunds, Selby, Sherborne, Shrewsbury, Tavistock, Thorney, Thornton,
Waltham, Westminster, Whitby, Winchcombe, Winchester (Hyde), and
York (St. Mary's); the Abbesses of Barking, Romsey, Shaftesbury, Wilton,
Winchester (Nunnaminster); and the Priors of Bromholm Coventry, Dun-
stable, and St. John of Jerusalem.

liamentary writs of the same period the widest variations appear from year to year. Of the bishops, the names of four only (Bath and Wells, Exeter, Lincoln, and London) are found on every occasion; but all save Canterbury were summoned more than ten times.[1] Among the religious, on the other hand, the fluctuations are much greater. Six received writs with unbroken regularity, twenty-seven were summoned ten times or more, but of the remaining twenty-three, thirteen were summoned on less than five occasions out of the possible twenty.

The most difficult problem in connexion with the summonses arises from the fact that, as noted in an earlier chapter,[2] a large proportion were apparently addressed to ecclesiastics from whom no military service was actually due to the Crown. We have seen that there are strong grounds for believing that the clerical tenants-in-chief *per servicium militare* as created by the Conqueror in 1070 received no subsequent accessions: yet six bishops and twenty-six religious, over and above the fifteen bishops and twenty-four religious who appear in the records of the twelfth century, were summoned at different times under Henry III and later to serve in the royal armies, several with great regularity. Among the bishops, Carlisle was summoned seventeen times and Rochester thirteen, while of the religious, the Abbess of Barking received fifteen individual summonses, the Abbots of Gloucester and Thorney each received fourteen, the Abbess of St. Mary's Winchester, twelve, and the Abbot of Crowland eleven. As early as 1225 a list of the ecclesiastics to be summoned for service, which is filed up with the scutage rolls of 2–15 Henry III, includes the names of the Bishop of Carlisle, and the Abbots of Whitby, Selby, St. Mary's York, Leicester, Shrewsbury, Battle, and Colchester, as well as those of the recognized military tenants.[3]

How is the policy of the Chancery in relation to the clerical tenants to be accounted for? That those summoned did not recognize military liabilities is, as we have seen elsewhere, capable of demonstration, and it is clear that, save in exceptional cases such as that of the Bishop of St. Davids, they made no

---

[1] The Archbishop of Canterbury was summoned only nine times in all between 1244 and 1385.　　　　[2] *Supra*, pp. 10 seq.
[3] Scutage Roll, No. 2, m. 19 d; cf. the list of 1229 (ibid., m. 21 d).

attempt to respond to the summons. Under Edward I a list of
the writs issued seems to have been consulted in the compilation
of the marshals' rolls, for the names of the recipients of individual summonses are duly entered thereon; but no record
of a proffer appears, and save on rare occasions the Crown seems
to have attempted no action against the defaulters. In 34 Edward I, it is true, the response was considered so unsatisfactory that the king ordered the sheriffs to inquire into the
service due from all ecclesiastics within their respective bailiwicks, and to cause all holding *per servicium militare* to appear
at the Exchequer to give an account of themselves and to hear
the judgement of the court.[1] Several religious, including the
Abbess of Barking and the Abbot of Netley were constrained,
under this order, to put in an appearance, but they denied the
liability to service and in the absence of any proof to the contrary, the Crown was compelled to accept their denial.[2] On
what principle or from what sources the Chancery selected the
ecclesiastics to be individually summoned there is no evidence
to show. The religious to whom special writs were addressed
were of all sorts and conditions. Augustinians, Cluniacs,
and Hospitallers were represented in addition to Benedictines.
Several of the houses—Chester [3] and Shrewsbury, for example
—were not of royal foundation, although changes in the allocation of the land had brought them in the course of time into
closer relation to the Crown. Some of the smaller foundations,
such as Dunstable, Eynsham, and Keynsham, can have held
little or no land in chief by any kind of tenure. It is impossible
to say whether their inclusion among the recipients of individual
writs was purely fortuitous, or whether it was the result of a
deliberate attempt on the part of the Crown to exact military
service where none was due.[4]

---

[1] Exch. L.T.R. Mem. Roll, No. 76, Brev. Ret. Hil., m. 69 d.

[2] Exch. L.T.R. Mem. Roll, No. 77, Rec. Mich., m. 14 and m. 15.

[3] I am indebted to the late Professor Tout for the information that,
excepting in 1303, Chester was always summoned when the king was
earl.

[4] Miss Elizabeth Kimball, in her interesting and important article on
'Tenure in Frankalmoign and Secular Services' (*E.H.R.* xliii. 341 seq.), suggests
a parallel in the various demands made by the Crown in the thirteenth century
on frankalmoign tenants, in the shape of *dona*, corrodies, &c. Such exactions
were, however, extra-feudal, and are therefore in an entirely different

Indeed, the one fact which clearly emerges from an analysis of the summonses issued to ecclesiastics is their entire unreliability as an index to the composition of the clerical element either in any given army or in the feudal host in general. Because a bishop or an abbot received a writ of summons it by no means followed that he either owed or rendered service. The numbers and personnel of the clerical tenants-in-chief *per servicium militare* can only be determined from the documents which record the response to the summons and not from the summonses themselves. The implications of this conclusion cannot now be considered, but, as will be shown later, they are of great importance, for the writs of summons have too often in the past been treated as an independent source, and many theories have been built up on their unsupported evidence.

II. THE FINES *PRO SERVICIO*

Under Edward I and later, it was usual to follow up the summons by writs authorizing the payment in certain circumstances of fines *pro servicio*. The sheriffs were directed to make proclamation that, by special royal grace, all ecclesiastics, women, and others 'ad arma minus potentes' might compound for their service; and a day, prior to the date assigned for the muster, was fixed for their appearance before the officials appointed by the king to assess and receive the compositions. Although no earlier writs seem to have survived, it is probable that, under Henry III and John, a broadly similar procedure was followed, for there is evidence that payment was usually made while the host was mustering.[1] General fining was not, however, sanctioned for every campaign. In 1311 permission to compound was restricted in the first instance to tenants holding less than half a fee, and it was only in virtue of a special royal concession that the Abbot of Peterborough, the Bishop of Exeter, and one or two other clerical tenants were allowed

category from attempts to extend feudal obligations to fiefs which were properly exempt.

[1] Cf. the evidence of the *Rotuli de Oblatis et Finibus*, especially for 1201 and 1205. In 1242 the fines were paid before the king's departure for Gascony. Cf. the heading in the pipe roll 'Fines militum ne transfretent . . . preter scutagia sua' (Pipe Roll, No. 86, *passim*).

to make fine for their service.[1] In 1327 the royal writ authorized composition by 'abbates, priores, abbatisse, prioresse et alii de clero' but not by the bishops,[2] from whom, therefore, the Exchequer refused to accept payment.[3] The clerical tenants-in-chief habitually transacted the business of fining by means of attorneys appointed 'ad hoc' under their letters patent;[4] their stewards or household officers, or, in the case of the religious, one of the monks of the house, who might or might not be an obedientiary, commonly acting in this capacity.[5] The fines were usually paid into the Exchequer, which, in the fourteenth century, followed the king north to York during the wars with Scotland;[6] but they were sometimes —and especially during the early years of Edward I's reign, when the king's household was absorbing an increasingly large share of public business—paid into the Wardrobe.[7] In either

[1] Exch. L.T.R. Misc. Roll, 1/13, m. 6; Exch. L.T.R. Mem. Roll, No. 81, Brev. Bar. Mich., m. 11, m. 1 d, m. 2 d. Writs under the privy seal to the treasurer and barons on behalf of the Abbot of Peterborough, the Bishop of Bath and Wells, and the Bishop of Winchester, authorizing them by special royal grace to fine for their service 'noncontrestant qe nous avions ordene qe nule fyn feust receu por service fors qe de meyns qe de my fet'. The like to the Bishop of Exeter 'a la requeste nostre cher et foial monsire Pierre de Gavaston' Counte de Cornewaille'.

[2] Exch. L.T.R. Misc. Roll, 1/13, m. 15.

[3] Ibid. The fine offered by the Bishop of Bath and Wells is crossed through and the note added: 'Vacat quia Thesaurarius et Barones non habuerunt warantum per breve superius irrotulatum ad capiendum fines de episcopis pro serviciis suis in exercitu predicto, etc.'

[4] See Exch. L.T.R. Misc. Roll, 1/13, especially m. 3, where the formula employed is: 'X per Y et Z attornatos suos per litteras suas patentes . . . finem fecit.' Examples of these letters of attorney occur in the St. Albans Cartulary, Cott. MSS. Tiberius, E. vj, f. 203 d, f. 193 d; *Register of Bishop John de Drokensford of Bath* (Somerset Record Society), p. 60; *Register of Bishop William Guisborough of Worcester* (Worcester Historical Society), p. 28.

[5] See Exch. L.T.R. Misc. Roll, 1/13, *passim*. We find instances of the cellarer or the sacristan acting as attorney in the case of religious houses, as well as ordinary monks. The bishops might be represented by their stewards, by 'clerici', or even by the parson or rector of one of the churches in their diocese. Occasionally, but very rarely, the great ecclesiastics made a personal appearance, e.g. in 28 Edw. I the Abbot of Ramsey appeared 'in propria persona sua' to make fine for his service (Exch. L.T.R. Misc. Roll, 1/13, m. 1).

[6] Ibid., *passim*. See also D. M. Broome, 'Exchequer Migrations to York in the Thirteenth and Fourteenth Centuries', in *Essays in Medieval History presented to Thomas Frederick Tout*.

[7] Such was the case in 5 and 10 Edw. I, *C.F.R.* i. 86 seq.; Exch. L.T.R.

case a formal acknowledgement of receipt was given, the Exchequer issuing, in the ordinary course, a tally, the Wardrobe letters of acquittance which might be reinforced by a notification of payment addressed to the treasurer and barons.[1] Occasionally the money due from individual tenants might be assigned by the Crown direct to its creditors. In 1277, for instance, several ecclesiastics, including the Bishops of Exeter, London, and Lincoln, and the Abbot of St. Edmunds, were ordered to pay their fines to certain merchants of Lucca to whom Edward was indebted.[2] In 1314 the Bishops of Ely and Lincoln, by command of the king, made payment to Peter Ferrand, merchant, 'in part satisfaction of the debts in which the king is bound to him for buying horses to his use'.[3] To secure acquittance in circumstances such as these might be a laborious proceeding. The Peterborough chronicle relates how, in 1282, the abbot's fine was assigned to the Luccanese merchants Henry de Podio and Baroncinus Gualtero. He paid in two instalments, for each of which he received a written receipt, which had then to be presented to and allowed by the Wardrobe as a preliminary to the issue of the necessary 'littera acquietancie' under the royal seal.[4] In 1314 the Archbishop of York made fine at the Exchequer in 100 marks for the expedition to Scotland. He was directed to pay the money to John Vanne, merchant, the king's creditor, and to obtain from him letters patent of receipt 'per quas Rex talliam fieri faciet Archiepiscopo allocand' in fine predicto'.[5]

On every fine exceeding ten marks in value the tenants-in-chief had, in accordance with what was already in the twelfth century a well-established custom, to pay an additional 10 per cent. as queen-gold.[6] Some attempt seems to have been made

---

Misc. Roll, 1/13, m. 11; *Johannis de Oxenedes Chronica*, R.S., Appendix, pp. 326 seq., Compotus Magistri Willelmi de Luda Custodis de Garderoba. Occasional payments into the Wardrobe are recorded at a later date, e.g. in 31 Edw. I, Exch. L.T.R. Misc. Roll, 1/13, m. 2 d.

[1] For these notifications to the barons of payment into the Exchequer see C.C.R., Edw. I, *passim*, and Exch. Mem. Rolls, Brev. Bar.

[2] *C.F.R.* i. 86 seq.

[3] Exch. L.T.R. Mem. Roll, No. 84, Brev. Ret. Trin.

[4] *Chronicon Petroburgense*, ed. Stapleton and Bruce (Camden Society), pp. 55 seq.   [5] Exch. L.T.R. Mem. Roll, No. 84, Brev. Ret. Trin.

[6] *Dialogus de Scaccario*, II. xxvi; *Red Book*, ii. 760.

under Edward II to question the validity of this principle
in the case of payments *pro servicio*,[1] but it broke down
on the question of precedent.[2] The 'aurum regine' was
apparently paid along with the fine into the Exchequer, from
whence it was subsequently collected by the queen's representative.[3]

The compositions for military service seem as a rule to have
been promptly settled in the thirteenth century, the bulk of the
money due being accounted for in the year of assessment.
Towards the end of the reign of Edward I, however, difficulty
began to be experienced in securing payment of the sums
promised, and several years frequently elapsed before they could
be collected.[4] If undue delay occurred, the sheriff, in the
normal course of Exchequer procedure, was made responsible
for levying the debt by distraint, or, in the last resort, by the
sale of the debtor's goods and chattels to the value of the sum
owed.[5] Not all that was promised was, however, paid. The fines
of the ecclesiastical tenants-in-chief were not infrequently
pardoned in whole or in part. In 1277, for instance, the Abbot
of St. Augustine's, Canterbury, was forgiven the fifty marks in
which he had fined for the one fee which he recognized.[6] In
the same year the Abbess of Shaftesbury was pardoned part
of her fine, thirty marks by the king's grace, and twenty at the

[1] Exch. L.T.R. Mem. Roll, No. 85, Rec. Hil., m. 5 d: Writ to the
Treasurer and barons on behalf of the Bishop of Ely, who has been granted
respite of payment of queen-gold on his fine for the army of 4 Edward II;
'Rex . . . volens informari utrum de finibus cum eo factis pro servicio Regi in
exercitibus suis Scocie debito aurum ad opus Isabelle Regine Anglie consortis Regis carissime levari debeat et de huiusmodi finibus solvi consueverit temporibus retroactis.'

[2] Ibid., loc. cit.: ' . . . datum est Regi intelligi quod huiusmodi aurum ad
opus prefate consortis Regis de huiusmodi finibus per ceteros prelatos et
magnates regni sui cum Rege factis pro serviciis suis Regi in huiusmodi
exercitibus debitis levari debet et hactenus levari consuevit.'

[3] Madox, *Exchequer*, i. 350 seq. For instances of actual payment see
Chron. Petroburgense, pp. 25, 55; Sparke, *Historiae Coenobii Burgi*, p. 171;
Cott. MSS. Vespas., E. xxi, f. 49 d; Cott. MSS. Tiberius, E. vi, f. 203.

[4] See Exch. L.T.R. Misc. Roll, 1/13 *passim*.

[5] See, for example, Exch. L.T.R. Mem. Roll, No. 64, Brev. pro Rege.
Trin. m. 19. Mandate to the Sheriff to levy the fines of divers persons for
the Welsh war of 10 Ed. I. Of the Bishop of Chichester, the sheriff reports
that he has taken of his goods and chattels to the value of the debt, but has
not yet found a purchaser.

[6] Exch. L.T.R. Mem. Roll. No. 58, Comm. Easter, m. 7 d.

instance of his son Alphonse.[1] In 1282 the Bishop of Norwich,[2] and in 1306 the Archbishop of York,[3] were exonerated from payment by special royal grace, and in 1323 Bishop Walter Stapledon of Exeter, the Treasurer, was pardoned his fine 'pro bono servicio quod . . . nobis impendit',[4] in accordance with Exchequer custom. In 1246 Henry III directed that the forty marks in which the Abbot of Westminster made fine for his service in the army of Gannoch, together with the scutage of his knights, should be assigned to the custodians of the building operations then proceeding in the abbey church.[5]

III. THE MUSTER

On the day and at the place appointed in the writ of summons the constable and marshal, or their representatives, appeared to receive the proffers of the tenants-in-chief. The proceedings, which might extend over several days or even weeks,[6] opened with the issue of a solemn proclamation to the effect that none should deny or conceal his service on pain of heavy forfeiture.[7] The tenants then came forward in their turn to make formal recognition of their liability, and to present their quota or notify their payment of a fine.[8] There can be no doubt that every lay lord was expected to appear in person at the muster, and that, at least in the early days of the feudal military system, personal attendance was rigorously exacted from all save women, minors, or the infirm. That this principle was ever valid in the case of the ecclesiastics is improbable; but it is nevertheless certain that in the eleventh century the great churchmen frequently led their military tenants to war. We have already seen that Abbot Ethelwig of Evesham acted in 1072 as the commander not only of his own contingent of five knights, but of those of

[1] *C.F.R.* i. 86.　　　　　　　[2] *C.C.R.*, 1279–1288, p. 268.

[3] *C.P.R.*, 1301–1307, p. 572.

[4] Exch. L.T.R. Mem. Roll, No. 92, Brev. Bar. Trin., m. 63.

[5] *C.C.R.*, 1242–1247, p. 387.

[6] In 5 Edw. I the majority of the proffers seem to have been made at Worcester between July 1st and 6th; but men were enrolled at Chester in the third week of July. In 10 Edw. I most of the proffers were taken during the first three weeks of August.

[7] *Parl. Writs*, i. 197; Chanc. Misc. 5/10, m. 4: 'Et proclamatum est . . . quod nullus sub gravi forisfactura servicium suum deneget, etc.'

[8] The usual formula is: 'X recognoscit servicium *y* militum pro quo satisfecit in garderoba Regis [*or*] pro quo finem fecit [*or*] faciend' per A, B, C.'

the several counties over which he exercised jurisdiction at the time.[1] Two years later we find him co-operating with Bishop Wulfstan of Worcester in defending the line of the Severn against the rebel advance.[2] Nor, apparently, was his an exceptional case. The Abingdon chronicler relates how the Conqueror sent a force against Malcolm of Scotland under the command of his son Robert, 'cum quo et plures Angliae primates quorum unus Abbas Ethelelmus fuit'.[3] Becket, when chancellor, participated vigorously in the campaign in Toulouse in 1159;[4] and as late as 1193 we learn from Jocelin of Brakelond that Abbot Samson of St. Edmunds, 'with several others of the English abbots', donned armour and led his knights in person, under his own banner, to the siege of Windsor. By that date, however, such behaviour was sufficiently unusual to earn the reprobation of the monks, who dreaded the establishment of a precedent, 'timens consequentiam, ne forte futurus Abbas cogatur in propria persona ire in expeditionem bellicam'.[5] The occupation of the clergy in war-like pursuits was in any case contrary both to the spirit and the letter of the canon law, and was probably rarely countenanced when once the actual period of conquest was past.[6]

Although, however, they ceased personally to attend the muster, the clerical tenants-in-chief commonly, if not invariably, sent an accredited representative to supervise, on their behalf, the making of the proffer. The Abbot of Peterborough, whose contingent of sixty knights was larger than that of any other religious house in England, delegated all his military

---

[1] *Supra*, p. 3.   [2] Round, *Feudal England*, p. 305.

[3] *Hist. Monasterii de Abingdon*, ii. 9.

[4] W. H. Hutton, *Thomas Becket*, pp. 43–4.

[5] Chron. Jocelini de Brakelond', *Chronicle of St. Edmunds*, R.S., p. 259.

[6] Cf. the decree of the Synod of Westminster of 1175, *Chron. Rogeri de Hoveden*, R.S. ii. 75, ex Consilio meldensi, A.D. 845: 'Quicunque ex clero videntur esse, arma non sumant, nec armati incedant, sed professionis suae vocabulum religiosis moribus ex religioso habitu prebeant. Quod si contempserint, tanquam sacrorum canonum contemptores, et ecclesiastice auctoritatis profanatores, proprii gradus amissione mulctentur, quia non possunt simul Deo et saeculo militare' (Hewitt, *Ancient Armour in Europe*, p. 114). At a later date Bishop Anthony Bek of Durham, who led a detachment at Falkirk, and Bishop Despencer of Norwich, who helped to put down the Peasants' Revolt of 1381 and led the Crusade in Flanders against the Clementines in 1383, are notorious examples of the fighting cleric.

responsibilities to a permanent official—the constable—who has not a few features in common with the *advocatus* of the Continent.[1] The office, which seems to have been created by Abbot John de Sais (1114–25) in the time of Henry I,[2] was hereditary in the family of de la Mare, tenants of the abbey in the counties of Northampton and Lincoln.[3] It carried with it the important duties of summoning and arraying, on receipt of the royal writ, the Peterborough knights, conducting them to the royal presence, and acting as their commander throughout the period of service in any theatre assigned to them 'infra regnum Anglie'. Incidental duties were the delivery, in person or by deputy, of the abbot's messages, and the maintenance of peace and order within the abbey precincts on the day of the installation of a new abbot; while at the inaugural banquet it was the special privilege of the constable to serve the abbot with his own hand from the first dish. In return for these services he claimed the reimbursement of all expenses incurred on the abbot's behalf, and an annual retaining fee of two robes or their equivalent in money; together with free maintenance in the abbey throughout the year for one war-horse and its groom, and free lodging 'ad adventus suos' for himself, three squires, five horses and their grooms, and two greyhounds. In addition, the gold and silver vessels from which the lord abbot was served on the day of his installation were considered the perquisites of the constable.[4] The office did not, apparently, retain its importance for more than about a hundred years. Brian de la Mare was seised of it at the beginning of the thirteenth century,[5] but on his death in 1227[6] it seems to have lapsed. The determining factor in its

[1] Round, 'The Knights of Peterborough', *Victoria County History, Northamptonshire*, i. 391 seq.; cf. C. Pergameni, *L'Avouerie ecclésiastique belge*, pp. 131 seq.

[2] See the transcript of the charter of Abbot John to Ralph de la Mare, *Chron. Petroburgense* (Camden Society), pp. 130 seq.

[3] Sparke, *Historiae Coenobii Burg*, i. 54: 'Galfridus de la Mare tenet duas hidas et dimid' terrae in Norhamtonscire, scilicet in Makeseie, Nortburch et Wodecroft. Et in Lincolnscire duas carucatas et dim' scilicet in Thurleby, et inde facit servicium trium militum.' The history of the family is traced in detail by W. T. Mellows, *Henry of Pytchley's Book of Fees* (Northampton Record Society Publications ii), pp. 85 seq. and notes.

[4] *Chron. Petroburgense*, pp. 130 seq.

[5] Ibid., loc. cit., Cott. MSS. Vesp., E. xxii, f. 1.

[6] *Chron. Petroburgense*, p. 9.

decline was doubtless the reduction in the abbey's *servicium*, combined with the fact that in the thirteenth century the abbots consistently compounded for their service; but a contributory cause is undoubtedly to be found in the family history of the de la Mares themselves. Between 1227 and 1290 the de la Mare fee seems to have passed through the hands of no less than seven different lords, of whom certainly the first and the last were minors when they succeeded.[1] In 1294 the seventh, Geoffrey, brought an action in the king's court against Abbot Richard of London for the recovery of the office held by his ancestors. After long delay an agreement was reached between the parties in 1296, Geoffrey quit-claiming Abbot William in consideration of the sum of sixty marks sterling.[2]

No other monastic house seems to have boasted an institution analogous to the Peterborough *constabulatum*. The Abbot of St. Albans habitually sent his contingent to the muster in charge of a representative, but the appointment was purely *ad hoc*. It might be filled by the abbot's seneschal or any other of his officials, or even by one of his monks,[3] and its responsibilities terminated as soon as the knights had been received by the constable and marshal and assigned to a unit.[4] We may,

---

[1] See the account of Geoffrey de la Mare's suit against the abbot, where the descent is traced from Brian to Geoffrey his son; to Brian his son; to Peter his brother; to Ralph his brother; to Geoffrey his brother; to Peter his brother; to Geoffrey his son, the claimant in 1294 (Cott. MSS. Vesp., E. xxii, f. i seq.). In 1228 Brian left a son over whose wardship there was a dispute between the abbot and the king (*Chron. Petroburgense*, p. 9; Sparke, *Hist. Coenobii Burgi*. 54). In 1282 Peter de la Mare left a son over whose wardship and marriage there was again a long contest, this time between the abbot and a certain Mabel of Kenington (*Chron. Petroburgense*, pp. 61, 72 seq.; Mellows, *Henry of Pytchley*, pp. 85 seq.).

[2] Cott. MSS. Vesp., E. xxii, ff. 1 seq.; Peterborough Cartulary, MSS. of the Society of Antiquaries, MS. xxxviii, f. 161 d.

[3] In 1257 brother John de Bulum was sent to the muster on the abbot's behalf (*Chron. Majora*, vi. 372 seq.). In 1265 the abbot was represented by his archdeacon and chamberlain (Chron. Willelmi de Rishanger, *Chron. Monasterii S. Albani*, R.S., p. 41).

[4] See the statement of the customs of the abbey in 1257: 'Senescallus autem abbatis vel alius nomine suo missus, debet praesentare capitales electos ad faciendum servicium regale coram marescallo ad recipiendum servicium domini regis ei concessum per eundem regem constituto' (*Chron. Majora*, vi. 373). Cf. Cott. MSS. Nero, D. i, f. 134 d: 'Propriis sumptibus debent [milites] ire ad locum destinatum, deputato tamen aliquo per abbatem qui eos representare debet marescallo domini regis, ut videatur si sufficienter armis compareant instructi.'

perhaps, discern a closer parallel to the Peterborough institution in the marshalsey of the bishopric of Winchester. In the thirteenth century the marshal of the bishop's household regularly accounts in the local pipe roll for the scutage of the episcopal estates; and he seems in addition to have exercised over the military lands and tenants of the bishop a general control, in some respects resembling that exercised by the king's marshal over the feudal host of the kingdom.[1]

The presence of a responsible person to supervise the enrolment of the proffer was a matter of considerable import, since the marshals' rolls, or alternatively the certificate of the commanding officer, afforded the sole proof of the performance of service.[2] The Bishop of Hereford, who in 1282 omitted to get the details of his proffer entered, had to appeal to the verdict of a jury of neighbours before he could satisfy the Crown that he had duly discharged his obligations.[3] In 34 Edward I Ralph de Gorges covenanted with the Abbot of Abbotsbury to perform the service of one knight due from the abbot's fee. Sir Ralph arrived five days late for the muster, with the result that his proffer was not enrolled on the marshal's roll, and that the abbot was prosecuted by the Exchequer for neglect of the summons. It was not until 1310 that he was able to secure from the constable a certificate of service, and to induce the Exchequer to release him from distraint.[4]

When the forces had assembled there was held the 'ostensio equorum et armorum', which concerned the interests of the tenants-in-chief no less closely than the proffer itself. Matthew Paris describes how, at the muster for the Welsh war of 1257, the men were warned to bear themselves well on parade, 'lest

[1] See, for example, Ecclesiastical Commission Various, nos. 159279, 159280, 159283, 159288, 159293, 159315, under the heading *Marchaucia*. Cf. H. Hall, *Winchester Pipe Roll of 1207*, Introd., p. xi.

[2] This is abundantly clear from the writs of quittance of scutage, &c., which run: 'Quia A. B. fecit servitium suum in exercitu Wallie anno X°, pro servicio x feodorum militum quod Regi tunc recognovit sicut per inspeccionem rotulorum Marescalcie de eodem exercitu Regi constat . . .', *or* 'sicut Edwardus princeps Wallie [*or* Aymer de Valence or some other of the king's captains or generals] testificatus est per suas literas *or* coram consilio regis, etc.'

[3] *Register of Bishop Swinfield*, p. 333.

[4] Ancient Petitions, E. 995; Exch. L.T.R. Mem. Roll, No. 77, Comm. Rec. Mich., m. 18 d.; No. 80, Brev. Bar. Trin. m. 6 d.

their lords, through their default, should suffer damage, and incur the royal displeasure'.[1] The constable and marshal were empowered to reject the services of all inadequately equipped knights or serjeants and to compel the lords to substitute others 'lege militari decenter armati'.[2] In 1197, it will be remembered, Archbishop Anselm received from Rufus 'turbatorie litere', fiercely upbraiding him for having sent to the Welsh war knights 'nec convenienter . . . instructi, nec ad bella . . . pro negotii qualitate idonei'; and ordering him to be prepared to do right in the matter according to the judgement of the king's court, whenever the king should think fit to summon him.[3] Later a similar fate appears to have overtaken Abbot Godfrey of Peterborough. In 1311 the king called upon him to furnish his service for the war in Scotland, and he accordingly dispatched Sir William la Zouche with horses and arms to the muster, at a cost of more than sixty marks. The king was, however, dissatisfied with the proffer and exacted from the abbot instead a fine of £200 and £20 queen-gold.[4] In 1257, on the other hand, we learn from Matthew Paris that the knights hired on behalf of the Abbot of St. Albans by Brother John de Bulum were received with approbation, although many others were censured or rejected.[5] Monk though he was, brother John had evidently a good eye both for horse-flesh and for the accoutrements of war! Twenty years later, in the first Welsh expedition of Edward I, the St. Albans contingent again acquitted itself with honour, the 'nobilis apparatus' of both men and horses earning the warm commendation of all in authority.[6]

---

[1] *Chron. Majora*, vi. 374.

[2] Cf. Cott. MSS. Nero, D. 1, f. 134 d, where it is stated that the Abbot of St. Albans is to be represented before the constable and marshal 'ut videatur si sufficienter armis compareant [milites] instructi, alioquin debent graviter amerciari et alii loco ipsorum in constabularia poni'.

[3] Eadmer, *Historia Novorum*, p. 37; E. E. Freeman, *William Rufus*, i. 572 seq.

[4] Sparke, *Historiae Anglicanae Scriptores Varii*; *Chron. Walteri de Whytleseye*, p. 172: 'et nihil placuit regi. Iterum rex scripsit abbati ut pecuniam pro servicio suo demanderet. Tunc autem abbas demandavit domino regi pro servicio sua ccxx li.' *Supra*, p. 60 n. 1.

[5] *Chron. Majora*, vi. 374: 'Et sic procuratum est per Dei gratiam quod nullus armigerorum die quo fuit armorum ostensio reprobatus fuerat vel repulsus, cum multi alii reprobarentur.'

[6] *Gesta Abbatum Sancti Albani*, R.S., i. 435: 'Dominus Stephanus de

Of the nature of the equipment demanded in the thirteenth and fourteenth centuries we learn comparatively little from the feudal military records themselves. Our knowledge of medieval arms and armour is derived rather from literary and pictorial sources, from coins and seals, from effigies, and later from monumental brasses. From these we see that the knightly panoply, after remaining essentially unchanged for some hundred years after the Conquest, underwent in the thirteenth century—perhaps as a result of experience gained in the Crusades—rapid and important modifications. The body armour of the *miles* in Norman and early Angevin times consisted simply of the mail shirt or hauberk, furnished later with sleeves fitting closely to the wrists and with a coif covering both head and neck; and the conical iron helmet fitted with a nasal and sometimes with a neck-guard. Leg-coverings designed to protect the outer part of the limb when the wearer was in the saddle were occasionally but by no means generally worn. No protection of any kind seems to have been provided at this date for the horse, which was probably of a fairly light and inexpensive breed. From the time of Richard I onwards, however, the elaboration of the defences of both horse and rider proceeded apace. The surcoat of linen or silk which came into general use in the reign of John was the most conspicuous feature of knightly costume for the next two centuries, but its military significance was negligible. Of greater importance was the universal adoption of the *gambeson*—a padded and quilted garment worn beneath the *lorica* or coat of mail; the evolution from the very imperfect leg-guards of the Norman period of complete mail hose; the extension of the sleeves of the hauberk to form first mittens and later gloves for the protection of the hands of the combatant; and the substitution for the light Norman head-piece of the heavy and cumbrous pot-helm which outlasted the thirteenth century. Finally, in the later years of the reign of Henry III the transition from chain

Chendut et quatuor armigeri . . . una cum ceteris . . . deputatis in nobili apparatu in equis et armis . . . ad servicium regale faciendum contra Wallenses eleganter sunt profecti. Ad ulteriora igitur anhelantes, apud Cestriam pervenerunt, ubi ad tantam honoris magnitudinem admittuntur, quod omnes videntes ipsos et equos suos ita strenue armatos, tale servicium apprime commendarunt.'

to plate began with the application to such exposed parts of the body as the elbows, knees, and shins of plates of metal strapped on above the mail. Simultaneously with these developments came the introduction of horse-armour. The light, flowing 'trapper' or *couverture* of linen or silk which figures so prominently in contemporary pictorial representations of warfare stands to the defences of the horse in much the same relation as that in which the surcoat stands to the armour of the knight—its purpose, that is, was ornamental rather than strictly utilitarian. More effective protection was afforded by the housings of mail or of gamboised and quilted textiles which came into fashion in the second half of the thirteenth century, and were gradually supplemented by *chamfrons* and body-plates of *cuir-bouilli* or metal, in much the same way as the mail of the knight was supplemented by *coudes*, *genouillères*, and *jambes* of solid iron.[1] The cost of equipment increased in proportion to its elaboration. Not only was the intrinsic value of the full knightly panoply much greater in the Plantagenet than in the Norman period; but the increase in the weight of the armour worn by both horse and rider necessitated the employment of mounts of an altogether more powerful and expensive type than had sufficed for the comparatively light-armed Norman *miles*. As Dr. Morris has shown, the heavy but highly-bred *dextrarius* of the time of Edward I might cost anything from 60 to 120 marks; while even the humbler *equus* was priced at from 20 to 40 marks.[2]

The increasing costliness of military accoutrements combined with the spread of the chivalric conception of knighthood to confine the knightly class within much narrower limits than had been recognized in the eleventh and twelfth centuries. In the later Middle Ages the title of *miles* came to be restricted to persons of some importance, who had gone through the elaborate ceremonial of admission to the knightly order, and was no longer loosely applied to any tenant who rendered mounted service for his *feodum militis*. In theory the knight was still the unit of the feudal host; but in practice, from the

---

[1] Hewitt, *Ancient Armour and Weapons in Europe*, pp. 341 seq. and *passim*. Cf. ffoulkes, *The Armourer and his Craft*; *Armour and Weapons*; Sir J. F. Laking, *Record of European Arms and Armour*.

[2] *Welsh Wars*, p. 49.

beginning of the thirteenth century onwards, the *milites* constituted but a dwindling fraction of any feudal army. The majority of the tenants-in-chief—certainly of the ecclesiastics—discharged their obligations at least in part by *servientes*, two of whom were accepted as the equivalent of one knight.[1] Thus, for example, the Abbot of Ramsey rendered service for his four fees in 1223[2] and in 1244 by three knights and two *servientes*, in 1241 by one knight and six *servientes*, in 1245 by two knights and four *servientes*,[3] and in 1310[4] and 1323[5] by eight *servientes*; the Abbot of St. Albans proffered for his six fees two knights and eight *servientes* in 1257[6] and 1282,[7] and one knight and ten *servientes* in 1277[8] and 1310;[9] the Bishop of Hereford, who recognized in the later thirteenth century five fees only, served in 1277 by three knights and four *servientes*,[10] in 1282 by two knights and six *servientes*,[11] in 1300[12] and 1303[13] by one knight and eight *servientes*, and in 1310[14] and 1323[15] by ten *servientes*; while the Archbishop of York (five fees) offered four knights and two *servientes* in 1282,[16] ten *servientes* in 1310,[17] and one knight and eight *servientes* in 1323.[18]

The exact connotation of the term *serviens* in this connexion is not easy to determine. Sir Charles Oman and Dr. Morris both regard the 'serjeant' of the thirteenth and fourteenth centuries as roughly the equivalent of the knight of the Norman period;[19] but there can be little doubt that in the details of equipment considerable latitude was permitted. If the majority of the men who were enrolled as *servientes* in the records of feudal service were equipped as 'troopers' with sword and lance, some at least carried the cross-bow or arbalest which had come into fashion under Richard I. In 1223 the Abbot of

[1] See the Marshal's Rolls, *passim*.
[2] Scutage Rolls, No. 3, m. 1: 'Gaufridus de Hemingford' se iij° cum ij servientibus pro abbate de Rames'.'
[3] *Ramsey Cartulary*, iii. 50–2.   [4] *Parl. Writs*, ii. 404.
[5] Chanc. Misc. 5/10, m. 1.
[6] Matthew Paris, *Chron. Majora*, vi. 373.   [7] *Parl. Writs*, i. 228.
[8] Ibid., p. 198.   [9] Ibid., ii. 405.   [10] Ibid. i. 197.
[11] *Register of Bishop Swinfield of Hereford*, p. 76.   [12] Ibid., p. 78.
[13] Ibid., p. 392; *Chanc. Misc.* 5/6, m. 2.   [14] *Parl. Writs*, ii. 404.
[15] Chanc. Misc. 5/10, m. 1.   [16] *Parl. Writs*, i. 228.
[17] Ibid. ii. 404.   [18] Chanc. Misc. 5/10, m. 4.
[19] C. W. C. Oman, *Art of War in the Middle Ages*, i. 367; Morris, *Welsh Wars*, pp. 50 seq.

Peterborough performed the service of six fees by one knight, seven serjeants and three *balistarii*;[1] and in 1257 the St. Albans contingent included at least two mounted cross-bowmen.[2] Armour probably showed as many variations as weapons. Mr. Morris has suggested that the normal equipment of a *serviens* was the same as that prescribed by the assize of 1252 or the statute of Winchester of 1285 for the second class of the national militia—viz. a hauberk and iron headpiece, as distinguished from the helm and complete covering of mail worn by the knight.[3] There are, however, indications that, at least in the thirteenth century, the mail shirt was not in universal use. Matthew Paris tells us that of the *armigeri* who served in 1257 for the Abbot of St. Albans 'quaedam cum armis lineis [i.e., presumably, the *gambeson*] quaedam ferreis contra hostes fuerunt praemuniti';[4] and again in 1277 only six of the St. Albans *servientes* seem to have worn mail.[5] The same probably holds good of the defences of the horse. The *serviens* was distinguished from the light horseman of the 'hobelar' type by the fact that he was required to ride a barded horse. Hewitt believed that this requirement did not come into force until the close of the reign of Edward I, since there is no mention in the statute of Winchester of horse-coverings of any description;[6] but it appears from other sources that horse armour was in general use among soldiers of less than knightly rank at least from the middle of the thirteenth century. The mounts of the St. Albans contingent in 1257 were barded,[7] and from the early marshal's rolls of Edward I it is clear that possession of an *equus coopertus* was already coming to be regarded as the *sine qua non* of serviential rank.[8] It is probable, however, that throughout the history of the feudal levy gamboised or pourpointed textiles or *cuirbouilli* were more commonly used than mail for the housings of horses in this class. Only four of the animals ridden by the St. Albans troopers who were so highly

---

[1] Scutage Rolls, No. 3, m. 1.
[2] Matthew Paris, *Chron. Majora*, vi. 373.
[3] *Welsh Wars*, p. 53.   [4] *Chron. Majora*, vi. 373.
[5] *Parl. Writs*, i. 198: '. . . servientes unde sex ferreo cooperti et alii [iv lineo?].'
[6] Hewitt, *Ancient Armour in Europe*, i. 341 seq.
[7] Matthew Paris, loc. cit.   [8] *Parl. Writs*, i. 197 seq. and 228 seq.

commended in 1257 were 'tam cum lineis armis quam cum ferreis . . . cooperti'.[1] Indeed, it is difficult to suppose that the moderately priced rounsey usually employed by the *servientes* [2] could have borne the weight of an iron covering in addition to that of a mail-clad rider. Matthew Paris estimated the value of the horses of the *armigeri* in 1257 at from four to ten marks each,[3] while the horse inventories of Edward I's reign show that later the average cost of a *runcinus* was from £5 to £8.[4]

Instances of the employment of men below the serviental rank for the discharge of knight-service are extremely rare. True, in 1323 the Abbot of St. Albans sent to the host twelve hobelars as the equivalent of four serjeants,[5] but the expedient was quite exceptional and required the special licence of the king. Its chief interest is that it affords an additional clue to the status of the serjeants, whose services were evidently considered to be worth three times those of the light horseman with the unbarded mount.

Did the numbers registered on the marshal's roll invariably represent the full strength of the contingent? Mr. Morris has shown that at least in the case of the earls and greater barons they did not. 'One thing is very clear,' he writes. 'When a baron recognized the service of x knights and registered the names of precisely x knights, we must allow for at least $2x$ troopers in attendance.'[6] As we have seen, the ecclesiastics rarely offered their full quota of knights. In the Edwardian period they usually discharged their service at least in part by *servientes*. Whether such knights as were present with the clerical contingents were normally accompanied by personal attendants or 'esquires' is not clear. In 1257 the two St. Albans *milites* seem to have had their own *armigeri* as distinct from those who rendered the service due from the remaining four fees of the abbot;[7] and in 1300 the Bishop of Hereford was

---

[1] Matthew Paris, loc. cit.   [2] Morris, *Welsh Wars*, p. 53.
[3] *Chron. Majora*, vi. 374 seq.   [4] Morris, loc. cit.
[5] Chanc. Misc. 5/10, m. 1. A copy of the king's writ of privy seal authorizing 'de nostre grace especiale' the substitution of 'douze hobelours' for 'quatre hommes d'armes' is appended.   [6] *Welsh Wars*, pp. 54-5.
[7] Matthew Paris, *Chron. Majora*, vi. 373-4. The knights were separated from the serjeants 'quod factum est ad cautelam ne armigeri militum essent stipendiati sicut et alii mercede conducti'.

registered as serving by Thomas de Birmingham knight and nine *servientes*, the presence of the ninth *serviens* perhaps being due to the chance enrolment under this head of Sir Thomas's *scutifer*.[1] The extra horses which occasionally figure in the proffers of tenants as recorded in the marshal's rolls may possibly indicate the presence of unregistered additional retainers. Thus in 1310 the Abbot of Hyde served by one knight and four serjeants with six barded horses;[2] in 1323 the Abbot of St. Edmunds offered two knights and eight serjeants with twelve barded horses;[3] the Bishop of Durham four knights and ten serjeants with eighteen barded horses;[4] the Bishop of Ely two knights and six serjeants with ten *equi cooperti*;[5] and the Archbishop of York one knight and eight serjeants also with ten covered horses.[6] It will be noted that in every case the number of extra mounts corresponds exactly to the number of knights present with the contingent. Some provision must, of course, always have been necessary for the transport of arms and armour. On the Ramsey fee the need was met by the creation of a special serjeanty. In the thirteenth century the Pyel family held the fee of Isham by the service of furnishing a pack-horse with saddle, canvas bag, and pin 'ad deferenda arma quatuor militum abbatie, ad quodlibet iter dictorum militum in servicium domini regis'.[7]

IV. CONDITIONS OF SERVICE

When the muster was complete the contingents were apportioned among the various captains and commanding officers. In general each seems to have been treated as a unit. In 1282, for instance, the two knights and six men-at-arms of the Bishop of Hereford were assigned to the command of Roger Mortimer, senior, under whom they fought at his castle of Builth in the upper Wye valley.[8] In 1277 the St. Albans retinue evidently served together through the campaign.[9] Occasionally,

---

[1] *Register of Bishop Swinfield*, p. 78.   [2] *Parl. Writs*, ii. 405.
[3] Chanc. Misc. 5/10, m. 1.
[4] Ibid., loc. cit.   [5] Ibid., m. 4.   [6] Ibid., loc. cit.
[7] *Ramsey Cartulary*, iii. 55; *Select Pleas in Manorial Courts*, ed. F. W. Maitland, pp. 62–3.
[8] *Register of Bishop Swinfield*, pp. 76, 333.
[9] *Chron. Monasterii Sancti Albani, Gesta Abbatum*, R.S., i. 435.

however, the *milites* were separated from the *servientes* in action. Thus we are told that in 1257 the *armigeri* of St. Albans were, on account of their vigour, specially selected by the marshal to serve under his command in the van of the army, one of their number being appointed to act as *constabularius* over his companions, 'cum duobus sibi adjunctis de servicio alieno'. The two knights fought in the rear with the lords Thomas de Gresley and Henry de Percy.[1]

Traditionally, of course, service in the feudal host was rendered by the tenant-in-chief for forty days only, at his own expense. It is probable, however, that the Crown acquiesced with reluctance in this inconvenient limitation; and in adopting the principle of the *quota* it doubtless had in view a proportionate extension of the period of service. When in 1197 Richard I summoned a tenth of the *servicium debitum* of England for service in Normandy it was with the intention that this picked force should serve for the duration of the war; and the Abbot of St. Edmunds, who had hired knights for forty days only, was glad to make fine with the king to secure release from any further obligation.[2] In 1212 the four knights of Ramsey were to be maintained by their fellow tenants as long as they were in the king's service.[3] As late as 1265 William de Rishanger has a grievous complaint to make against Henry III on somewhat similar grounds. In response to the royal summons the Abbot of St. Albans and many other religious sent their contingents for service against the sons of De Montfort to Northampton. There the king detained them 'fere per sex hebdomadas', but at the end of that time, instead of discharging them, he exacted for every knight forty marks as the condition of release from further service.[4] Clearly, however, this was a case of barefaced extortion. It is probable that under Henry III, as under Edward I and later, the forty days principle was generally, if unwillingly, admitted by the Crown.[5]

---

[1] Matthew Paris, *Chron. Majora*, vi. 373–4.   [2] *Supra*, p. 43.

[3] 'Rex Rogeri de Nevill', etc. Precepimus tibi quod quatuor militibus de abbatia de Rames' qui sunt in servicio nostro . . . inveniri facias rationabiliter necessaria sua a militibus tenentibus de predicta Abbatia qui remanserunt in partibus suis quamdiu fuerint in predicto servicio nostro' (*Rot. Litt. Claus.* i. 123 a).

[4] *Chron. Monasterii Sancti Albani*, Chron. Willelmi de Rishanger, p. 41.

[5] Cf. the writ on behalf of the Abbot of Ramsey in 1268: '. . . Abbas de

On the expiry of the term of compulsory unpaid service, the king, at least from the later thirteenth century onwards, frequently took the feudal retinues into his pay. In 1277 the St. Albans contingent served altogether for eight weeks—'for forty days at their own costs and thereafter at the king's expense';[1] and in 1282 the men of the Bishop of Hereford were in action 'for forty days and more'.[2] None might depart from the host without the express permission either of the king or of the officer in command of the detachment concerned,[3] who, it would seem, issued a certificate of performance of service corresponding to the 'litere acquietancie' issued by the Wardrobe in acknowledgement of payment of a fine.[4]

The tenant-in-chief who failed to appear at the muster or who proffered less service than was properly due from his fee, rendered himself liable to heavy penalties. Distraint was the recognized means of enforcing obedience to the summons, and under Henry III the Chancery rolls show that it was not infrequently employed. In 1242, for example, the sheriffs were instructed to distrain all tenants who had omitted to answer the summons to Winchester in the previous April, to appear at London on July 15 ready to cross to the king in Gascony.[5] The punishment for default was the much graver one of disseisin. As we have seen, Richard I in 1197 ordered the seizure of the estates of the Bishops of Lincoln and Salisbury because of their refusal to render service in Normandy; and at least in the latter

---

Rameseia per preceptum nostrum fecit nobis servicium suum . . . per quatuor milites a crastino assumptionis Sancte Marie . . . per quadraginta dies . . .' (*Ramsey Cartulary*, ii. 295). In 1258 the abbot's knights were to be paid four shillings 'quolibet die quadraginta dierum . . . cum stant in servicio domini regis' (*Select Pleas in Manorial Courts*, pp. 50 seq.). In 1260 the knights of St. Albans admitted that they were bound to remain for forty days in the king's service at their own expense. Cott. MSS. Nero. D. 1, f. 134 d.

[1] *Gesta Abbatum*, i. 435. [2] *Register of Bishop Swinfield*, p. 76.

[3] In 1277 the St. Albans contingent returned home 'a domino regi licenciati, gratias exhibente' (*Gesta Abbatum*, i. 435). In 1282 the men of the Bishop of Hereford, on the completion of their service, 'secuti sunt dominum Rogerum [de Mortuomari] predictum usque ad manerium suum de Kingslene, et inde eciam de licencia sua ad propria redierunt' (*Register of Bishop Swinfield*, p. 76).

[4] See, for example, the certificate of Nicholas de Segrave to the Bishop of Hereford in 1303 (*Register of Bishop Swinfield*, p. 394).

[5] *C.C.R.*, 1237–1242, p. 486.

instance the order was executed.[1] In the next year Abbot
Samson of St. Edmunds hastened to make his peace with the
king, 'fearing to lose seisin of his barony for his default, as
befell the Bishop of London (?) and many of the barons'.[2]
Under John the penalty was enforced on several occasions,
although none of the ecclesiastics or greater barons suffered;
while under Henry III no less than twenty-one tenants, of
whom the Abbess of Wilton was one, were temporarily dis-
seised for failure to answer the summons to serve in Wales in
1223.[3] Edward I in 1297 threatened to confiscate the estates
of those magnates who attempted to evade service in Gascony,
and to bestow them upon others more amenable to his will.[4]
The threat, it need hardly be said, was impossible of execution,
although the ringleaders of the opposition were deprived of
office. Neglect, as distinct from defiance, of the royal summons
seems commonly, in the Edwardian period, to have gone entirely unpunished. True, the Abbot of Tavistock who, as
already noted, offered neither service nor its money equivalent
in 1277, was fined five marks for his default,[5] but the Archbishop
of Canterbury, the Abbot of Westminster, and some others
who consistently evaded their obligations, escaped even this
light punishment.[6]

Concealment of service was, at least in theory, heavily
penalized. In 1277 the Abbot of Pershore fined for the service
of two fees, but in 1282 he made fine for one only 'servicio
alterius feodi quod prius recognoscerat maliciose concelando in
decepcionem curie et exheredacionem suam manifestam'. He
was summoned before the Exchequer in 1294 to answer for
his deception, and since he could not deny that he had formerly
recognized two fees, he was ordered to pay the fifty marks fine
due from the second for the army of 10 Edward I, and for his
transgression was amerced 'ad voluntatem regis'.[7] The Abbot

---

[1] *Supra*, p. 42.   [2] *Chron. Jocelini de Brakelond*, p. 63.
[3] *Rot. Litt. Claus.* i. 572. Order for the restitution to the Abbess of Wilton
and others of the lands seised into the king's hand for default of service.
[4] Walter of Hemingburgh, *Chronicon*, R.S., ii. 121.
[5] *Supra*, p. 61.   [6] *Supra*, pp. 61, 62.
[7] Exch. L.T.R. Mem. Roll, No. 65, Brev. pro Rege, Trin., m. 98 d;
No. 66, Comm. Mich., m. 1; No. 77, Comm. Rec. Mich., m. 18 d. See also
the case of the Prior of Coventry, who recognized the service of four fees in

of Hyde was guilty of a somewhat similar misdemeanour about the same date.[1] Amicia de Columbiers, who under Henry III held the manor of Congbourne of the abbot by the service of three knights, granted a third part to the king to be held as one fee. Henry accordingly conceded to the abbot a proportionate reduction of his *servicium*, and the allowance was duly made in the pipe roll of 49 Henry III. Subsequently, under Edward I, the then Abbot of Hyde put in a further claim for release from the service of one knight on account of the same transaction: 'et sic falso petiit dupplicem allocacionem de uno et eodem servicio'. The deception was detected by the barons of the Exchequer who, it is interesting to discover, condemned the abbot to prison.[2] The sentence was, however, a purely formal one, for we read that the culprit was afterwards replevied and eventually fined in forty shillings for his transgression.

The right of the Crown to demand the service of its vassals was exercised only within clearly defined limits. For instance, it was recognized that unpaid service could not properly be demanded on more than one occasion in a single year.[3] Under Edward I it was further established that the feudatories were bound to serve only when the king in person was present with his army. How far back the principle extends it is not easy to determine. It does not seem to have been observed in the early Norman period, for the Abingdon chronicler tells us that the Conqueror called out the feudal host for service against Malcolm of Scotland, and dispatched it under the command of his eldest son Robert.[4] In the thirteenth century the Abbot of Evesham produced for confirmation a charter purporting to belong to the reign of Henry I, in which the lands of the abbey were to be held by the service of four and a half knights 'in expedicione,

5 and 10 Edward I, but fined on two only (Exch. L.T.R. Mem. Roll, No. 64, Comm. Mich., m. 10 d; Brev. pro Rege, Mich., m. 52).

[1] Exch. L.T.R. Mem. Roll, No. 64, Comm. Easter, m. 19 d.

[2] 'Ideo compertum est quod eat ad prisonam.' The entry is headed 'De Abbate de Hida liberando ad prisonam'.

[3] This rule was broken by Henry III in 1230 when two summonses were issued for service in France and two scutages were imposed. The army crossed in the first place to Brittany and subsequently moved on into Gascony (Mitchell, *Taxation under John and Henry III*, p. 183).

[4] *Hist. Monasterii de Abingdon*, ii. 9.

me presente',[1] but whether this was a privilege peculiar to the house or merely a special application of a general principle is not clear. The question of the obligation to service in the absence of the king first assumed prominence under Edward I in connexion with the proposed expeditions to Gascony in 1294 and 1297 respectively. In June of the former year Edward summoned his feudal tenants to serve in France,[2] at the same time authorizing the payment of fines at the exorbitant rate of 100 marks the fee by ecclesiastics and others desirous of compounding.[3] The simultaneous outbreak of a serious revolt in Wales necessitated, however, the countermanding of the original summons, and the diversion of the main army to the new centre of disaffection; and the king, instead of crossing in person to Gascony, relinquished the command to John of Brittany, Earl of Richmond, who had already sailed with a small advance-force.[4] Actually, therefore, no full muster of the feudal host took place; but the Exchequer nevertheless continued to press for payment of the fines which had been assessed after the issue of the summons, as if the occasion had been a *bona fide* one.[5] The bearing of the events of 1294 upon the famous dispute over foreign service of three years later has not hitherto been fully appreciated. Mr. Morris arrived at the mistaken conclusion that the Gascon army served for pay, and not on a feudal basis,[6] and he failed, in consequence, to realize that the tenants-in-chief were, in point of fact, supplied in 1294 with a grievance which does much to explain and justify their subsequent opposition to the royal demands. When in 1297 Edward proposed to the lay magnates assembled at Salisbury that he in person should lead the main feudal army in an attack upon France through Flanders, while a detachment under the constable and marshal operated in the south from Gascony, his suggestion provoked the bitter altercation so vividly

---

[1] *C.Ch.R.* i. 257, 3 March 1241. [2] *Parl. Writs*, i. 259.
[3] Ibid., p. 393.
[4] Sir James Ramsay, *Dawn of the Constitution*, pp. 408 seq.
[5] *Infra*, p. 101.
[6] Morris, *Welsh Wars*, p. 276: '. . . the writs of summons to the expedition to Gascony in 1294 were, in appearance, formal demands on feudal allegiance . . . [but they] cannot but have been mere invitations to professional soldiers to raise cavalry for the king's pay, though couched in feudal language.'

described in the pages of Hemingburgh.[1] Hereford and Norfolk, smarting, it is true, under a sense of personal injury, but with the fiasco of 1294 also fresh in their minds, flatly refused to cross to Gascony unless Edward himself accompanied them, alleging that by the terms of their office they were bound to serve only in the king's presence. The obligation of the English tenantry to unpaid service in Flanders they further expressly denied, on the ground that no precedent could be found for any such demand.[2] So widespread was the discontent which the king's policy had aroused, and so strong the support accorded to the contumacious earls, that Edward found himself compelled to surrender on the main points at issue. He deprived the ringleaders of office, but he was obliged to abandon the project of a Gascon expedition, and to concede 'post multas et varias altercationes' that none should serve in Flanders save at the costs and charges of the king.[3] The baronage was not slow to follow up its victory. In 1301 the fines for the Scottish expedition were assessed on the definite understanding that they should not be paid 'nisi ipse Rex exercitum suum in Scocia habeat'.[4] A few years later the Abbot of Evesham, relying ostensibly on the prescriptive right of his house, but doubtless inspired by the successful resistance of 1297, petitioned the king for release from payment of the 450 marks demanded from him for the army of Gascony of 1294. The treasurer and barons were accordingly directed to scrutinize the charters of the abbey and to do justice in the matter, the words 'habito respectu ad statum domini regis' being added in a last attempt to save the dignity of the Crown.[5] No immediate action seems to have been taken on this order; but in 1305 all who had made

---

[1] Walter de Hemingburgh, *Chronicon* (English Historical Society), ii. 121 seq.

[2] Bartholomew Cotton, *Historia Anglicana*, R.S., pp. 325 seq.: 'la ne deyvent nule service fere, pur ceo ke eus ne lur predecessors ne lur auncestres unkes en cele terre servise ne firent'. See the list of grievances presented to the king in 1297.

[3] *Hist. Anglicana*, loc. cit.: 'Eodem anno post multas et varias altercationes concessit rex omnibus qui debebant sibi servicium . . . non teneri ire secum in Flandriam nisi ad vadia et pro stipendiis dicti domini regis.'

[4] Exch. L.T.R. Misc. Roll, 1/13, m. 1.

[5] Ancient Petitions, 406; *Rot. Parl.* i. 461 b; Exch. K.R. Mem. Roll, No. 79, Brev. Bar. Mich., m. 6 d.

fine for their service in 22 Edward I were summoned to appear before the Exchequer 'to show cause why distresses should not be made upon their lands and chattels for the sums outstanding'.[1] Early in the next reign the seal was set on the baronial victory when all fines assessed for the army of 1294 were formally remitted 'pro eo maxime quod . . . Rex personaliter non fuit in guerra predicta nec dictum servicium communiter factum erat'.[2]

V. CASTLE-GUARD

With the duty of serving in the feudal host was often coupled the duty of garrisoning the royal castles; and many of the great ecclesiastics were bound to service of this kind. The knights of Abingdon, as early as the date of Domesday Book, rendered castle-guard at the king's castle at Windsor;[3] the knights of Peterborough rendered it at the castle of Rockingham;[4] the knights of St. Edmunds at the castle of Norwich;[5] the knights of Cerne at the castle of Corfe.[6] Originally the Abbots of Ely owed ward to the castle of Norwich, but under Henry I the newly instituted bishop bought for his knights the privilege of serving instead within the isle of Ely.[7] At St. Edmunds, at the close of the twelfth century, the fifty *milites* discharged their service in *constabilie* or groups of ten, each of which served for a period of three months.[8] At Cerne all the ten knights enfeoffed on the abbey lands were bound to render castle-guard at Corfe at the king's command for one month in the year, although the fief owed alternatively the service of only two knights (later reduced by charter of Henry II to one) in the

[1] Exch. L.T.R. Mem. Roll, No. 75, Brev. Ret. Easter, m. 79 d.

[2] Exch. L.T.R. Mem. Roll, No. 82, Brev. Bar. Mich., m. 1 and *passim*. In 16 Edw. II the fines for service in Scotland were made 'condicionaliter, videlicet quod si dominus Rex exercitus suum in Scotiam contra Scotos habuerit' (Peterborough Cartulary; Cott. MSS. Vesp. E. xxii, f. 49 d; Exch. L.T.R. Misc. Roll, 1/13, m. 14).

[3] *Hist. Monasterii de Abingdon*, ii. 3, 90, 153.

[4] *Rot. Litt. Claus.* i. 297. Writ to the constable of Rockingham re the performance of castle-guard by the knights of Peterborough, 27 Jan. 1217 (*Chron. Petroburgense*, pp. 41, 130 seq.).

[5] *Chron. Jocelini de Brakelond*, pp. 48 seq.

[6] *Red Book*, i. 212.

[7] *Pipe Roll*, 31 Hen. I, p. 44; *Monasticon*, i. 482.

[8] *Chron. Jocelini de Brakelond*, loc. cit.

host.[1] By the latter half of the twelfth century, however, money
payments were already beginning to take the place of service,
since the Crown found it more convenient to entrust its castles
to the keeping of a permanent garrison. When Abbot Samson
in 1196 engaged in his famous dispute with his knights, one
of the points at issue was the amount they were accustomed to
pay towards the castle-guard of Norwich.[2] Under John the
tendency towards commutation was accelerated, chiefly, it
would appear, because the king preferred to employ mercenaries
to man his castles, rather than to trust to his own subjects,
whose loyalty was doubtful. In this as in other directions, he
abused his right, and the twenty-ninth clause of the Charter of
1215 was specially designed to protect the interests of tenants
liable to the duty of castle-guard. It provided, first, that a money
payment should not be exacted if the tenant were prepared to
serve in his own person or by a proper substitute; and secondly,
that men who had served in the field should be relieved of
garrison duty 'secundum quantitatem temporis quo per nos
fuerit in exercitu'.[3] This clause, which was repeated in a slightly
modified form in the reissue of 1217,[4] seems to have done little
to check the development of the principle of commutation.
By the later Middle Ages the duty of castle-guard had been
universally converted into rent, in which form it continued to
be rendered not only until the abolition of feudal tenures at the
Restoration, but until well into the eighteenth century.[5]

In the Edwardian period the tenants-in-chief attempted to
use the obligation to garrison duty to justify the disparity between the number of fees for which they rendered service in
the host, and the number of their traditional *servicium debitum*.
As we have seen in an earlier chapter, the Abbot of Abingdon

---

[1] *Red Book*, loc. cit.: 'Quisque autem istorum debet facere wardam ad
preceptum vestrum apud castellum de Corfe uno mense per annum, vel
si vobis placuerit habere inde milites ad exercitum, interim dimissa wardia,
ij milites ad servicium vestrum invenient.'

[2] *Chron. Jocelini de Brakelond*, loc. cit. Henry I made an agreement
with the Abbot of Peterborough, whereby the latter's knights were to
commute their castle-guard at Rockingham at the rate of four shillings the
fee (W. T. Mellows, *Henry of Pytchley*).

[3] McKechnie, *Magna Carta*, pp. 333-4.

[4] Ibid., p. 334, and n. 3.

[5] J. H. Round, 'Castle Guard', *Archaeological Journal*, lix. 144 seq.

claimed in 1302 that of his thirty-three fees thirty were quit of all liability for service in the field, since they paid annually to the constable of Windsor £30 as the commutation of castle-guard.[1] A similar plea was advanced thirteen years later on behalf of the whole body of Crown tenants, when it was asserted in Parliament that all fees owing and performing ward at the king's castles were exempted thereby from knight-service.[2] The claim seems in general to have had no historical basis. It is true that at Cerne, in the twelfth century, castle-guard appears as the alternative to service *in exercitu*,[3] but this was apparently a privilege peculiar to the house. At Abingdon, Peterborough, or St. Edmunds it was clearly a parallel and not an alternative obligation. The weakness of their case was evidently realized by the tenants-in-chief, for the argument advanced in 1315 was not subsequently pressed. It finds no place in the Exchequer proceedings of that year or in the later parliamentary petitions.

VI. SCUTAGE

It remains to consider the conditions governing the imposition of scutage. Strictly speaking, of course, it was for the king alone to decide whether a scutage should or should not be taken in connexion with any given campaign. He had an indubitable right to the corporal service of his tenants-in-chief, and it was an act of grace to allow the commutation of that service into a money payment. Throughout the twelfth century we may safely conclude that theory and practice coincided, and that the royal will alone determined both the occasion and the rate of the levy. John's intolerable abuse of the whole feudal military organization led, however, in the early thirteenth century, to the introduction of an element of consent quite foreign to the original conception of scutage. In McKechnie's words, John 'elevated the scutage from a weapon reserved for emergencies into a regular source of revenue'.[4] During a reign of only sixteen years he exacted no less than eleven scutages, in contrast to the seven which his father had taken in a reign of thirty-five and the three with which his brother, despite a

---

[1] Exch. L.T.R. Mem. Roll, No. 64, Brev. pro Rege, Mich., m. 52.
[2] *Rot. Parl.* i. 292, No. 17.
[3] *Supra*, p. 102, n. 2.   [4] McKechnie, *Magna Carta*, p. 74.

reputation for insatiable rapacity, had contented himself in a reign of ten.[1] The indignation which this policy aroused was greatly increased by the fact that the levies were frequently imposed on specious occasions, and not in connexion with bona fide expeditions. In 1201, for instance, the host was assembled at Portsmouth ready to cross to Normandy, but was subsequently disbanded with the exception of a small picked force.[2] In 1204 and 1205 the same thing occurred, the bulk of the forces being dismissed without serving;[3] while in 1209 the army was led against the Scots, but a treaty was concluded at Norham before hostilities actually commenced.[4] The Welsh expedition of 1211 was no less of a fiasco, for the king, hearing that the barons were meditating insurrection, dismissed the assembled troops, and retired to Nottingham Castle.[5] Not only were scutages thus imposed with unprecedented frequency and on the flimsiest pretexts, they were assessed at a greatly enhanced rate. The first levies of the reign (in 1199, 1201, 1202, and 1203) saw a return to the two marks common under Henry II; in 1204 the rate rose to two and a half marks, while for the Irish campaign of 1210 as much as three marks the fee seems to have been exacted.[6] The consequent grievances of the military tenants were further increased as a result of John's practice of demanding heavy fines either in place of or in addition to the scutage; and of the reduction which was simultaneously being effected in the amount of corporal service rendered. A tenant owing nominally fifty or sixty knights actually furnished by the time of John a contingent of only five or six; yet if he wished to secure exemption from service he had to pay scutage at a high rate upon the full number of his fees, or a fine which might amount to three or four times the value of his scutage. Thus the actual was very much higher than the nominal rate of commutation, and there was, moreover, no limit to the power of the Crown to increase it.[7]

[1] See, for the scutages of Henry II and Richard I, Baldwin, *Scutage and Knight Service in England, passim*; for that of John, Mitchell, *Taxation*.
[2] Roger de Hoveden, *Chronicon*, R.S., iv. 163.
[3] Ralph de Coggeshall, *Chron. Anglicanum*, R.S., p. 153.
[4] Kate Norgate, *John Lackland*, p. 133.
[5] Coggeshall, *Chron.*, p. 164.   [6] Mitchell, *Taxation*.
[7] So Mr. Mitchell, op. cit. His view is, however, criticized by Mr. Powick (*E.H.R.* xxx. 535).

These considerations do much to explain such manifestations of discontent as the refusal of the northern barons in 1213 to serve in Poitou,[1] and the prominence assumed by questions relating to military service and scutage both in the negotiations preceding the Charter of 1215 and in the Charter itself. The so-called 'Unknown Charter of Liberties', which was probably formulated somewhere between 1213 and 1215, attempted to limit the action of the Crown by fixing the normal rate of scutage at one mark the fee, with the proviso that it might in special circumstances be increased 'consilio baronum regni'.[2] The solution offered by Magna Carta was yet more drastic. The famous twelfth clause brought the scutage, properly exigible by the Crown as of right, into the category of the 'extraordinary' or voluntary aids; and provided that it should not henceforth be levied 'nisi per commune consilium regni nostri'.[3]

It is probable that the framers of the charter of 1215 went farther in this particular than they intended. Their purpose was not to contravene a fundamental feudal principle by claiming the right to grant or to refuse a scutage, but merely to guard against the repetition of the abuses of which John had been guilty, and to see that henceforward scutage should be taken only when it was justly due, and at a uniform and reasonable rate. When, therefore, the death of John and the accession of a minor placed the control of the government virtually in the hands of the baronage, they were content to abandon the demands embodied in clause twelve of the original charter, and to substitute for them in the reissue of 1217 the much vaguer declaration: 'Scutagium de cetero capiatur sicut capi solebat tempore regis Henrici avi nostri.'[4] Nevertheless, the provision of 1215 left its mark upon the subsequent history of the scutage. Although there is no evidence that the baronage at any time claimed the right to refuse a levy when one was properly due, it was henceforward customary to put the scutage in charge in consultation with the *magnum concilium* or the parliament,

---

[1] Coggeshall, p. 167; Walter of Coventry, *Memoriale*, R.S., ii. 217–18.

[2] *E.H.R.* viii. 288; ix. 119, 326; xx. 719, Clause VIII: 'Et si scutagium evenerit in terra una marca argenti capietur de feodo militis; et si gravamen exercitus contigerit, amplius caperetur consilio baronum regni.'

[3] McKechnie, *Magna Carta*, pp. 231 seq.

[4] Ibid., Appendix, Charter of 1217, c. 44; Charter of 1225, c. 37.

which was thus enabled to control to some extent both the occasion and the rate of the impost.[1]

A further modification of the conditions governing the imposition of scutage which was effected between the twelfth and the fifteenth century was in regard to the time at which the levy was put in charge. In early days it seems, as a rule, to have been decided on at the opening of the campaign—an arrangement convenient both for the Crown for whose use the proceeds were immediately available, and for the tenants-in-chief, who were informed in advance of the conditions on which they might absent themselves from the host. With the appearance of the fine, and the growth of the principle of assent, however, a tendency developed to postpone the assessment of the scutage until the campaign was over.[2] The logical outcome of this tendency is apparent in the Edwardian period, when scutage was levied merely as an afterthought, several years frequently elapsing between the conclusion of the campaign and the imposition of the scutage in connexion with it. The scutage for the Welsh War of 1277 was not put in charge until 1279;[3] that for the expedition of 1282[4] until 1285; that for the Scottish campaigns of 1300 and 1303 until 1305–6;[5] while the

---

[1] e.g. the scutage of Brittany of 1230 was put in charge in consultation with the earls and barons at Northampton (Madox, *Exchequer*, ii. 607); the scutage of Poitou in the same year with the advice of the magnates present with the host (*Wendover*, iv. 218–19); the scutage of Gascony in 1242 was agreed upon by the 'commune concilium' (Exch. L.T.R. Mem. Roll, 27 Hen. III, m. 4); and the same was true of the scutages of 1246 and 1257 (Scutage Rolls, Nos. 7 and 8).

[2] Most of the early scutages seem, from the date at which the account appears in the pipe roll, to have been put in charge when the host was summoned, or soon after. Towards the end of his reign and throughout that of Henry III, scutage was, with rare exceptions, put in charge at or near the end of the campaign, e.g. the scutage for the Welsh War of 1223 is accounted for in the pipe roll of 1224 (Pipe Roll, No. 68); that for the army against Falkes de Bréauté in 1224 was put in charge at the close of the siege of Bedford (*Wendover*, iv. 99); writs for the levy of the scutage of Kerry 1228 were issued after the king's return from the campaign in October (*C.C.R.*, 1227–1231, pp. 79–81); the scutage of Elveyn was put in charge in September 1232, just before the expedition ended (Scutage Roll, No. 2).

[3] *C.C.R.*, 1272–1279, p. 522.

[4] Florence of Worcester, *Chronicon*, R.S., ii. 235; Pipe Roll, No. 132, *passim*.

[5] Exch. L.T.R. Mem. Roll, No. 76, Comm. Rec. Hil., m. 20; K.R., No. 79, Brev. Bar. Easter, m. 15 d.

levies for the Scottish wars of 34 Edward I and 4 Edward II
were not imposed until 1314[1] and 1319[2] respectively, and that
for the expedition of 1 Edward III until 1337.[3]

In the thirteenth century the procedure for the collection of
scutage was as follows. As soon as a levy had been determined
upon, writs in that sense were issued to the treasurer and
barons,[4] and to the sheriffs,[5] to whom was entrusted the general
supervision of the collection. A list of the tenants whom
performance of service or payment of a fine had qualified to
collect the scutage of their sub-vassals for their own use was at
the same time compiled from the evidence of the marshal's rolls
and the rolls of fines,[6] and writs *de scutagio habendo* were issued
to all whose names appeared thereon. The production of a
writ of this type ordinarily sufficed, until the attempted revolution in the incidence of the scutage under Edward I, to secure
for the tenant complete acquittance as regards the Crown;[7]
and from 1194 onwards the names of all recipients were entered
in the scutage account on the pipe roll under the heading 'Isti
habent quietantiam per brevia regis'. As we have seen, isolated
instances occur, especially under John, of tenants charged with
and even paying scutage in spite of the previous offer of service
or a fine.[8] These are clearly, however, exceptions to the general
rule. The full number of knights' fees in the thirteenth century
has been estimated at rather more than 6,500; but, as Mr.
Mitchell has shown, the number on which scutage was charged
rarely exceeded two-thirds of this total, and varied within

---

[1] *C.Chanc.R., Various*, p. 384.   [2] Ibid., p. 393.

[3] *C.F.R.* v. 52–4.

[4] See, for example, the writs for the levy of the scutage of 1277 (Exch.
L.T.R. Mem. Roll, No. 52, Comm. Easter, m. 4).

[5] Cf. the writs to the sheriffs in the same year (*C.F.R.* i. 108–9).

[6] In 1305, when the scutages of 28 and 31 Edw. I were put in charge, the
constable and marshal were directed to send into the Chancery their records
of the proffers made, and the treasurer and barons were ordered to furnish
lists of the fines *pro servicio* (*C.C.R.*, 1302–1307, p. 262; Exch. L.T.R. Mem.
Roll, No. 76, m. 36 d). The same procedure was followed in 1314 for the
scutage of 34 Edw. I (Exch. L.T.R. Mem. Roll, No. 85, Brev. Bar. Mich.,
m. 8).

[7] See, for instance, the instructions issued to the sheriffs for the levy of
the scutage of Gascony of 1242. They were to collect from all 'qui quidem
brevia nostra . . . non tulerint de habendo scutagio suo' (Close Rolls,
1237–1242, p. 486).   [8] *Supra*, p. 47.

exceedingly wide limits from year to year.[1] The carelessness
of the tenant-in-chief in omitting or delaying to secure a writ
of quittance might result in his being assessed for scutage, and
part of the supposed debt might even be collected; but afterwards the amount charged would normally be written off, and
the sum exacted either returned to him or credited to some
other account.[2] With those who had served or fined the sheriff
had properly no dealings, unless it were to present their claim
to acquittance at the Exchequer, or to certify the Crown of the
number of their fees, which, from 1211 onwards, was regularly
entered on the roll.[3] Even with the tenants who were liable
for scutage he had few direct dealings. The greater lords
collected the scutage of their sub-tenants by their own bailiffs,
and paid it direct into the Exchequer by the hand of their
steward or some other of their officials. Thus in the thirteenth
century we find the Abbot of Peterborough claiming, in virtue
of his franchise, the right to collect 'per ministros suos' all
scutages and aids due from his fee, and to respond for them in
person.[4] Under Edward I the sheriff of Norfolk and Suffolk,
charged with the levy of certain sums due from the Abbot of
St. Benet's, Holme, for various fines and scutages, successfully
represented to the treasurer and barons that the Abbot held of
the king *per baroniam*, and that his steward was therefore
properly answerable for his debts.[5] Only the lesser tenants,
as a rule, paid through the medium of the sheriff, who responded
accordingly in the pipe roll.[6]

Save in exceptional circumstances the sheriff had no dealings
at all with the under-tenants. Sometimes, in virtue of a 'writ
of aid', he might assist the lord with distraint to collect from
them the scutage for which he (the lord) was to respond 'per
manus suas' at the Exchequer;[7] occasionally he might collect

---

[1] Mitchell, *Taxation*, pp. 318 seq.

[2] See examples given by Mitchell, op. cit., pp. 50 seq.

[3] *Red Book*, i. 126.

[4] Peterborough Cartulary, MSS. of the Society of Antiquaries, xxxviii,
ff. 148 seq.; Cartulary of Abbot William of Peterborough, Cott. MSS. Vesp.
E. xxii, f. 75 d.

[5] Exch. L.T.R. Mem. Roll, No. 75, Rec. Mich., m. 12.

[6] The formula runs: 'Idem vicecomes reddit compotum de *x*. li. de Abbate
de *Z* de *y* feodis.'

[7] Examples of these writs are numerous under John and Henry III, e.g.

and pay in the sums due in respect of the outlying fees of a great estate situated in another country,[1] but only if, as in 1242, his instructions gave him special authority to do so[2] would he enter the lands of the tenants-in-chief and collect from the sub-tenants direct. If the tenant-in-chief opposed payment the sheriff might distrain or even disseise him; but normally he would not proceed to levy the debt from his dependents. Thus in 1204 the lands of the Archbishop of York were seised into the king's hand 'occasione scutagii que ipse debet domino regi';[3] but no attempt was made to collect from his men. On the contrary, as soon as the archbishop gave an undertaking to pay, his estates were restored, and his knights and free tenants were distrained by the sheriff to render him the scutage for which he was personally to respond at the Exchequer.[4] In the thirteenth century, indeed, the under-tenants were pro-tected in the king's court itself from any such extension of the royal authority. If a man charged with scutage at the Exchequer could prove by inquest or otherwise that he did not hold *in capite*, the demand upon him was remitted.[5] The intervention of a royal official was, in any case, unlikely to be welcomed either by the great feudatories, who had from the first to contend against the frequent attempts of the Crown to establish a direct contact with the occupants of the lower rungs of the feudal ladder; or by these latter, who had to fear therefrom a modifica-tion of their status.

---

in 1199 and 1205 writs were issued on behalf of the Archbishop of York (Madox, *Exchequer*, i. 680, note *n*; *Rot. Litt. Claus.* i. 46); in 6 Hen. III on behalf of the Abbess of Shaftesbury and the Abbot of Peterborough (Exch. L.T.R. Mem. Roll, 6 Hen. III, m. 2 and 2 d); in 7 Hen. III on behalf of the Abbot of St. Benet's, Holme (Exch. L.T.R. Mem. Roll, m. 6 d); in 9 Hen. III on behalf of the Abbot of Westminster (Exch. L.T.R. Mem. Roll, m. 2), &c.

[1] e.g. in 1205 the sheriff of Berkshire accounted for 2 marks for one fee of the Abbot of Hyde, the bulk of whose lands lay in Hampshire (Pipe Roll, No. 7, John Berks, m. 6 d).

[2] The writ for the collection (May 1242) orders the sheriff 'quod de omnibus feodis militum que tenentur de tenentibus de nobis in capite in balliva tua, et que ipsi de nobis tenent in capite, que quidem brevia nostra tibi non tulerint de habendo scutagio suo, etc. . . . scutagium nostrum colligi facias' (Close Rolls, 1237–1242, p. 486).

[3] *Rot. Litt. Claus.* i. 116.   [4] Ibid., loc. cit.

[5] See examples given by Mitchell, *Taxation*, pp. 52, 59, 67, 74, 81, 100, 116, 319 seq.

In the Edwardian period, however, the conditions governing the levy of scutage were completely revolutionized as a result of the attempt of the Crown to convert the scutage into a general tax exigible without regard to the performance of service or the payment of a fine. Under Edward II a new method of collection was instituted, based upon that which was habitually employed in the collection of taxes upon movables, and occasionally in the case of the regular feudal aids. By a series of commissions issued in November 1314 two or more 'collectors' were appointed in place of the sheriffs in the several counties or county-groups of England, to levy the scutages of 28, 31, and 34 Edward I;[1] a similar system being adopted in 1319 for the scutage of 4 Edward II and in 1337 for that of 1 Edward III.[2] Their instructions empowered the collectors to levy the appropriate amount from every fee held of the king in chief *ut de corona*, or of escheats and honours in the king's hand, or of his purchase, within their respective bailiwicks. Thus at the same time that the sheriff was ousted from his former position in relation to the feudal imposts, an attempt was made to give general validity to the principle of direct collection which had been tentatively and unsuccessfully applied to the great scutage of Gascony of 1242. The burden of the baronial protests and petitions of the reign of Edward II is that the under-tenants are being distrained to render to the Crown the scutage to which their immediate lords are properly entitled.[3] Just as the scutage had lost its original significance as the commutation of feudal service and had become a mere expedient for raising revenue, so the machinery for its assessment and collection had been assimilated to that employed in the levy of the national taxation which was gradually superseding the old feudal sources of income.

In order to facilitate the collection of its dues and to strengthen its hold upon the entire military system the Crown was careful to keep a record not only of the obligations of its immediate tenants, but of the services owed to those tenants in their

---

[1] *C.F.R.* ii. 216.   [2] Ibid. iii. 9; v. 52–4.
[3] Exch. K.R. Mem. Roll, No. 88, m. 145; L.T.R., No. 85, Hil. Rec. m. 7; *Rot. Parl.* i. 292, No. 17; Cole, *Documents Illustrative of English History*, p. 7; *Rot. Parl.* i. 383.

turn by their dependents. For this purpose, as we have seen,
it supplemented the evidence of the Exchequer rolls by means
of periodical 'inquests of service', of which the first and most
important was that instituted by Henry II in 1166.[1] In 1212
John held an inquiry into tenures in order to fill in the gaps
left by the *carte* of his father's day, and, in particular, to ascertain the location as well as the ownership of all fees.[2] Under
Henry III not only were the Red Book lists compiled by
Alexander Swereford,[3] but fresh inquests were held in connexion with both the aid to marry of 1235 and the scutage of
Gascony of 1242.[4] The returns were sometimes made by the
tenants-in-chief themselves—as in 1166 and 1235—but usually
they were made by the sheriffs, working from hundred to
hundred, with the assistance of specially empanelled juries.[5]
These efforts notwithstanding, the difficulty of keeping track
of the allocation and distribution of fees had, by the Edwardian
period, become acute, owing in part to the normal process of
change resulting from the application of the principle of
hereditary descent, in part to the steady increase of subinfeudation. The situation was further complicated by the
dispute over the incidence of the scutage, and by the long
interval which was frequently allowed to elapse between the
date of the expedition and that of the levy imposed in connexion
with it. In 1284–5 Kirby's Quest was held in the hope of
obtaining information likely to facilitate the collection of the
royal dues,[6] and five years later the statute *Quia Emptores* was
enacted with the object of simplifying feudal relationships to
that same end.[7] For all the Scottish scutages, and for the several
aids imposed by Edward I and Edward II inquests were held
as of course; but they were now conducted by the collectors,
to whom the sheriffs and all the subordinate local officials were
ordered to be intendant.[8] All attempts to obtain reliable and
accurate information were, however, unavailing. The efficiency
of the machinery declined in proportion as its complexity
increased. By the fourteenth century the whole feudal super-

---

[1] *Red Book*, i. 186 seq.   [2] Ibid. i. 469 seq.; *Book of Fees*, i. 52 seq.
[3] *Red Book*, i.   [4] *Book of Fees*, i. 405 seq.; ii. 637 seq.
[5] e.g. in 1212 and 1242.   [6] See *Feudal Aids, passim*.
[7] *Statutes of the Realm*, i. 106.   [8] *Supra*, p. 110, nn. 1 and 2.

structure was rapidly disintegrating, and the very expedients devised to check the process of dissolution served only to hasten it. By sanctioning free substitution *Quia Emptores* gave a tremendous impetus to the buying and selling of land, thus finally shattering that tenurial stability which was the *sine qua non* of the effective working of the feudal military organization.[1]

[1] For further details concerning the collectors and their work see *E.H.R.* xxxviii. 19 seq.

CHAPTER IV

THE RELATION BETWEEN THE TENANTS-IN-CHIEF AND THE SUB-TENANTS ON THE ECCLESIASTICAL FIEFS

I. SUBINFEUDATION ON THE CLERICAL ESTATES

IN the last three chapters our attention has been concentrated upon the relation between the king and his immediate vassals, as being, in Round's words, 'the primary relation that determined all below it'.[1] We must now turn to the more obscure but no less interesting problem of the relation between the tenant-in-chief—'the "middleman" of the feudal system'[2]—and his sub-tenants. Every great estate was a replica in miniature of the kingdom. Just as the Conqueror distributed or regranted the conquered lands in return for specified services, so the grantees in their turn parcelled out their holdings among their personal followers in order to secure the wherewithal to discharge their obligations towards the Crown. Hence every demand made by the king for service from his tenants-in-chief, was passed on by the tenants-in-chief to their own vassals, who supplied the contingents which their lords led to war, or paid his scutage if he compounded for his service.

It was Round who, in his illuminating studies in *Feudal England*, first clearly distinguished between the two stages in the establishment of military tenures in England—the first, the assessment of the service to be rendered by the tenants-in-chief, both lay and ecclesiastical, for the lands which they held of the Crown; the second, the plotting out of the land into 'knights' fees', as a result of the process of subinfeudation on the several fiefs—and who demonstrated that the second stage was accomplished as a result of the independent action of the baronage, and not of the royal initiative.[3] For a lord permanently to maintain the requisite number of knights for the royal service in his household or upon his demesne was both costly and inconvenient; and most of the greater tenants, whether lay or ecclesi-

---

[1] *Feudal England*, p. 247. [2] Ibid., p. 248.
[3] Ibid., pp. 246 seq.

astical, preferred to convert their military followers from 'stipendiarii' into 'tenentes per servicium militare' by making them grants of land. Naturally there was no uniformity in the process of subinfeudation, since the determining factor was the personal convenience or inclination of each individual tenant-in-chief; but such evidence as is available shows that already in the reigns of the two first Norman kings considerable progress had been made in the creation of knights' fees.

As usual, the bulk of our information concerns the clerical estates. It is probable that in the years immediately following the assessment of the church fees in 1070 few sub-tenancies were created. We know, for instance, that at Ely, down to the time of Abbot Symeon, who was appointed in 1082, the abbey's knights were maintained 'infra aulam ecclesie' at a regular wage, their food being supplied to them daily by the cellarer.[1] At Abingdon Abbot Athelelm (1072-84) at first employed *stipendiarii*;[2] so at Peterborough did Abbot Thorold (1069-98);[3] while in Domesday Book we find twenty-five houses in the vicinity of the abbey of Westminster assigned to the use of the abbey's knights, who, if they did not feed at the abbot's table, were certainly maintained at his expense.[4] Even Bishop Wulfstan of Worcester (d. 1095) adopted, according to his biographer, the Norman custom, and retained a body-guard who served in return for their board and an annual payment.[5] A system which was attended in any circumstances by grave disadvantages proved, however, peculiarly ill-adapted to the needs of churchmen. As the monks of Ely quickly found, the standing entertainment of a band of roistering knights was an intolerable burden on a peace-loving community,[6] and even

---

[1] *Liber Eliensis*, p. 275. Quoted by Round, *Feudal England*, p. 300.

[2] 'Taliter itaque regni tumultuantibus causis, domnus Adellelmus abbas locum sibi commissum munita manu militum secure protegebat; et primo quidem stipendiariis in hoc utebatur' (*Hist. Monasterii de Abingdon*, ii. 3).

[3] This may be inferred from the sentence 'Turoldus vero sexaginta et duo hidas terre de terra ecclesie Burgi dedit stipendiariis militibus' (*John of Peterborough*, ed. Giles, quoted by Round, *Feudal England*, p. 300, n. 234).

[4] J. Armitage Robinson, *Gilbert Crispin*, pp. 37 seq.

[5] 'Nam et consuetudines Normannorum non omittebat, pompam militum secum ducens, qui stipendiis annuis cotidianisque cibis immane quantum populabantur' (William of Malmesbury, *Gesta Pontificum*, p. 281).

[6] 'Quod intollerabiliter et supra modum potuit vexare locum' (*Liber Eliensis*, p. 275).

the sacrifice of part of the abbey's demesne was not too high a price to pay for release. Accordingly, Abbot Symeon granted to these disturbers of monastic tranquillity 'quasdam terras Sancte Etheldrede in feodum . . . ut in omni expeditione regi observarent, [et] ecclesia perpetim infatigata permaneret'.[1] Athelelm of Abingdon also, when once the disturbances following on the Conquest were over, found it expedient to establish on the lands of the abbey the knights he had hitherto maintained at his own expense;[2] while according to the *carta* of the Bishop of Worcester in 1166, Bishop Wulfstan, before his death in 1095, had enfeoffed no less than $37\frac{1}{2}$ knights out of the fifty due from his holding to the king.[3] There is evidence that subinfeudation was proceeding simultaneously on other church fees. Abbots Ethelwig (d. 1077) and Walter (1077–86)[4] of Evesham; Abbot Geoffrey of Tavistock (died *c.* 1088);[5] Abbot Paul of St. Albans (1077–93);[6] Baldwin of St. Edmunds (1065–

---

[1] Liber Eliensis, loc. cit.

[2] '. . . et primo quidem stipendiariis in hoc utebatur. At his sopitis incursibus . . . eisdem donativis prius retentis, abbas mansiones possessionum ecclesie pertinentibus inde delegavit, edicto cuique tenore parendi de sue portionis mansione' (*Hist. Monasterii de Abingdon*, ii. 3). Compare the list of knights given on pp. 3–7, with the abbey's tenants as given in Domesday Book, ff. 258–9; Round, p. 306.

[3] *Red Book*, p. 300. The return is made under three heads:
Wigornensis ecclesie isti sunt feoffati antiquitus . . . summa xxxvij milites et dimidium.
Isti sunt feoffati a tempore Samsonis Episcopi . . . summa iiij milites.
Isti sunt feoffati de dominico a tempore Theophi Episcopi . . . summa iiij milites.
The implication clearly is that the $37\frac{1}{2}$ were enfeoffed by Wulfstan. See also the hidated survey of the Gloucestershire manors of the Bishop of Worcester, which Round believes to be of pre-Domesday date (*Feudal England*, p. 294). The bishop's *milites* are there said to hold 15 hides of the manor of Westbury-on-Trim.

[4] Round, pp. 300 seq.; quoting the Evesham Cartulary. Cott. MSS. Vesp. B. xxiv, f. 8; *Chron. Abbatie Eveshamensis*, R.S., p. 96, &c. Abbot Ethelwig: 'de hiis terris quas . . . suo tempore acquisivit, quibusdam bonis hominibus pro magna necessitate et honore ecclesie dedit, et inde Deo et sibi fideliter quamdiu vixit serviebant.' Abbot Walter persisted in enfeoffing knights 'contradicente capitulo'.

[5] See the clause in the charter of Henry I to William Bishop of Exeter and Richard fitz Baldwin: 'Prohibeo ne aliquis preter monachos ipsas terras amplius teneat vel alias aliquas que de dominio ecclesie fuerunt, exceptis illis quas Gaufridus Abbas dedit ad servicium militare' (*Monasticon*, ii. 496).

[6] In 1244, when the St. Albans service was in dispute, it was stated on the abbot's behalf that his knights 'feofati fuerunt per Paulum abbatem de

98) and Gilbert Crispin of Westminster (1082–1117) can all be proved to have enfeoffed knights. In the two latter cases contemporary charters of feoffment have actually survived. Among the muniments of Westminster is preserved a charter tentatively assigned by Dr. Armitage Robinson to the year 1083, in which Abbot Gilbert grants Tothill to William Baynard to be held by the service of one knight;[1] while Mr. Douglas has recently discovered in the Black Book of St. Edmunds the copy of a grant made by Abbot Baldwin to one of the knights of the Conqueror.[2] No less certain is it that Lanfranc had, before the death of William I, already enfeoffed on the Canterbury estates the full number of knights for which he was answerable to the king. Not only do the *milites* of the archbishop figure prominently in the great Domesday Book,[3] but the contemporary 'Domesday' of the Christchurch monks supplies a parallel list in which are set forth not merely the names of the tenants, but also the service due from each.[4]

Where the lawlessness of the hired knights was not an incentive to subinfeudation, the nepotism of bishops and abbots frequently supplied a motive. Thorold of Peterborough, we are told, squandered the abbey lands among his kinsmen, and the knights he brought with him at his institution.[5] A list of the abbey's military tenants appears under a special heading in Domesday Book, and detailed particulars of the conditions of tenure in the reign of Henry I are furnished by the Peterborough 'Liber Niger'.[6] According to one authority even the

dominico Sancti Albani ad faciendum omnia forinseca servicia, etc.' (Matthew Paris, *Chron. Majora*, vi. 439).

[1] J. Armitage Robinson, *Gilbert Crispin*, p. 37 seq.

[2] *E.H.R.* xlii. 245 et seq.   [3] Domesday Book, f. 4.

[4] 'De Militibus Archiepiscopi', 8th Report on Hist. MSS. i. 316; A. J. Macdonald, *Lanfranc*, p. 151.

[5] 'Quoniam ipse abbas Turoldus non solum non addidit sed etiam terras bene congregatas male distraxit, et dedit eas parentibus et militibus suis qui cum eo venerant, ita ut vix tercia pars abbacie remaneret in dominio.' *Henry of Pytchley's Book of Fees*, ed. W. T. Mellows, pp. xlvi seq. Mr. Mellows, in this very valuable survey, shows that the version given in Sparke, *Historiae Coenobii Burgi*, p. 54, is corrupt, and embodies a gloss by Walter of Whittlesey (*c.* 1274) upon the original of Hugh Candidus (1115–78).

[6] See the list of the abbot's knights in Domesday Book, Northampton, f. 221 b. Cf. *V.C.H. Northampton*, i. 390 seq.; Round, *Feudal England*, pp. 157 seq. For the list temp. Henry I see Soc. of Antiquaries MSS. no. lx; Mellows, *Henry of Pytchley, ut supra*.

feoffments made by Athelelm of Abingdon were the result not, as his panegyrist maintains, of necessity,[1] but of the abbot's desire to lavish the possessions of his house upon the members of his own family, whom he summoned for the purpose from Normandy.[2] Abbot Walter of Evesham and his successor Robert persistently granted away to their relatives the lands of the abbey, in spite of the protests of the chapter;[3] Guimond of Tavistock (1088–1102) similarly enriched his connexions, and in particular his brother William, at the expense of the monks;[4] while in 1166 the Archbishop of York in his *carta* ascribed the excess of knights upon his lands to the nepotism of his predecessors, who 'non pro necessitate servicii quod debent, sed quia cognatis et servientibus suis providere volebant, plures quam debebant Regi feodaverunt'.[5] Nor were the abbots and bishops themselves the only offenders. There is evidence that the Conqueror not infrequently compelled his ecclesiastical tenants-in-chief to provide for his own nominees. Thus at Peterborough, Thorold, despite his protests, was made to enfeoff Eudes, the king's 'dapifer', with property at Easton, although the land had already been assigned by him to another;[6] while in Domesday Book we find a certain Picot entered as holding land in Cambridge of the Abbot of Ely 'by the king's command',[7] and one of the tenants of the Bishop of Salisbury's Wiltshire manor of Potterne described as 'miles jussu regis'.[8] The charter of feoffment of Abbot Baldwin of St. Edmunds,

---

[1] *Hist. Monasterii de Abingdon*, ii. 3.

[2] Ibid., p. 233: 'Misit . . . in Normanniam pro cognatis suis, quibus multas possessiones ecclesie dedit et feoffavit, ita ut in anno lxx de possessionibus ecclesie eis conferret.' Quoted by Round, p. 302.

[3] *Chron. Abbatie Eveshamensis*, pp. 96–8. Cott. MSS. Vesp. B. xxiv. Quoted by Round, *Feudal England*, p. 32. Compare the plaint of the Evesham annalist. Wrottesley, *Burton Cartulary*, p. 2: 'Hic notantur milites et liberi tenentes Abbatie de Evesham multi injuste feoffati, pauci vero juste.'

[4] See the charter of Henry I to the abbey (*Monasticon*, ii. 496).

[5] *Red Book*, p. 413. Paul of St. Albans was also accused of nepotism: 'Multa autem et alia parentibus suis de substantia ecclesiae (in laesionem conscientiae suae) indignis et litteraturae ignaris, et origine ac moribus ignobilibus, quae non possunt scribi, delapidando bona ecclesiae, inconsulte distribuit, et occulte.' But the chronicler charitably adds: 'Sed idcirco ignoscendum fuit ei, quia multo plura bona fecit quam damna ecclesiae irrogaret' (*Gesta Abbatum*, i. 64). [6] *Chron. Petroburgense*, p. 168.

[7] Domesday Book, Cambridge, i. ff. 191, 200.

[8] Ibid., Wilts., f. 66.

already mentioned, is another case in point. Here we have a certain Peter, described as 'Willelmi Regis miles', received by the abbot as his feudal man 'with the permission of the king'. The document not only affords additional evidence of the Conqueror's practice of endowing his followers at the expense of the Church; it testifies to the close supervision exercised by him over every detail of the working of the feudal machinery which he had constructed. The claims of the abbot upon his vassal are strictly subordinated to those of the king; and the obligation of Peter to serve for his lord is absolutely conditioned by the previous royal command. At a later date the vacancy of a bishopric or an abbacy offered to the king or to the custodian appointed by him an excellent opportunity of rewarding friends or dependents without cost to himself. When the archbishopric of Canterbury was in hand after the death of Lanfranc, William Rufus bestowed many fiefs upon followers of his own.[1] Even so respectable a person as Bishop Roger of Salisbury, when acting as custodian of the abbey of Abbotsbury, did not scruple to grant away, without the consent of the monks, two hides of the abbey's land to a certain Nicholas de Meriet 'ad maritandam quandam neptem suam';[2] while during a vacancy at Middleton he converted certain 'terre censuales' into knights' fees against the will of the community.[3]

In the early Norman period, when the fief still retained something of its original beneficiary character, the lord appears to have exercised wide powers of revocation. We are told that Abbot Walter of Evesham, instigated by his young kinsmen who were themselves hungry for land, deprived most of the knights enfeoffed by his predecessor of their holdings.[4] With greater justification the Abbot of Middleton secured the reversal of the unauthorized innovations made on the estates of

[1] Eadmer, *Historia Novorum*, p. 46. The king begged Anselm that 'terras ecclesie quas ipse rex defuncto Lanfranco suis dederat pro statuto servicio, illis ipsis hereditario jure tenendas, causa sui amoris condonaret'.

[2] *Red Book*, i. 211.

[3] Ibid., p. 210. See also the case of the Bishop of Chichester and the Count of Eu, p. 200.

[4] *Chron. Abbatie Eveshamensis*, pp. 96–8: '. . . noluit homagium a pluribus bonis hominibus quos predecessor suus habuerat suscipere eo quod terras omnium, si posset, decrevit auferre.' . . . 'dicitur quod fere omnes milites hujus abbatie hereditavit'.

his church by Bishop Roger;[1] while the monks of Tavistock obtained from Henry I a charter restoring the lands which had been granted away by the simoniacal Abbot Guimond.[2]

That attempts to check the process of subinfeudation were in the main ineffectual, is, however, abundantly clear from a study of the returns made by the ecclesiastics in 1166. These show that of the forty clerical tenants-in-chief, the Abbot of Middleton alone had made no enfeoffments, preferring to furnish from his demesne the two knights he owed the king.[3] Two other religious—the Abbot of Winchcombe and the Prior of Coventry—had enfeoffed less than their total service; the former retaining one of his two knights 'in dominio',[4] the latter $2\frac{1}{6}$ out of his full quota of ten.[5] The number of those who had enfeoffed more than their *servicium debitum* is, by contrast, remarkably large, especially among the bishops. For instance Canterbury, with a service of 60 knights, acknowledged a total enfeoffment of $84\frac{3}{4}$; Durham, owing 10 knights, had enfeoffed 68 +, of whom 64 had been created before 1135;[6] Ely, owing 40, had enfeoffed $72\frac{3}{4}$, of whom $56\frac{1}{4}$ were of the old feoffment; Exeter, owing $17\frac{1}{2}$ had enfeoffed 35 +; Lincoln, owing 60, had enfeoffed 104, all but two having been created before the death of Henry I; London, with a *servicium* of 20 knights, had created $36\frac{1}{3}$; and York, owing originally only 7, had enfeoffed no less than 43 +, of whom all save a few small fractions were 'de veteri feoffamento'.[7] Among the religious, the most striking

---

[1] *Red Book*, i. 210: 'Postmodum vero bone memorie R. predecessore meo constituto abbate, per justitiam regis Henrici et consilio prefati Episcopi [Rogeri] feoda predicta ad antiquum statum revocata sunt. Et quos Episcopus constituit milites facti sunt censuarii.'

[2] *Monasticon*, ii. 496.

[3] *Red Book*, i. 210: 'Servicia que vobis ecclesia nostra debet de dominio suo persoluit.'

[4] Ibid., p. 287: 'Ecclesia de Winchcumba habet unum feodum de veteri feodamento . . . et super dominia j. feodum militis.'

[5] Ibid., p. 324: 'Prior de Covintria habet de veteri feoffamento fefatos vij milites et tertiam partem militis et duas quintas partes militis et xmam partem. Et super dominium ejus quantum sufficit ad perficiendum x milites.'

[6] The large number of enfeoffments on the Durham estates is probably accounted for by the bishop's palatinate status and his responsibility for the defence of the borders.

[7] The only two bishops who had not in 1166 enfeoffed more knights than they owed the king were Bath and Coventry.

figures are those which appear on the returns of St. Edmunds, which, with a *servicium debitum* of 40 had by the death of Henry I enfeoffed 52¾ knights, and of Westminster which, owing 15, returned 23 + as of the old feoffment.[1]

By the end of the reign of Henry I, therefore, if not in the time of the Conqueror himself, there had been created on both lay and clerical estates a class of military sub-tenants in which the French or Norman element was as overwhelmingly preponderant as it was among the tenants-in-chief. The testimony of chronicles and cartularies to the wholesale importation by the Norman prelates of their foreign kinsfolk and dependents is supported by the evidence of such contemporary records as have survived. The authors of the Historical MSS. Commission Report give it as their opinion that of the names which appear on the list of Lanfranc's knights preserved in the Christchurch 'Domesday', only about one in ten is English.[2] The Peterborough list yields an equally small proportion of English names. One of the most interesting of the rare examples of military tenure by a member of the conquered race occurs on this fee. Coleswegen of Lincoln, called by Freeman 'the Conqueror's English favourite',[3] and a man of considerable influence in the locality, held land of Abbot Thorold in Riseholme in 1086 by knight-service, and was succeeded in the holding by his son Picot.[4] The 'Swainus' who, under Henry I, held three virgates and an acre in Northamptonshire on condition of serving 'cum militibus', and the Godwinus de Uptona who held three virgates on similar terms, were probably also of English origin.[5] The Domesday survey of the Bishop of Salisbury's Wiltshire estates gives us a further instance, for we learn that the knight who held 'iussu regis' of the bishop's manor of Potterne was an Englishman.[6] Such cases are, however, undoubtedly exceptional, and

---

[1] *Supra*, p. 20.   [2] Hist. MSS. Commission, 8th Report, i. 316.

[3] Freeman, *Norman Conquest*, iv. 219.

[4] Domesday Book, i. f. 345 b: 'In Risun habuit Elnod iiij bovatas terre ad geldum . . . nunc habet Colswan de Abbate Turoldo.' 'Descriptio Militum', *Chron. Petroburgense*, p. 175: 'Picotus filius Colswaini habet dimidiam carrucatam in Rison, quam abbas dedit patri suo.'

[5] *Chron. Petroburgense*, pp. 172, 173.

[6] Domesday Book, Wilts., f. 66: 'De eadem terra hujus manerii tenent ij Angli vj hidas et unam virgatam terre. Unus ex eis est miles jussu regis et nepos fuit Hermanni episcopi.'

do not affect the general conclusion that in the post-Conquest period the class of military sub-tenants was predominantly of French or of continental derivation.

Granting that continuity of personnel was rare, is there any indication of the continuity of Anglo-Saxon tenurial conditions among the military sub-tenants of the post-Conquest period? Although the theory that the Conqueror's assessment of his tenants-in-chief was influenced by earlier conditions has been long since exploded, the attempts to connect the *feodum militis* of the twelfth century with the five-hide unit of pre-Conquest days, or at least to establish some principle of uniformity, has only with reluctance been abandoned.[1] All such efforts break down, however, in face of the evidence of the records, from which it clearly appears that the knight's fee varied indefinitely in area not only from fief to fief, but even upon the same estate. The *carte* of 1166 show us, it is true, the five-hide principle apparently prevailing on the lands of the Bishop of Salisbury[2] and the Abbot of Westminster;[3] but elsewhere no uniformity is discernible. The abbey of Shaftesbury had fees varying in extent from 4 to 6 hides;[4] the knights of St. Albans held between them 40 hides, of which $5\frac{1}{2}$ made up the first fee, 7 the second, $8\frac{1}{2}$ the third, 6 the fourth, $5\frac{1}{2}$ the fifth, and $7\frac{1}{2}$ the sixth.[5] At Abingdon in one instance 19 hides were held by the service of four knights, in another 6 were held by the service of two, in yet another thirteen by the service of $1\frac{1}{2}$; while a single fee might comprise seven, nine, or even ten hides.[6] At Malmesbury we find 25 hides rendering the service of two knights to the abbot and $\frac{3}{4}$ to the king, 4 hides rendering 1 knight to the abbot and $\frac{1}{2}$ to the king, 3 hides and 3 virgates, $\frac{1}{2}$ to the abbot and $\frac{1}{4}$ to the king, and 5 virgates, $\frac{1}{4}$ to the abbot and $\frac{1}{8}$ to the king.[7] Much has been made of the fact that at Ramsey the knight's fee was, for the purpose of assessing the relief due from the smaller free tenants, reckoned as equal to four hides;[8]

---

[1] See Maitland, *Domesday Book and Beyond*, &c.
[2] *Red Book*, i. 237–8.   [3] Ibid., p. 188.   [4] Ibid., p. 214.
[5] Cott. MSS. Nero, D. i, f. 63, f. 171.
[6] *Hist. Monasterii de Abingdon*, iii. 4 seq.
[7] *Registrum Malmesburiense*, R.S., i. 245 seq.
[8] *Ramsey Cartulary*, iii. 47: 'Feodum integrum soluit ad relevium centum solidos. Una hida que est quarta pars feodi, viginti et quinque solidos . . .'

but if the holdings of the individual knights are examined it will be found that no such uniformity as this rule implies existed in practice. In the twelfth-century list of the abbey's *milites* the fees vary in extent from 5 to $10\frac{1}{2}$ hides.[1] At Peterborough, on the other hand, the area of the military holdings was, as Round has pointed out,[2] peculiarly small. We find $4\frac{1}{4}$ knights due from $10\frac{3}{16}$ hides, 3 due in one instance from $13\frac{1}{6}$, in another from $7\frac{3}{4}$ hides, and even $1\frac{1}{2}$ due from $2\frac{1}{2}$.[3] Clearly the process of subinfeudation on individual fiefs was no more determined by the Saxon five-hide principle than was the Conqueror's assessment of the tenants-in-chief.[4] In either case the determining factor was the caprice or the convenience of the lord.

II. THE MACHINERY FOR THE EXACTION OF SERVICE, FINE, AND SCUTAGE

We have seen that the number of knights enfeoffed on any given estate rarely tallied exactly with the number owed to the king. Occasionally fewer were created, but usually the tenants-in-chief enfeoffed more than were actually due. In the course of the thirteenth century the surplus, already considerable in 1166, became proportionately much larger as a result of the reduction effected in the *servicia debita* of most of the greater tenants, both lay and ecclesiastical. Where money payments such as scutage or aid were concerned, the lord simply reaped the profits from the extra feoffments, but when corporal service was in question the settlement of its incidence presented a complicated administrative problem. On what principle, for instance, did the Archbishop of York select the twenty (later five) knights he owed to the king from among the forty odd enfeoffed upon his lands; or the Bishop of Lincoln the sixty (later five) due from his 104 fees? The most obvious solution was to institute a system of rotation, the knights serving in turn in the royal army. We may conjecture that some such tradition in regard to corporal service underlay the assertion of the military tenants of St. Edmunds in 1196, that the twelve enfeoffed in excess of the abbot's *servicium* 'debent adjuvare

---

[1] *Ramsey Cartulary*, iii. 218 seq.   [2] *V.C.H., Northampton*, i. 392.
[3] *Chron. Petroburgense*, 'Descriptio Militum', pp. 170 seq.
[4] Cf. Sir Paul Vinogradoff, *English Society in the Eleventh Century*, pp. 42–8.

alios xl. ad wardas faciendas et ad scutagia, similiter et ad auxilium abbatis'.[1] In the case of the Abbots of Ramsey, St. Albans, and Malmesbury, and the Bishop of Hereford, the evidence is abundant and decisive.

The system prevailing at Ramsey has recently been investigated in detail by Dr. W. O. Ault of Boston,[2] and it will suffice here to summarize briefly the conclusions at which he has arrived, after a careful study of the printed cartulary and the few surviving rolls of the honour court of Broughton. The abbey, which may originally have acknowledged a larger *servicium*,[3] recognized, under Henry II and later, four knights only. In 1166 the abbot made his return to the great inquest of service on the basis not of knights' fees, but of hides, adding in explanation: 'Homines faciunt iiij milites in communi ad servicium domini regis. Ita quod tota terra abbatie communicata est cum eis per hidas ad predictum servicium faciendum.'[4] This statement led earlier investigators such as Baldwin[5] and Maitland[6] to conclude that no knights' fees had been created on the Ramsey estates; but Mr. Ault has clearly established that this was not the case. Not only does the cartulary contain examples of early Norman charters of enfeoffment,[7] but it includes a return, roughly contemporaneous with the *carta* of 1166, in which the holdings of the abbey's tenants are expressed in terms of *feoda militum*.[8] This list shows a total of thirteen knights, all of the old feoffment, and this total, according to Mr. Ault's calculations, was increased within the next century to sixteen or nineteen.[9] Of these, whenever a royal summons was issued, four were elected or assigned in rotation by the knights and free-holders assembled in the honour court of Broughton to serve for their companions. The expenses of the chosen four

[1] *Chron. Jocelini de Brakelond*, pp. 20, 48 seq.
[2] *Private Jurisdiction in England*.
[3] Cf. the writ of William Rufus reducing Ramsey's service on festivals from ten knights to three (*Ramsey Cartulary*, i. 235).
[4] *Red Book*, i. 37 seq.   [5] *Scutage and Knight Service*, p. 11.
[6] *Select Pleas in Manorial Courts*, p. 50. Round, with greater caution, contents himself with the statement that the case of Ramsey is peculiar and that further inquiry is necessary (*Feudal England*, p. 298).
[7] *Ramsey Cartulary*, i. 248, ii. 259; *supra*, p. 41.
[8] Ibid., iii. 218 seq.
[9] Ault, *Private Jurisdiction in England*, p. 69.

were paid throughout the forty days of feudal service from the date of their assignment to a unit, at a rate which varied at the discretion of the court. The money was raised by a 'hidage' assessed at a proportionate rate, not, it would seem, upon the remaining knights' fees, but upon all the non-military lands of the abbey, with the exception of the small holdings of cottars or crofters and certain privileged tenements.[1] In 1257, on the occasion of Henry III's expedition against Llewelyn ap Griffith, the court decreed that the four knights designated to serve for the abbey should receive four shillings each a day, each hide contributing to their maintenance two shillings.[2]

The case of St. Albans has frequently been cited as affording a parallel to that of Ramsey. Although, however, the system there followed was in its main outlines similar to that described above, there were certain important differences of detail. No thorough investigation of the conditions of knight-service at St. Albans has hitherto been made. The information used for purposes of illustration by Maitland in his introduction to the *Select Pleas in Manorial Courts* was derived exclusively from the printed chronicles of the abbey—in particular from the 'Additamenta' to the *Chronica Majora* of Matthew Paris, and the *Gesta Abbatum* of Walsingham. For the purposes of the present treatise this has been supplemented from the unprinted cartularies of the abbey preserved in the British Museum, among which the famous 'elephant' manuscript—Cott. MSS. Nero, D. i.—and the partially burnt manuscripts Otho. D. iii and Tiberius, E. vj, have yielded particularly valuable evidence.

The service of St. Albans, like that of Ramsey, was strikingly small in proportion to the wealth and extent of the monastic lands. In 1166 the abbot acknowledged a *servicium* of six knights only[3]—a total which remained constant throughout the thirteenth and fourteenth centuries. Instead, however, of following the example of their brethren at Ramsey and enfeoffing from four to five times as many men as they owed the king, the abbots of St. Albans in the Norman period created

---

[1] Maitland, *Select Pleas in Manorial Courts*, Pleas in the Court of the Honour of Broughton, pp. 50 seq.; Ault, *Private Jurisdiction*, pp. 70 seq.

[2] Ibid., loc. cit. That the system goes back at least to the early thirteenth century is clear from the writ of John to Roger de Nevill', given *supra*, p. 95, n. 3.   [3] *Red Book*, i. 359.

six fees only. Whether or no they enfeoffed originally six
integral fees, by 1166 only one—that held of the abbot by
Hugh Wake—was held as a single unit.[1] The remaining five
were already divided between two or more tenants.[2] In the
course of time the sub-division, as the appended tables will
show, tended to increase. The Wakes left the performance of
their service to their five military sub-tenants, who in the
thirteenth century were treated as the immediate vassals of the
abbot.[3] The fee of Croxley and Oxhey, originally shared by
two families, was divided in the later thirteenth century into
a number of fragments, as a result of the death, without male
heirs, of Roger de Croxley, tenant of $\frac{13}{17}$ of the whole. Roger
left to succeed him three daughters: Petronilla, who married
Hugh de Amuneville; Beatrice, who married John de Shelford;
and Joan, who married Thomas de Wauncy.[4] Of these three,
Beatrice and her husband died without heirs and their share
of the Croxley lands eventually reverted, between 1260 and
1290, to the abbot.[5] Joan and Thomas de Wauncey left three
daughters—Joan, Agnes, and Alice, who married respectively
Ralph de Glynley, Roger le Tailleur, and Richard de Tinge-
wicke.[6] Owing, perhaps, to the difficulties resulting from the
minute subdivision of the manors, consequent upon the inheritance by each of a third of the third which had belonged to their
mother, the de Wauncy heiresses finally surrendered their
respective shares of the Croxley inheritance to Abbot John,
who is found responding for them in 1327.[7] In the meantime
Petronilla de Amuneville and her husband had also left only
daughters to succeed them. The elder, Petronilla, married
Nicholas de Oxhey, tenant of the remaining $\frac{4}{17}$ of the fee, and
had by him a son, Richard, who succeeded to the Oxhey lands.[8]
The younger, also named Petronilla, married Hugh de Vynon,

[1] Ibid., loc cit.: 'Nullum vero militem habemus qui plenum servicium j
militis faciat, praeter Hugonem de Wach, qui de nobis tenet feodum j
militis.'   [2] See appended table.
[3] The Wakes were tenants of Peterborough also; and their relations to
the abbot there were the same as at St. Albans (Mellows, *Henry of Pytchley*,
pp. 81 seq.).   [4] Cott. MSS. Tiberius, E. vi, f. 180.
[5] *Gesta Abbatum*, i. 475–6.   [6] Cott. MSS. Tiberius, E. vi, f. 180.
[7] See appended table; *Gesta Abbatum*, ii. 120 seq.
[8] Cott. MSS. Tiberius, E. vi, f. 180; *V.C.H.*, *Hertford*, ii. 454 seq. under
Oxhey.

and seems to have transmitted her share of the Croxley tenement by the marriage of her daughters to Nicholas de Whethamsted and John de Westwick,[1] who responded therefor in 1303.[2]
This is, of course, an extreme case, but subdivision also proceeded far on the Batchworth and Britwell fee. The de Batchworth inheritance, which originally represented $\frac{7}{11}$ of the whole,
was divided in the early fourteenth century into two portions;
while that of Britwell, which represented the remaining $\frac{4}{11}$, was
partitioned among three tenants, of whom the abbot was one.[3]

The result was to compel the abbots to adopt a scheme of
rotation broadly similar to that in force at Ramsey. We have no
specific evidence of the working of the system before 1244,[4]
but the fact that subdivision already existed on most of the St.
Albans fees in 1166 makes it probable that it was even then
in operation. In 1257 a dispute over the service due in Wales
led to a formal declaration of the custom of the abbey in
military matters. Matthew Paris relates in a familiar passage
how, in the courtyard under the ash-tree within the abbey
precincts, in the presence of Lawrence de Broke, the king's
justice 'ad deliberandum gayolam', William de Welmulle,
steward of the liberty of St. Albans, William de Todwyke,
coroner of the county of Hertford, and various obedientiaries
of the house, Sir Roger de Meridon declared on behalf of his
fellows, that, on receipt of the royal summons, all the immediate
tenants of the abbot *per servicium militare* ought to assemble
and elect one man in turn from each of the six fees, to perform
service for his coparceners either in person or by deputy.
Towards the expenses of the contingent while on service, each
fee ought to contribute at the rate of six marks, every tenant
paying according to the extent of his holding; so that each of
the 'capitales electi' ought to receive six marks less the amount
due in respect of his own tenement. If he expended more than

[1] Cott. MSS. Tiberius, E. vi, f. 180; *V.C.H., Hertford*, ii. 454 seq. under
Oxhey.   [2] See table, *supra*, p. 125.
[3] See table, *supra*, p. 125. Sir Ralph Munchansy received Harpesfield;
the abbot received Pinchfield in Rickmansworth 'ex dimissione [? J. de
Brut]welle'. Cott. MSS. Tiberius, E. vi, f. 229.
[4] The first detailed record of service is for the Scottish campaign of 1244
(Matthew Paris, *Chron. Majora*, vi. 437). Note the use in 1257 of the
expression 'Consuetudo autem est *et fuit ab antiquo*' (*Chron. Majora*, vi. 375).

the sum allowed him the responsibility was his own; and he alone must be answerable for any damage incurred by the abbot by reason of his default.[1]

In this version of the 'customs of the barony' the abbot seems to have acquiesced with some reluctance. The main point at issue was the rate of the contribution by the main body of military tenants towards the expenses of the men serving. The fixed quota of six marks, for which Roger de Meridon contended, represented a daily allowance of two shillings only— a sum which, as the Ramsey assignment of the same date clearly proves, was wholly inadequate to the needs of the later thirteenth century. The claims of the tenants prevailed in practice, however, over the will of the lord. An elaborately constructed table in Tiberius, E. vi, which shows the sums due from various fractions of a fee ranging from $\frac{1}{2}$ to $\frac{1}{60}$, indicates that the abbot had capitulated, in spite of a marginal note to the effect that the custom 'quam ab antiquo pretendunt tenentes' had never been formally approved.[2] In the same cartulary is a rough draft of the amounts to be paid by the individual tenants, perhaps in connexion with Edward I's Welsh war of 1277.[3]

As at Ramsey, the existing material is insufficient to enable us to discern the exact principle upon which the system of rotation worked. The appended table shows the incidence of the *corpus*, in so far as it can be traced with certainty, between 1244 and 1327.

It will be seen that of the tenants of the first fee, all but the almoner of St. Albans make one appearance each; on the second fee Oxhey is twice represented, Croxley five times; on the third, Batchworth appears four times and Britwell three; on the fourth all except Sarratt render service at least once, while Langley and La Hyde each make two appearances; the fifth fee is represented six times by the tenants of Westwick, four times by the tenant of Shephall; and the sixth twice by Norton, twice by Childwick Magna, once by Codicot, and not at all by Munden. The gaps in the evidence are too numerous to justify the formation of any general conclusions from these data; but casual references suggest that, at least where sub-division had not

1 Ibid., pp. 438 et seq.
2 Cott. MSS. &c., f. 231 d.   3 Ibid., f. 180.

proceeded too far, the rotation of service was determined by the proportionate extent of the various holdings comprising the fee. At Westwick and Shephall, for instance, the de Gorhams and their successors the de Veres held two-thirds of the whole, the remaining third belonging to the de Munpinzons and their successors the de Brokes. In the thirteenth and fourteenth centuries it was clearly the rule that the former, as tenants of the major portion, should serve on two out of every three occasions. In 1282 the abbot did the service for William de Gorham, who was at the time a minor in his custody, and a note was added in the record to the effect that 'erit primus in futuro dominus Willelmus de Gorham, quia pro ceteris bis debet facere'.[1] Similarly in 1327 Alfonse de Vere was elected to represent the fee, on the understanding that 'iterum proxima vice faciet idem corpus, quia ipse tenet duas partes illius scuti'.[2] The contribution of the coparceners to the expenses of their 'capitalis electus' seems to have been modified in accordance with this allocation of service. In 1327 it was provided that Ralph de Broke, instead of paying the two marks technically due from his holding, should pay on each occasion upon which de Vere performed service 40 shillings, or the equivalent of half a fee.[3] A similar arrangement may originally have existed upon the Croxley and Oxhey manors. In 1257 we find Richard de Oxeye contributing not the 20 shillings properly exigible for his fourth part of the fee, but 2 marks—the equivalent of a third.[4] This seems to suggest that the de Croxleys as tenants of three-fourths of the fee, served three times to the once of the de Oxheys, just as the de Gorhams served twice to the once of the de Brokes.[5]

What was the nature of the assembly which administered the military system of the abbey of St. Albans? Maitland saw in

---

[1] Cott. MSS. Nero D. i, f. 173.

[2] Ibid., f. 148 d.   [3] Ibid., loc. cit.

[4] *Chron. Majora*, vi. 372 seq.: 'Ricardus de Oxaie consensit ad solvendum duas marcas pro parte sua, videlicet quarta parte scuti eunti pro ipso capitaliter et partionariis suis in exercitum regis.'

[5] At a somewhat later date the de Oxhey tenement paid only 20 shillings or even 18 shillings, but the change may be accounted for by the subdivision of the Croxley holding which had taken place in the interval and probably necessitated a reorganization of the method of rendering service. Cott. MSS. Tiberius, E. vi, f. 180.

it a court for freeholders parallel to the Abbot of Ramsey's honour court at Broughton.[1] His opinion has, however, recently been questioned by Professor Levett, who, after a detailed study of the courts and court-rolls of the abbey, remains unconvinced of the existence of any special court for freeholders on the St. Albans estates. She admits the existence of a central *curia* held 'infra Abbathiam' or 'sub fraxino', but adduces ample evidence to show that it was 'only the manorial court sitting elsewhere'. The assembly under the ash-tree in 1257, upon which alone Maitland appears to have based his conclusion, she shows to have been of an exceptional character, and to have had more affinity to the abbot's council than to the ordinary three-weekly court held within the abbey precincts.[2] From the extant records relating to military service it seems clear that, at least in the thirteenth century, the six knights were elected and the incidence of the *corpus* was determined not by a court, but simply by an assembly of the tenants *per servicium militare* convened *ad hoc* whenever the king called out the feudal array. In 1257 it was said to be the custom of the abbey that, upon receipt of the royal summons, all the military tenants should be called together 'ad unum locum' to designate their representatives.[3] According to a somewhat later entry the seneschal was to cause them to assemble for the purpose 'in abbathia'.[4] We are told that in 1260, before the expedition to Wales, they met 'ad sanctum Albanum in maiori ecclesia';[5] while in 1327 the 'capitales' are said to have been elected 'secundum consuetudinem' in the *curia* of the abbey beneath the ash-tree.[6] The terminology employed to describe these meetings does not suggest that they had any of the characteristics of a court. We find nothing at St. Albans to correspond to the 'milites et libere

---

[1] Maitland, *Select Pleas in Manorial Courts*, p. xlvi.

[2] A. E. Levett, 'The Courts and Court Rolls of St. Albans Abbey', *Transactions of the Royal Hist. Soc.*, 4th Series, vol. vii, pp. 52–76 *passim*.

[3] *Chron. Majora*, vi. 373 seq.

[4] This seems to be the sense of an almost indecipherable entry in the burnt MS. Tiberius, E. vi, f. 265 d. Upon receipt of the royal summons 'tunc debet Senescallus . . . ire omnes tenentes per servicium militare . . . pareant in Abbathia et ipsi eligent . . . scuto unum per ordinem qui faciet [corpus?] . . .' Cf. f. 230.   [5] Cott. MSS. Nero, D. i, f. 134 d.

[6] Ibid., m. 148 d. 'Et venerunt milites sex secundum consuetudinem per breve regis in curia Sancti Albani sub fraxino.'

tenentes de curia de Broucton' '. The St. Albans knights were elected to serve for the abbot and their coparceners, and not, as was the Ramsey contingent, 'pro domino abbate et communa curie';[1] they presented themselves 'prompti et parati ad servicium faciendum' not in the court, as at Ramsey, but 'ad parcam Sancti Albani';[2] while the nearest equivalent of the phrase 'per consideracionem curie' which constantly recurs in the Broughton rolls is the 'secundum consideracionem et visum parium suorum' employed in the St. Albans cartulary in 1282, apropos of the corporal service due from Ralph Pirot.[3] Maitland's misconception probably arose from the ambiguous use of the word *curia* in the St. Albans records. A study of the context establishes that when the term is employed in connexion with the meetings of the abbey's military tenants it denotes not a judicial assembly, but the place—viz. the outer courtyard of the monastery—in which the meetings were held.[4]

The system of rotation which prevailed at St. Albans was, therefore, distinguished from that followed at Ramsey in four main particulars. First, since only that number of fees had been created which was due to the king, the rotation was between the various tenants of each fee and not, as at Ramsey, between the tenants of the different fees. Secondly, while at Ramsey the expenses of the abbey's contingent were furnished by a levy upon the non-military tenants, at St. Albans only those who held *per servicium militare* were bound to contribute. Thirdly, at St. Albans the rate of contribution was, despite the opposition of the abbots, fixed in the thirteenth century at six marks the fee, whereas at Ramsey it varied from time to time according to the discretion of the court of Broughton. Fourthly and lastly, while at Ramsey the whole procedure was administered by a court of knights and freeholders meeting at regular intervals and exercising powers of distraint, at St. Albans, in spite of the rather hasty judgement of Maitland to the contrary, the rotation process seems in general to have been

---

[1] *Select Pleas in Manorial Courts*, p. 50.
[2] Cott. MSS. Nero, D. i, f. 134 d.   [3] Ibid., f. 173.
[4] A. H. Thompson, *English Monasteries*, chapter v. The meeting of 1257 is described as being held in the presence of Lawrence de Broke, &c., 'sedente sub fraxino in media curia' (*Chron. Majora*, vi. 438). In 1327 we are told 'venerunt milites . . . in curia Sancti Albani' (*supra*, p. 129, n. 6).

controlled by an *ad hoc* assembly of the military tenants of the abbey, disputes being dealt with by a special tribunal such as that of 1257, or referred to the royal courts.

At Malmesbury we find yet further local variations of the rotation principle. Here, as at Ramsay and St. Albans, the abbot's *servicium debitum*—in this case of three knights only— remained constant from the twelfth to the fourteenth century. The abbot made no return to the great inquest of 1166,[1] but, probably to repair this omission, his knights made a formal recognition of their respective obligations in the *curia regis*, at some date between 1168 and 1174. The record, which is preserved in the Malmesbury register,[2] reveals a curious double assessment of the abbey's tenants *per servicium militare*. For the purpose of reckoning the homage, relief, and aids due to the abbot they were assessed at a much higher service than they were expected to render on the abbot's behalf to the king. It is probable that originally their total obligation under the latter head was for just those three knights which comprised the abbot's *servicium debitum*, but already under Henry II the eleven military tenants acknowledged between them a service of $8\frac{3}{4}$ knights due to the abbot, and of $3\frac{1}{3}$, $\frac{3}{8}$ due as *regale servicium*. A second list, which is dated by Round between 1257 and 1311 and which gives the extent of the various holdings in hides as well as in knights' fees, raises the second total to $3\frac{2}{3}$, $\frac{1}{8}$ knights;[3] while the return for the inquest of 1242, which is included in the Book of Fees,[4] shows fifteen tenants or groups of tenants, holding in all $3\frac{3}{4}$, $\frac{1}{3}$, $\frac{1}{5}$, and $\frac{1}{16}$ fees, which appear in the appended table.[5]

From an entry in the register under the heading 'Turni ad faciendum regale servicium in exercitu regis',[6] it is clear that, in the thirteenth century, these fractional holdings were, for the purpose of rendering corporal service, combined into several groups. Round, generalizing rather hastily from this single reference, concluded that there were three such groups, each of which, whenever a feudal summons was issued, was

---

[1] In 1172 the sheriff of Wilts., in charge of the abbey's revenues during the vacancy, accounted under the heading 'de hiis qui cartas non miserunt' for the scutage of the Malmesbury knights (*Pipe Roll*, 18 Hen. II, pp. 160–1).

[2] *Registrum Malmesburiense*, R.S., i. 277–8.   [3] Ibid., pp. 245 seq.

[4] *Book of Fees*, ii. 732 seq.; cf. the lists in *Registrum*, ii. 389, 392.

[5] *Infra*, p. 132.   [6] *Registrum*, i. 248.

Names of Tenants.	Fraction of fee held.	Name of Tenants.	Fraction of fee held.
1. Roger de Dauntsey	$\frac{3}{4}$	9. Miles de Morle and	
2. Adam de Puriton	$\frac{3}{4}$	Ralph de Hurle	$\frac{1}{4}$
3. Geoffrey de Siffrewast		10. Richard le Bret and	
[Avene]	$\frac{1}{2}$	three coparceners	$\frac{1}{4}$
4. Beatrix Muredag		11. Robert Maureward	$\frac{1}{8}$
(? Maudut) [Somer-		12. Richard, son of	
ford].	$\frac{1}{3}$	William [la Legh]	$\frac{1}{8}$
5. William de Hankinton	$\frac{1}{4}$	13. William le Theyn	$\frac{1}{10}$
6. Payn de la Legh and		14. Henry Husee	$\frac{1}{10}$
Fraricus de Diche-		15. Thomas de Cherle-	
ford [Brinkeworth]	$\frac{1}{4}$	ton	$\frac{1}{16}$
7. John Matravers	$\frac{1}{4}$		
8. Walter le Escot and			
three coparceners	$\frac{1}{4}$	Total	$3\frac{3}{4}, \frac{1}{3}, \frac{1}{5}, \frac{1}{16}$

bound to furnish one knight.[1] The records of the service rendered on several occasions under Edward I and II, which are
contained in the second volume of the printed register,[2] and
which seem to have escaped Mr. Round's attention, prove him
to have been mistaken in both particulars. In the first place,
they show that the number of groups was not three but four,
the holdings being combined in the following order, without
regard to their extent:[3]

First Group.		Second Group.		Third Group.		Fourth Group.	
Somerford (4)	$\frac{1}{3}$	Dauntsey (1)	$\frac{3}{4}$	de Matravers		Morle (9)	$\frac{1}{4}$
Avene (3)		Brinkeworth (6)		(7)	$\frac{1}{4}$	le Bret (10)	$\frac{1}{4}$
(Avon)	$\frac{1}{2}$	(Brinkworth)	$\frac{1}{4}$	le Scot (8)	$\frac{1}{4}$	le Theyn (13)	$\frac{1}{10}$
				Maureward(11)	$\frac{1}{8}$		
Hankinton (5)	$\frac{1}{4}$	Puriton (2)		la Legh (12)		Husee (14)	$\frac{1}{10}$
		(Purton)	$\frac{3}{4}$	(Leigh)	$\frac{1}{8}$		
	$1\frac{1}{12}$		$1\frac{3}{4}$		$\frac{3}{4}$		$\frac{7}{10}$

In the second place they show that each group, instead of
furnishing one knight whenever service was rendered, furnished in its turn all three knights due from the abbot to the
king. As in the case of Ramsey and St. Albans our information
is very incomplete, but entries in the register enable us to trace

---

[1] J. H. Round, 'Knight Service of Malmesbury Abbey', *E.H.R.* xxxii.
249 seq.   [2] *Registrum*, ii. 404–5, 407, 416, 391.
[3] The numbers in brackets afford a key to the list of fees given above.

the operation of the system of rotation as between the different groups in the following years:

Date.	Group rendering Service.
1295.	1. Somerford, Avene, Hankinton.[1]
1300.	1. Somerford, Avene, Hankinton.[2]
1303.	2. Dauntsey, Brinkeworth, Puriton.[3]
1306.	4. Morle, le Bret, le Theyn, Husee.[4]
1316.	2. Dauntsey, Brinkeworth, Puriton.[5]

Whether, as at Ramsey and St. Albans, the remaining tenants contributed to the maintenance of the knights discharging their *turnus* does not appear from the records; but the nature of the arrangements for the discharge of the abbey's service renders it probable that they did. Conclusive evidence as to the means whereby the system of rotation was controlled and administered is also wanting. A certificate (dated by Round between 1280 and 1290) of the knights and freeholders of the abbey, testifying that John Comyn, lord of Newbold and Walcote ($\frac{1}{6}$ of a fee) and his predecessors, had done their share of the *regale servicium* in company with their fellows, suggests that, as at St. Albans, the control was vested in the whole body of military tenants.[6] It scarcely seems, however, to justify Mr. Ault's opinion that there existed at Malmesbury a court for freeholders parallel to the Ramsey honour court.[7]

The distinguishing features of the Malmesbury system are, therefore, first, the double assessment of the military tenants; and secondly, their association in sets of three or four for the performance of corporal service. A group of tenants whose holdings probably represented in the aggregate less than a single knight's fee was thus required to furnish, on one out of every four occasions, three fully-equipped knights or their equivalent in *servientes*.

The case of the bishopric of Hereford is of peculiar interest, in the first place because it is the only episcopal fee upon which it has been possible to trace in any detail the conditions of knight-service prevailing in the later Middle Ages; in the second place because of the reduction of its *servicium debitum* in the course of the thirteenth century from 15 knights to 5. Since the barony was situated on the turbulent Welsh marches its

---

[1] *Registrum*, ii. 391.   [2] Ibid., p. 404.   [3] Ibid., loc. cit.
[4] Ibid., loc. cit.   [5] Ibid., pp. 416–17.   [6] Ibid. i. 250.
[7] Ault, *Private Jurisdiction*, p. 76.

military organization retained its vigour long after that of most of the more favourably placed ecclesiastical estates had ceased to function; and the fine series of episcopal registers—now fortunately available in print—is exceptionally rich in material bearing on the feudal obligations of the see.[1]

The bishop who, before 1166, had regularly responded for 15 knights,[2] returned in his *carta* of that year 14 as of the old feoffment and $4\frac{1}{2}$ as of the new.[3] In the inquest of 1212 he was credited in all with 18 fees,[4] while in two lists which are preserved in the register of Bishop Richard de Swinfield under the date 1304, the total varies between $21\frac{1}{2}$ and $22\frac{1}{2}$.[5] As early as 1166 at least four of these fees were partitioned among groups of tenants, in one case as many as nine being included in a single group;[6] and at the beginning of the fourteenth century the liabilities of the various holdings were apportioned on the following plan:

Tenement.	Service.	Tenement.	Service.
1. Hamme Lacy [Holme Lacy]	$2\frac{1}{2}$ or 2	12. Walford [Walford]	1
2. Parva Herefordia [Little Hereford]	2	13. Caple [How Caple]	1
3. Sapy et Pirie [Sapey and Perry]	2	14. Hasele [Adzor]	1
4. Ullingwyk [Ullingswick]	1	15. Yadefen [Edvin Ralph]	1
5. Brokintone [Brockmanton]	1	16. Robertus de Brokehampton et sociis sui	
6. Morton [Moreton]	1	17. John de Baderun et socii sui	1
7. Preston [Preston]	1	18. Wallyntone, Masinton, Nathynton, Ruddok of Underdoune [Wellington, Mainstone]	1
8. Bishopestone [Bishopstone]	1		
9. Burges [Bridge Sollers]	1	19. Stanford [Bishop Stanford]	$\frac{1}{2}$
10. Childestone [Chilstone]	1	20. Mora Alani [Allens More]	$\frac{1}{2}$
11. Dudley et Eglinton [Didley]	1		

---

[1] See in particular the registers of Bishops Thomas de Cantilupe [1275–82], Richard de Swinfield [1283–1317], and John de Trillek [1344–61].

[2] *Red Book*, i. 16, 24. [3] Ibid., pp. 278–9. [4] Ibid., p. 495.

[5] Ibid., pp. 403 seq.

[6] *Red Book*, loc. cit.:

Radulfus Foliot et Radulfus Pere et Radulfus filius Ernoldi .j. militis.

Arnulfus de Estnover, et Hugo, et Willelmus filius Gerini et Johannes et Willelmus de Alchurges, et Godefridus Ruddoc faciunt .j. militem.

Ricardus de Huntelande et Baderon .j. militis.

Johannes de Stanford et Radulfus de Munesleia, et Willelmus de Froma, et

The method whereby corporal service was rendered seems to have been roughly similar to that in force at Ramsey, save that the tenurial was here more strongly emphasized than the personal element. Whenever a royal summons issued, five of the twenty odd fees were assigned, according to a formal scheme of rotation, to furnish the five knights due from the bishop to the king. No evidence of the operation of the system is available before the reign of Edward I, but the fact that surplus fees were early created on the episcopal estates and that tenure of single fees by groups of tenants was frequent, suggests that it originated not later than the middle of the twelfth century. The first reference *eo nomine* to the rotation process occurs in 1310 in a certificate of Bishop Swinfield, acknowledging the receipt of thirteen marks in discharge of arrears of service due from the Abbot of Gloucester's tenement in Ullingswick, with the proviso that the payment shall not release the abbot from his obligation to pay scutage in future, '*cum ad suum turnum militarem venerint*'.[1] In 1316 a similar phrase is employed in a bond executed by Robert Petit, Lord of Dudley, in which he recognizes the service of one knight's fee, adding: 'de que feu ieo dey le dit mon Seygnour le eveske aquiter devers nostre seygnour le roi auxsi souvent *cum mon tourn escherra*, enfesaunt mon serviz cum mes autres pieres le frount'.[2]

The entries in the episcopal registers enable us to determine the incidence of the 'turn' on four occasions only.[3] Little can be gathered from the very inadequate data available. The 'turn' of 1316, so far as it can be reconstructed, appears to be identical with that of 1277. From this it might be concluded that the grouping of the fees was stereotyped, as at Malmesbury; but on this hypothesis the appearance of Walford both in 1282 and 1300 would be difficult to account for.

There is nothing in the registers to show whether any contribution was exacted from the remaining military tenants for the support of those serving, nor is there any indication of the

Walterus et Robertus de Cradeleia, et Gilbertus Cletera, et Bernardus de Brochantone, et Ricardus de Huntelande, et Rogerus de Wallia faciunt servicium .j. militis.

[1] *Cartularium Monasterii Sancti Petri Gloucestrie*, R.S., iii. 226.
[2] *Register of Bishop Swinfield*, pp. 508 seq.
[3] See appended table, *infra*, p. 136.

1277.[1]	1282.[2]	1300.[3]	1316.[4]
(2) Hereford Parva	(1) Hamme Lacy	(1) Hamme Lacy [1 fee]	(2) Hereford Parva
?	(12) Walford	(12) Walford	—
(13) Caple	(8) Bishopstone	(6) Morton	(13) Caple
(11) Dudley	(4) Ullingswick	(14) Hasele	(11) Dudley
(3) Sapy	(7) Preston	(18) Ruddok	—

nature of the machinery by which the rotation of service was controlled. It is probably safe to conclude that, as at St. Albans and elsewhere, the whole body of the tenants *per servicium militare* acted as custodians of the traditions and interpreters of the custom of the barony in military matters, although not necessarily constituting a court such as existed at Ramsey.[5]

No specific evidence of the existence elsewhere of conditions of service similar to those described above is as yet available. Round has, indeed, shown that on the lands of the Bishop of Chichester in the later twelfth century, reliefs were paid 'per consuetudinem episcopatus', not upon the knights' fee, but at the rate of one mark the hide, on the Ramsey parallel.[6] This, in conjunction with the fact that in 1166 most of the bishop's fees were already held by groups of from four to ten tenants,[7]

[1] *Register of Bishop Swinfield*, p. 76. The service was rendered by John de la Mare, Nicholas de Wormele, William de Caple, knights, with Robert and Thomas Petit, and John and Robert de Sapy. Of these I have been unable to identify Nicolas de Wormele. He may have been a substitute.

[2] Ibid., loc. cit. and p. 333 : '...fuerunt assignati pro servicio quinque militum per quadraginta dies faciendo . . . dominus Johannes Daniel miles pro Bissopestone, dominus Johannes Tregoz pro villa de Hammelacy miles, Johannes de Hortele serviens pro Ullingwik, Johannes dominus de Waleford serviens pro villa sua predicta, et Robertus Wyve serviens pro Prestone.'

[3] Ibid., p. 78: 'Servicium factum fuit in Scotia . . . per feoda de Waleford, Mortone, Hasele et per unum feodum de Hamme Lacy et feodum de Ruddok.'

[4] Ibid., pp. 508 seq. Bonds executed by William, lord of Caple, Reginald de la Mare, lord of Little Hereford, and Robert Petit, lord of Dudley, for the discharge of the service due from them in the army summoned to Newcastle against the Scots.

[5] Note the use of the phrase 'mes autres pieres' in the bond of Robert Petit above, p. 135. Cf. also the procedure employed in military matters at St. Edmunds (*Chron. Jocelini de Brakelond*, pp. 20, 48, 63) and at Peterborough (*Chron. Petroburgense*, pp. 24–5).

[6] J. H. Round, 'The Knight Service of Malmesbury Abbey', *E.H.R.* xxxii. 252.

[7] *Red Book*, i. 198–200.

may, he suggests, be taken as an indication that there was in operation at Chichester a system of election for the discharge of knight-service in the field comparable to that in use at Ramsey or St. Albans. In the absence of corroborative information[1] this cannot be regarded as anything more than a plausible speculation; but since, as we have seen, most of the bishops and many of the religious early enfeoffed more knights than they owed to the king, it is probable that the principle of rotation was far more commonly applied than has hitherto been recognized.

We must now turn to examine the working of the system of commutation as between the tenants-in-chief and the sub-tenants. Whenever the lord compounded for his service by the payment of a scutage the levy fell back upon his dependants, who were bound to assist him in the discharge of his obligations to the Crown, whether he elected to offer money or men. So long as only that number of knights had been enfeoffed which was due to the king, the application of this principle presented no difficulties; but where more than the *servicium debitum* had been created, the allocation of the proceeds of the surplus fees constituted a problem somewhat similar to that which arose in connexion with corporal service. The tenants-in-chief consistently maintained that, as the original feoffors, they were entitled to the profits of the extra feoffments; but their position was exposed to attack from two different quarters. On the one hand the Crown, from 1168 onwards, made persistent efforts to divert the profits from the baronial to the royal coffers, by claiming payment not upon the traditional *servicium debitum*, but upon all lands held by military tenure; and on the other, the sub-tenants, as is clear from the famous dispute at St. Edmunds in 1196,[2] were disposed to apply to the scutage the same principles that applied to corporal service, and to insist that, whatever the number of fees created, they were bound to render to the lord only that amount of service for which he was traditionally responsible to the king. Against both contentions the tenants-in-chief were able, on the whole,

---

[1] No episcopal registers are available for this period, so that it is difficult to test Dr. Round's theory.

[2] *Chron. Jocelini de Brakelond*, pp. 20, 48 seq.

to maintain a successful resistance. The Crown was, as we have seen elsewhere,[1] unable to effect any permanent increase in the number of fees for which its immediate vassals responded at the Exchequer, while the sub-tenants failed equally in their attempt to limit the amount of service for which they were answerable to their lords. In 1196 Abbot Samson, after a long tussle, compelled his knights to make individual acknowledgement of their liability towards him, and set the seal upon his victory by conducting them one and all to London at his own expense, there to make formal recognition of their service in the king's court. Henceforward, as Jocelin de Brakelond exultantly points out, the Abbot stood to gain from every scutage at the 20-shilling rate, a profit of £12 from the twelve fees created in excess of his *servicium* of forty.[2] When in 1235 the then abbot made his return to the inquest for the aid to marry Henry III's sister Isabella, he was careful to point out that of the twelve surplus fees of St. Edmunds 'nulli respondent, nec unquam responderunt, nec respondere debent nisi soli abbati Sancti Edmundi'.[3] In the same way, the Bishop of Hereford at the end of the thirteenth century claimed the proceeds from all fees created in excess of his *servicium debitum* of fifteen, contending that: 'illos milites ultra xv predictos semper habuit Episcopus de lucro ad cameram suam, unde illi adhuc appelantur milites de camera episcopi'.[4] The surplus fees of the Bishop of Hereford numbered, as it happens, only from three to eight, but enormous profits must have been reaped by ecclesiastics such as the Bishop of Durham, who in the twelfth century had enfeoffed more than six times the number of knights he owed the king; the Archbishop of York or the Bishop of Exeter who had created twice as many as were included in their *servicia debita*; or the Bishop of Lincoln who

---

[1] *Supra*, Chapter I.

[2] *Chron.*, pp. 48 seq.: 'Superatis ergo omnibus militibus, ex tali victoria tale lucrum poterit abbati, nisi abbas voluerit aliquibus parcere; quociens xx solidi ponentur super scutum, remanebunt abbati xij libre, et si plus vel minus ponatur, plus vel minus ei remanebit secundum debitam porcionem.'

[3] *Book of Fees*, i. 385.

[4] *Register of Bishop Swinfield*, pp. 414 seq. The surplus knights of the Abbot of Peterborough were similarly described as 'knights of the abbot's chamber' (Mellows, *Henry of Pytchley*, pp. 134, 136, 143, 148).

in 1166 had already more than one hundred knights enfeoffed, of which he owed only sixty to the king.[1]

Not only did the payment of scutage entitle the lord to reimburse himself from his sub-tenants: the performance of corporal service also procured him the right to impose a levy for his own use upon such of his fees as had not been represented in the proffer. Where, as at St. Albans, there were no surplus enfeoffments, and all the tenants of each fee contributed to the maintenance of the men serving, the writ *de scutagio habendo* must obviously have been meaningless; but, in the majority of cases, especially after the reduction of the *servicia debita* under John and Henry III, it undoubtedly conferred a valuable privilege. In the later thirteenth and fourteenth centuries, for instance, the Bishop of Lincoln could purchase for the service of five knights the right to collect scutage from between ninety and a hundred fees; the Bishop of Winchester, the Archbishop of York, and the Abbot of Peterborough from some seventy, forty, and sixty fees respectively; while the service of three knights would entitle the Abbot of Abingdon to the proceeds of thirty fees, and the Abbot of Glastonbury to the profits of forty or more.[2]

What was the position when the lord made fine for his service? The fine was the result of an individual bargain between the king and his immediate vassal, and the responsibility for it could not, therefore, properly be shifted on to the sub-tenants. If a scutage were levied in connexion with the campaign for which payment was made the lord could obtain a writ authorizing him to reimburse himself to the extent of a levy at the current rate upon the fees held of him; but for any surplus he alone was answerable.[3] If the number of his feoffments were large, the burden upon him would probably, in these circumstances, not be excessive; whether, as in the earlier thirteenth century, he offered a lump sum arbitrarily assessed without regard to the number of his fees, or, as in the Edwardian period, paid at a fixed rate upon the fees of his reduced *servicium*. Thus, under Edward I and later, the Abbot

---

[1] See table *supra*, Chapter I, p. 19.
[2] See tables *supra*, Chapter I, pp. 32, 33.
[3] See Scutage Rolls, *passim*; Mitchell, *Taxation*, pp. 331 seq.

of Peterborough, fining perhaps in 100 to 250 marks on his
five fees, could hope to recover, in virtue of the writ *de scutagio
habendo* to which his fine entitled him, some 160 marks by a
levy at the usual 40-shilling rate upon the sixty odd fees created
on his lands. The Bishop of Lincoln, fining at the same rate,
actually stood to gain by the transaction, since his hundred odd
fees would yield him more than three hundred marks of scutage.
The Abbot of Abingdon, whose fine for three fees might vary
from 60 to 150 marks, could recover at least 80 from a scutage
on his thirty or more enfeoffments.[1] If no scutage were levied
the tenant-in-chief had, in strict feudal law, no means of even
partially reimbursing himself; but even here a way was often
found, in practice, of shifting some portion of the burden on
to the under-tenants. On several occasions under Henry III
fines were assessed before it was known whether a scutage
would subsequently be levied.[2] Most of those offered were
small, and were made with the proviso that scutage should be
paid in addition, if it were afterwards current. Where large
sums were proffered it was on the understanding that part
should be pardoned if no scutage were imposed; or that the
tenant should be granted a reasonable aid from his dependents
to enable him to pay. Thus in 1233, for the campaign against
Richard Marshal, the Bishop of Lincoln fined in £100 on condition that, if scutage did not run, 'habebit literas vicecomiti
directas de habendo rationabili auxilio de predictis feodis ad
finem illum acquietandum'.[3] For the Scottish war of 1244 he
offered 60 marks and the scutage of his fees, should scutage
be current; on the understanding that any of his knights who
would not assent to the fine or agree to pay their share, should
be distrained to render corporal service.[4] Later, for the Welsh
campaign of 1257, in spite of the fact that a scutage was afterwards imposed, Henry III issued letters to the tenants of
various ecclesiastics and others who had compounded for their

---

[1] See tables *supra*, Chapter I, pp. 32, 33.
[2] e.g. in 1233, 1241, 1244, 1253.   [3] Pipe Roll, No. 78, Lincoln.
[4] Fine Roll, No. 41, pt. i, m. 4; Mitchell, p. 240. The Sheriff of Northampton is instructed 'quod milites ipsius episcopi qui prefato fine assentire
vel portionem ipsos de prefato fine contingentem solvere noluerint distringat
ad veniendum in predictum exercitum, allocato predicto episcopo in prefato
fine servicio predictorum militum qui in predictum exercitum venerint'.

service, exhorting them to make their lords a liberal aid towards the liquidation of their fines *pro servicio*.[1]

The lot of the lesser tenant-in-chief who fined was, whether a scutage was levied or not, invariably harder than that of the tenant with many fees. On the one hand he seldom secured any such reduction of his liabilities as the majority of the greater tenants obtained, and so his assessment was proportionately higher than theirs; on the other hand his opportunities for reimbursing himself were necessarily more restricted. For instance, the Abbot of Chertsey, who recognized throughout a *servicium* of three fees, might have to pay as composition for his service in the later feudal period, anything from 60 to 150 marks; but from a levy of scutage in the ordinary course upon the four fees created on his lands he could not hope to raise more than £8. The Abbot of Evesham, fining in from 90 to 225 marks on the 4½ fees of his *servicium debitum*, had only five fees from which to reimburse himself; while the Bishop of Chichester, the fine for whose 2½ fees would amount to between 80 and 125 marks, could collect only about £24 towards that total from his twelve or more feoffments.[2] The result in these and similar cases was that a disproportionately large share of the expense had to be borne by the tenant-in-chief in person; and it is not surprising to find that on individual baronies provision was occasionally made for a more equitable distribution of the burden. An example is afforded by the abbey of St. Albans. Here the abbots had obtained no reduction of their original *servicium debitum* of six knights, nor, as we have seen, had they ever enfeoffed more than that number. Hence, while in the later thirteenth and fourteenth centuries their fines *pro servicio* would probably amount to between 120 and 300 marks (a sum larger than could be exacted from any other ecclesiastical estate except the bishopric of Durham and the abbey of St. Edmunds), a scutage on their military tenants according to the normal plan would have allowed them to recover no more than £12. To safeguard themselves against

---

[1] *C.P.R.*, 1247–1258, pp. 599, 600. Letters were directed to the tenants of the Bishop of Chichester, the Prior of Coventry, the Abbot of Abingdon, the Abbot of Evesham, and the Abbot of St. Benet's, Holme.

[2] See tables *supra*, Chapter I, pp. 32, 33.

such losses the abbots seem from the first to have insisted that the responsibility for fines no less than for service or scutage should be accepted by the under-tenants. Whether the fine was assessed by the Exchequer as a lump sum, or at a fixed rate *per feodum*, the total was subsequently divided equally between the six fees, every tenant of each fee contributing according to the extent of his holding.[1] The St. Albans cartulary (Cotton MSS. Tiberius, E. vi) contains tables for calculating the amounts payable by various fractions of a fee ranging from $\frac{1}{2}$ to $\frac{1}{40}$, when the whole was assessed at £20.[2] Sometimes the entire sum seems to have been paid by the tenant whose turn it was to perform the *corpus*. This was certainly the case on the Westwick and Shephall fee which, as we have already seen, had its individual method of discharging its corporal service. Sir William Melksop (tenant of Shephall) offered a fine of £20 in 1303,[3] Sir William de Gorham (tenant of Westwick) a fine of 20 marks and 2 marks queen-gold in 1306,[4] and Sir Alfonse de Vere (tenant of Westwick) a further fine of £20 in 1327,[5] the coparceners apparently contributing at the ordinary 6-mark rate which was current when service was rendered.[6] Both methods of fining might be employed in a single year, for in 1303 and again in 1306 the tenants of the Taillebois fee combined on the traditional plan to furnish their share.[7] Copies of the bonds executed by the tenants of various fees in 31 and 34 Edward I in recognition of their liability towards the abbot have been preserved, together with the acknowledgements of receipt subsequently issued by the latter.[8]

[1] Cott. MSS. Nero, D. 1, f. 148 d: 'Si vero fiat finis pro toto scuto omnes equaliter contribuent secundum porciones.' Cott. MSS. Tiberius, E. vi, ff. 230, 265 d.

[2] f. 230 gives the completed table; f. 265 d gives a list of the tenants with their appropriate payments. The folios are badly damaged, and the explanatory note can only be partially deciphered.

[3] Cott. MSS. Nero, D. 1, f. 173; Exch. L.T.R. Mem. Roll, No. 73, Brev. Bar Easter, m. 35.   [4] Cott. MSS. Tiberius, E. vi, f. 203.

[5] Cott. MSS. Nero, D. i, f. 148 d.   [6] Ibid., loc. cit.

[7] Cott. MSS. Nero, D. i, f. 173; Cott. MSS. Tiberius, E. vi, ff. 196, 211 d.

[8] Cott. MSS. Tiberius, E. vi, ff. 193 d, 195 d, 196, 202 d, 203, 211 d. Letters of the tenants of the fee of Taillebois in 31 Ed. I, with the abbot's acknowledgement of receipt from Stephen de Reymes, the nuns of Sopwell, and William de Ockhirst. Letters of John de Gorham for 34 Ed. I, with the

When the St. Albans custom originated cannot easily be determined, but it is probable that it dates at least from the beginning of the thirteenth century. The pipe rolls show that from 1201 onwards the abbots frequently paid fines, and as early as the Welsh expedition of 1245 there is entered in the cartulary against the tenants of several fees the note: 'inveniunt unum militem denarios dando'.[1]

Other ecclesiastics followed the example of the Abbot of St. Albans in shifting the responsibility for the fine on to their under-tenants. In 1316 we find the knights whose turn it was to render corporal service for the Bishop of Hereford entering into a formal engagement to pay their share of the fine made by the bishop with the king.[2] Here there is no suggestion of a general contribution by the military tenants such as was traditional at St. Albans. The entire burden evidently fell upon the five knights who had been elected for the occasion to perform the *corpus*.

At Malmesbury the procedure seems to have been similar, for in 1295 we find the king, at the instance of Hugh de Vere, pardoning to William de Laveham (tenant of Avene) and to the abbot through him, half of the fine of 100 marks in which William was bound to the abbot and the abbot to the king for the service of one knight in the army of Gascony.[3]

As to the methods employed by the mesne lords in assessing and collecting the scutage of their under-tenants we have singularly little detailed information, although the general outlines are sufficiently clear. Just as the Crown in order to facilitate collection from the tenants-in-chief found it necessary to keep itself informed of the number and location of their fees, so the tenants-in-chief in their own interest were obliged to keep a careful record of the descent and the services of the lands held of them by military tenure. Most of the extant cartularies and many of the episcopal registers include feodaries drawn up

abbot's acknowledgement of receipt. Note of sums due from the Croxley and Oxhey fee.

[1] Matthew Paris, *Chron. Majora*, vi. 437.

[2] *Register of Bishop Swinfield*, pp. 508 seq. Bonds executed by William, Lord of How Capele, Reginald de la Mare, Lord of Little Hereford, and Robert Petit, Lord of Dudley.

[3] Exch. L.T.R. Mem. Roll, No. 66, Comm. Mich., m. 6.

from time to time to afford a basis for the levy of scutage and of the various feudal incidents.[1]

No mesne lord could levy a scutage upon his tenants unless it were current throughout the realm. If corporal service could be demanded only in virtue of a royal summons, so also its commutation could be exacted only at the instance of the Crown.[2] The collection, when the necessary authorization had been procured, was usually controlled by the bailiffs of the tenant-in-chief, to whom, as a rule, belonged the general supervision of the conditions of military tenure.[3] At Peterborough, we learn from a late entry in the cartulary, the 'ballivi feodales' of Oundle and Aston, who served the court of Castor, collected from the fees of the abbey in the counties of Northampton, Warwick, and Leicester, and responded for the proceeds at the abbatial exchequer at Peterborough; while the bailiffs of Nassaburgh collected and responded for the scutage of the Lincoln and Huntingdon fees.[4] On the lands of the Bishop of Bath the bailiff of the liberty of Wells acted in the fourteenth century as collector of the bishop's scutage from his Somersetshire fees, and apparently also as receiver for his whole estate.[5] At Hereford, those of the bishop's tenants who held fees of the new feoffment seem to have paid not through the bailiffs, but directly into the episcopal 'camera' at Bromyard; while at Peterborough similar arrangements were made, the knights of the new creation responding personally in the abbot's chamber.[6]

[1] The Peterborough and St. Albans cartularies are particularly rich in material of this kind. Note particularly the list of fees with their descents in the Peterborough Cartulary (MSS. of the Society of Antiquaries, MS. lx, ff. 159 seq.) in which each group is headed by a thumb-nail sketch in pen and ink of the head of a knight. See Mellows, *Henry of Pytchley's Book of Fees, passim.*

[2] See the letters to the sheriffs in 1243 directing them to inquire 'qui magnates . . . sive episcopi sive alii tallagium vel scutagium auctoritate sua propria super liberos homines suos assiderunt et ab eisdem ea ceperunt contra consuetudinem Anglie' (Close Rolls, 1242–1247, p. 69).

[3] Note, for instance, their role at St. Albans, where in 1260 they testify on the abbot's behalf to the customs of the barony. Cott. MSS. Nero, D. 1, f. 134 d. At Peterborough the duties of the feudal bailiffs included the summoning of the tenants of the abbey to render their service (Sparke, *Historia Anglicana*, Scriptores Varii, Chron. Walteri de Whytleseye, p. 134).

[4] MSS. of the Soc. of Antiquaries, MS. lx, f. 169 d.

[5] *Register of Bishop John de Drokenesford*, pp. 89 and 192.

[6] *Register of Bishop Swinfield*, pp. 403 seq.; Mellows, *Henry of Pytchley*, p. 148, n. 1.

On the Winchester estates the entire business of collection was
in the hands of a single official, the marshal, who exercised a
general control over the military affairs of the bishopric.[1] No
series of local accounts of scutage, other than those of the
Winchester marshal which appear on the episcopal pipe roll,
have as yet come to light.[2] Further examples will no doubt
be discovered as the mass of extant local records is gradually
sifted and arranged, but it is improbable that any considerable
number survives. Ministers' accounts of a period antecedent
to the fourteenth century are comparatively rare. No parallel
in medieval administrative history has as yet been found to
the fiscal system of the bishops of Winchester—closely modelled
as it was on the central administration; and no set of financial
records analogous to the Winchester pipe rolls is known to
exist. True, many of the accounts of monastic obedientiaries
have been preserved, and are already sufficiently accessible to
have formed the basis of Mr. R. H. Snape's recent study of
English Monastic Finances in the later Middle Ages. The general,
if not the invariable practice in the case of the greater religious
foundations was, however, to keep the lands and revenues of
the abbot distinct from those of the convent, and wherever
such an arrangement existed it was upon the former that the
whole burden of feudal obligations rested.[3] Hence it fell to the
abbatial household and its officials, and not to the obedientiaries
of the house, to collect and account for the scutage of the
abbey lands. Indirect information regarding the administrative
methods employed by both abbots and bishops is not wanting;
but no body of records of any ecclesiastical household appears
to have survived for the period when scutage was a living institution. In spite, however, of the difficulty of concrete illustration,
the procedure of assessment and collection can be readily
conjectured, and occasional survivals of private accounts of aids
afford useful analogies. The particulars in the great Peterborough cartulary of the sums received for the aid of 1254 by
the hands of Brother Richard de London' show that payment

[1] *Supra*, p. 87.
[2] The list headed 'de Scutagio Baronum' in the Malmesbury Cartulary
(i. 276) might be regarded as a further example of the local scutage account;
but it is impossible to say to what levy it refers, or even whether it relates to
a scutage proper or to an aid. See p. 146, n. 7, *infra*.   [3] *Infra*, pp. 163 seq.

was there acknowledged by means of the wooden tally,[1] but at
St. Albans the written acquittance seems to have been in general
use,[2] at least in the fourteenth century. In case of undue delay
in settlement the bailiffs had power to distrain upon the debtor,
and, as a last resort, to sell his goods to the value of the sum
owed. Bracton's note-book affords many examples of such
action in the early years of Henry III.[3] If the authority of the
bailiff did not suffice, it might, in the thirteenth century, be
reinforced on purchase of a writ of aid by that of the sheriff.[4]

The incidence of the scutage did not cease with the immediate
vassals of the mesne lords. These collected in their turn from
their own sub-tenants. Thus we find the Prior of Dunstable,
who paid scutage in 1286 to Amaury de St. Amand, of whom
he held by knight-service, himself securing payment from the
Abbot of Woburn, from his own monks, and from a number
of lesser tenants who owed between them in the one case 8s.,
and in the other 3s. 5¼d.[5] At St. Albans Roger de Meridon,
who held a share of the Childwick fee, had under-tenants who
owed him scutage as he owed service to the abbot.[6] The
obligation might extend even to the villein tenements, for at
Malmesbury, in the thirteenth century, we find the abbot, as
'custos' of the Matravers fee, collecting 8s. 4d. scutage 'de
dominico et villenagio eiusdem feodi'.[7] In such cases there was,
of course, no question of corporal service. They merely help
to illustrate the extraordinary complexity of the feudal machinery
of which the Crown was the centre and pivot; and to explain

---

[1] MSS. of the Soc. of Antiquaries, MS. lx, f. 248 seq.

[2] *Supra*, p. 142, n. 8.

[3] See, for instance, pls. 202, 333, 390, 447, &c. Cf. Johannes Glastoniensis,
Historia de Rebus Glastoniensibus, ed. Hearne, p. 226.

[4] *Supra*, p. 108; *infra*, p. 150.

[5] *Annales Monastici*, *Annals of Dunstable*, p. 325.

[6] Cott. MSS. Otho, D. iii, m. 102 d.

[7] Malmesbury Cartulary, i. 276, 'De Scutagio Baronum'. The whole
entry is interesting, but puzzling. I have been unable to discover the levy
to which it relates. It appears to be of late thirteenth century or early fourteenth century date, but since the rate is 40 shillings the fee it might refer
to any of the later scutages of Henry III, or to any of those of the Edwardian
period. The aids of 1253 and 1302 present further possibilities. The amount
constitutes a further difficulty since, counting the personal contribution of
the abbot, it reaches a total of £12, representing 6 fees as against the
abbot's recognized *servicium* of 3.

the widespread discontent which could be aroused by a policy such as that of John or of Edward I.

III. THE WORKING OF THE MACHINERY IN THE THIRTEENTH AND FOURTEENTH CENTURIES

We must now turn to consider the extent to which the machinery for the exaction from the sub-tenants of service or its money equivalent was actually functioning in the thirteenth and fourteenth centuries. We have seen the necessity, in the case of the ecclesiastics, for modifying to some extent Maitland's conclusion that the feudal military organization as between the Crown and its immediate tenants was already virtually obsolete by the accession of Edward I. Down to the end of the first quarter of the fourteenth century the clerical tenures-in-chief continued to furnish, at least for Welsh and Scottish campaigns, their quota of cavalry, or its equivalent in the shape of fines *pro servicio*. It remains to be seen how far this activity was reflected in the ranks of the military sub-tenants.

That reluctance to render corporal service early manifested itself among these latter, is a well-recognized fact, and nowhere was the disinclination more apparent than on the clerical fees. The great men who held land by military tenure of bishops or abbots were impatient of the obligations upon them and did not hesitate to take advantage of their power to disregard them; while the lesser tenants were affected by that process of 'ruralization' which Baldwin describes as following rapidly upon the completion of the Conquest.[1] Disputes between lord and vassal were facilitated by the general absence of documentary evidence with regard to the conditions of enfeoffment, and already in the Norman period they were of frequent occurrence. For instance, we learn from the Abingdon Chronicle that under Henry I Abbot Faritius (1100–17) had trouble with three of his knights. William, the king's chamberlain, who held a fee of the abbey at Leia (? Lea), refused, when first Faritius was installed, to render to him either homage or service, and when Henry called out the host against his brother Robert, the abbot was obliged to send another in his place. Subsequently, however, he

[1] *Scutage and Knight Service in England*, p. 15.

succeeded in forcing the recalcitrant William to perform the de-
ferred homage, and to acknowledge his obligation to furnish
the service of one knight 'in omni loco ubi ceteri homines
ecclesie faciunt servicium militum', exacting from him in addition £10 as the price of his previous default.[1] A second dispute
occurred with regard to the service due from Godcelinus de
Riviera for land at Beedon. Godcelinus declared that he owed
there for only two knights, but the abbot claimed the service
of three. Eventually the latter gained his point, but only after
the king had issued to Godcelinus a writ ordering him to make
submission on pain of losing his tenement.[2] In the same way
Faritius secured the intervention of the Crown to compel
Robert Mauduit, who held land of the abbey at Weston, to
acknowledge the service which his predecessors had rendered
in the time of Abbot Athelelm;[3] while later, when the knights
refused in a body to render the castle-guard at Windsor to
which they were bound by their tenure, they were constrained
to do so by a royal writ.[4] Thus, although in every case the
abbot was ultimately successful in asserting his rights, it is
significant that on three out of four occasions his victory was
won only with the assistance of the king.

This tendency towards the weakening of the bond between
the mesne lord and his vassals, which was already apparent in
the comparatively settled conditions of the early Norman reigns,
was naturally immensely accelerated during the nineteen years
of anarchy when Stephen occupied the throne. After the
restoration of order by Henry II we find that many of the great
ecclesiastics had to appeal to the king to compel their tenants
to render to them the services which they had recognized in
the days of Henry I. Writs in this sense were issued by Henry

---

[1] *Hist. Monasterii de Abingdon*, ii. 128.

[2] Ibid., pp. 129, 92. The king's writ ran as follows: '. . . Precipio ut
faciatis Faritio abbati de Abbendona tale servicium de feudo quod de eo
et de abbatia sua tenes, quale fratres tui fecerunt antecessori suo A. Quod
nisi feceritis, ipse abbas inde te constringat per feudum tuum . . .'

[3] Ibid., pp. 135, 91.

[4] Ibid., p. 90: 'Henricus, Rex Anglie, omnibus baronibus Abbatie de
Abbendona, salutem. Volo et vobis firmiter precipio ut faciatis wardam
meam de Windresores sicut solebatis facere tempore Rainaldi Abbatis et
tempore fratris mei, et sicut Abbas Faritius vobis precepit, et sitis ei obedi-
entes.'

or his consort Eleanor at different times to the knights of Abingdon and Malmesbury, with the proviso 'et nisi feceritis, justiciarii mei faciant'. The *carte* of 1166 also abound in testimony to the disintegrating influences of the 'nineteen long winters'. Among the clerical tenants-in-chief, the Abbots of Glastonbury,[1] St. Edmunds,[2] and Westminster,[3] and the Abbess of Shaftesbury,[4] together with the majority of the bishops, reported fees in dispute. The Archbishop of York wrote of his knights: 'ex hiis sunt quidam a quibus plus servicii exigo quam ipsi modo faciant';[5] the Bishop of Exeter returned that, 'sicut a multis audivi', the Earl of Gloucester, Earl Hugo, and the Earl of Hertford held of him by military tenure, but they neither recognized nor performed any service;[6] the Bishop of Salisbury reported of Walter Waleran, who had rendered the service of an entire fee to his predecessors that he now responded for half only—'quia ipse Walterus servicium dimidii militis a tempore guerre mihi difforciat', and of Peter de Lavintone that, whereas he had formerly recognized the service of one knight, he now rendered nothing.[7] The Abbot of Westminster, who returned several fees as in dispute, reported that, in particular, the Earl of Gloucester had rendered the service of two knights 'usque ad extremum exercitum Wallie', but that he had since denied the obligation.[8]

From this time forward the inability of the mesne lords to exact the service of their tenants without the assistance of the Crown becomes increasingly apparent. In 1196 Abbot Samson of St. Edmunds engaged in the famous contest with his knights over his claim to the profits of the abbey's surplus feoffments. Doubting the sufficiency of the recognition made in the court of St. Edmunds, he carried the case before the royal courts, where each of his tenants made formal acknowledgement in writing of his obligations towards the abbot.[9] Yet only two years later we find the St. Edmunds knights denying their liability

---

[1] *Red Book*, i. 222 seq. [2] Ibid., pp. 392 seq.
[3] Ibid., p. 188. [4] Ibid., p. 213. [5] Ibid., pp. 412 seq.
[6] Ibid., p. 250. [7] Ibid., pp. 237 seq.
[8] Ibid., p. 188. Cf. the *carte* of the Bishops of Bath, Ely, Hereford, London, Norwich, Winchester, and Worcester.
[9] *Chron. Jocelini de Brakelond*, pp. 48 seq.; *Feet of Fines*, 8 Ric. I (Pipe Roll Soc.), pp. 40 seq.

for corporal service overseas, so that Abbot Samson was compelled to hire men for the Norman campaign at a total cost of £124. In return, however, he obtained the king's favour, and a royal writ empowering him to distrain his men 'ad reddendum ei servicium regis quod ipse fecerat pro eis'. In virtue of the writ he was able to recoup himself by a levy at the rate of two marks the fee upon all who held of him *per servicium militare*.[1] About the same time we find the Evesham annalist lamenting the recalcitrance of the abbey's knights, who 'nullum servicium faciunt ecclesie nisi servicium Regis et hoc tepide'.[2] Yet here the abbot was accustomed, as his *carta* of 1166 informs us, to pay the expenses of his contingent while it was on service.[3]

In the thirteenth century it was the normal procedure for cases between lord and tenant relating to the performance of service or the payment of scutage to be dealt with in the *curia regis*. Bracton's *Note-book*[4] furnishes numerous examples of litigation of this type in the early years of Henry III's reign as between the lay feudatories and their dependants; while the close rolls show us in 1231 the Bishop of Lincoln suing his tenant, William de Ferrariis, in the royal courts for payment of his share of the scutages of Kerry and Brittany,[5] and in 1232 the Abbot of Abingdon initiating similar proceedings against Peter fitz Herbert.[6] Further testimony to the gradual weakening of the feudal bond is afforded by the increasing number of 'writs of aid' issued by the Chancery under John and Henry III on behalf of mesne lords who required the assistance of the sheriff in distraining their tenants for service or scutage. In 1199[7] and again in 1205,[8] the sheriffs of various counties were directed to aid the Archbishop of York with distraint to collect the scutage for which he was to respond at the Exchequer. In 1218 the Bishop of Lincoln was reported as owing the scutage of seven knights 'quos non potest distringere . . . ut baillivus

---

[1] *Chron. Jocelini de Brakelond*, pp. 63 seq.

[2] Quoted by Wrottesley from the Evesham Cartulary. *Burton Cartulary*, p. 2.   [3] *Red Book*, i. 301.

[4] Ed. F. W. Maitland. See especially pls. 190, 202, 288, 333, 390, 447, 727, 789, 1049, 1214, 1226, 1674, 1687.

[5] *C.C.R.*, 1227–1231, p. 512.   [6] Ibid., 1231–1254, p. 154.

[7] Ibid.; Madox, *Exchequer*, i. 680, n. *n*.

[8] *Rot. Litt. Claus.* i. 46. The sheriff is to distrain 'ubi ipse districcionem facere non poterit'.

suus dicit'.[1] Between 1222 and 1225 the Abbess of Shaftesbury, the Abbots of St. Benet's, Holme, of Westminster, and of Peterborough had writs of aid;[2] and in 1242 the latter again received assistance 'ubi non sufficiat ad distringendum milites suos'.[3]

The Ramsey cartulary and court rolls illustrate the growing difficulty of exacting corporal service. They show that almost every summons from 1242 onwards was the occasion of controversy between the abbot and his military tenants. In 1242 Sir William de Englefield, Matthew de Leyham, John de Brauncestre, and John de Harpesfeud were elected, according to the custom of the barony, to serve in Gascony. All save the first, who sent his two sons to represent him, denied their liability. Abbot Ranulph sued Matthew de Leyham in the king's court in the following year, and compelled him to acknowledge his obligation to find 'unum militum in servicio domini regis ad custum militum de eodem baronia', but of the other two the cartulary simply notes 'restant adhuc implacitandi'.[4] In 1244, when an army was sent into Scotland, the four men elected in the honour court duly performed their service;[5] but it appears that, shortly before, the abbot had been obliged to prosecute one of their number—Vital Engayne, tenant of Dillington—to force him to recognize his liability.[6] In 1245 John de Harpesfeud refused to serve in Wales, although he was designated to perform the *corpus* by his fellow-tenants; and the abbot had to send to the muster two *servientes* in his stead.[7] Ten years later the four knights elected in the honour court of Broughton to serve in Scotland declined to set forth, and the abbot had to find substitutes and meet the expenses of the expedition from his own purse. The note in the roll—'ideo conquerendum domino rege'—has a half-hearted ring, and even if the threatened proceedings were taken, they were clearly of little avail.[8]

At the same time the Abbot of St. Albans was having trouble

[1] Exch. L.T.R. Mem. Roll, 2 Hen. III, m. 6 d.

[2] Madox, i. 677, n. *a*; Exch. L.T.R. Mem. Roll, 7 Hen. III, m. 6 d.; 9 Hen. III, m. 2; 6 Hen. III, m. 2 d.

[3] Exch. L.T.R. Mem. Roll, 27 Hen. III, m. 3.

[4] *Ramsey Cartulary*, iii. 50, ii. 360.

[5] Ibid., iii. 51.

[6] Ibid. ii. 356.   [7] Ibid. iii. 52.

[8] W. O. Ault, *Court Rolls of Ramsey Abbey*, p. 13.

with his knights. In 1244 the six 'capitales electi' protested before the marshal at Newcastle that the abbot was bound to pay their expenses during the journey to the place of muster and until they were assigned to a unit. An altercation lasting several days ensued, but eventually the abbot's proctor made good his case and the men discharged their service without further protest.[1] 1257 was a year of crisis both at Ramsey and at St. Albans. At Ramsey the knights elected to serve in Wales refused to go, and although, when distrained at the instance of the court of Broughton, they 'made peace' with the abbot, the latter was obliged himself to furnish the necessary contingent and to pay its expenses from his own coffers.[2] At St. Albans also a number of the military tenants denied their liability for service, and the abbot, who on this occasion was properly bound to serve for the Croxley fee only, had to provide the entire quota at a total cost of more than 100 marks.[3] Subsequently, however, in the famous assembly under the ash-tree within the abbey precincts, the recalcitrant tenants made grudging recognition of their obligations, and some at least offered full satisfaction to the abbot for the service he had rendered on their behalf.[4]

The subsequent history of these two clerical fees may be briefly dealt with. The cartulary throws little light on the military activities of Ramsey between 1257 and 1294. We know that service was rendered by the abbot in 1268, although no particulars are available;[5] but the marshal's and fine rolls show that he fined for his service in the two Welsh wars of Edward I.[6] When in 1294 the Broughton court rolls give us another glimpse of the working of the abbey's scheme of rotation, we see that the breakdown which was already threatened under Henry III is complete. A sworn inquest was apparently necessary to determine the identity of the abbot's military

---

[1] Matthew Paris, *Chron. Majora*, vi. 439.

[2] *Select Pleas in Manorial Courts*, pp. 50 seq.; *Ramsey Cartulary*, i. 52: 'Qui quatuor districti ad faciendum dictam expeditionem fecerunt pacem cum domino Abbate. Qui pro eis destinavit, suis sumptibus, dominum Gilbertum de Deneford' et alios tres milites.'

[3] Matthew Paris, loc. cit., vi. 374.   [4] Ibid., vi. 438–9.

[5] *Ramsey Cartulary*, ii. 295.

[6] *Parl. Writs*, i. 198, *C.F.R.* i. 85; *Parl. Writs*, i. 228, Exch. L.T.R. Misc. Roll, 1/13, m. 11.

tenants and to settle the incidence of the *corpus* for the Gascon expedition of Edward I, and not even the distraint repeatedly ordered by the court sufficed to induce those elected to recognize or perform their service. Eventually the abbot was obliged to send to the muster a knight and six *servientes* at his own cost.[1] The only subsequent occasions upon which he offered service were Edward II's Scottish expeditions of 1311 and 1323, when fining was not permitted except as a special concession. Neither contingent, if the names of the men who served may be accepted as evidence, seems to have been provided by the Ramsey military tenants.[2] Clearly the system which had furnished the abbey's quota down to the middle of the thirteenth century had ceased to function at its close.

The St. Albans military organization preserved its vitality longer than did that of Ramsey, although in the later thirteenth century it did not work without friction. In 1260, in an assembly held in the abbey church, the tenants *per servicium militare* repeated the attempt made in 1244 to insist that, when the host was summoned, the abbot should afford the six 'capitales electi' 'adequate sustenance' until their term of service actually began. They admitted, however, that they were bound to serve for the traditional forty days, and to accomplish the return journey, at their own costs. Against their claim the abbot's bailiffs maintained 'quod dictum servicium totaliter debent facere sumptibus suis propriis, tam in eundo quam redeundo et in exercitu morando'; and they seem to have succeeded in carrying their point, at least for the time being.[3] In 1265 we learn that the abbot sent six knights at the king's summons to Northampton,[4] although we do not know by what means they were furnished; and in 1277 the St. Albans chronicler jubilantly records the due performance of their service by the abbey's tenants. In consequence, the abbot escaped with a total expenditure for his six fees of barely fifty marks, 'salvis sibi equis et tota apparatu', whereas many ecclesiastics were compelled to fine at that rate upon each of the fees of their *servicium debitum*.[5]

[1] *Select Pleas in Manorial Courts*, pp. 76 seq.
[2] *Parl. Writs*, ii. 404; Chanc. Misc. 5/10, m. 1.
[3] Cott. MSS. Nero, D. i, f. 134 d.
[4] *Chron. Willelmi de Rishanger, Chron. Monasterii Sancti Albani*, p. 41.
[5] *Gesta Abbatum*, i. 435.

In 1282 the system again seems to have functioned on the whole satisfactorily, although Ralph Pirot refused to render the service for which he was responsible as a tenant of the Taillebois fee, and had to be impleaded in the king's court.[1] The fact that the abbot responded for three of the remaining fees was due, not to any breakdown of the principle of rotation, but to his recent acquisition of a portion of the Croxley inheritance, and to the nonage of the heirs of the Britwell and Gorham tenements.[2] In 1300 the nuns of Sopwell, whose turn it was to furnish the service of the Taillebois fee, omitted to discharge their obligation, and the abbot had to find a substitute;[3] while in 1303 Nicholas de Whethamsted for Croxley and Oxhey and the tenants of the Taillebois fee were both reported to be in default, although the latter afterwards made fine with the abbot.[4] As to the method whereby the contingents which served in the Scottish wars of 4 and 16 Edward II were furnished, the cartulary is silent;[5] but since in the latter year the abbot was only able to make up his total of six knights by employing hobelars, it seems evident that the traditional machinery was beginning seriously to weaken.[6] As late as 1327, when the abbot fined for his service in Scotland, an attempt was made to assess the fine according to the customary plan, upon the under-tenants; but sub-division had been proceeding apace in the last half-century, and the attempt was only partially successful. By the death of Abbot Hugh no more than £40 out of a total of £120 had been paid, and of this sum half was certainly contributed by the abbot himself.[7]

Nevertheless, St. Albans constitutes a notable exception to the generally-accepted rule that by the latter half of the thirteenth century the feudal military organization as between mesne lords and their tenants had ceased to function. Although after 1250 the under-tenants rarely discharged their obligations in person, it remains true that they continued to furnish by the provision of substitutes or of money the bulk of the service for which the abbot was responsible to the king.

---

[1] Cott. MSS. Nero, D. i, f. 173.   [2] Ibid. and table *supra*, p. 125.
[3] Ibid., loc. cit.   [4] Ibid., loc. cit.
[5] *Parl. Writs*, ii. 404; Chanc. Misc., 5/10, m. 1.
[6] Ibid.   [7] Cott. MSS. Nero, D. i, f. 148 d.

Nor was the case of St. Albans unique. Both at Malmesbury and at Hereford there is, as we have seen elsewhere, ample evidence that the machinery for the exaction of military service from the sub-tenants was working well into the fourteenth century,[1] although, as at St. Albans, the tenants seem for the most part to have preferred to discharge their liabilities indirectly. How general such activity was among the clerical fees cannot easily be determined, but it is probable that, where a large service was owed and enfeoffments were many, decline set in more rapidly than where the service was light and the sub-tenancies few. The abbeys of St. Edmunds and Peterborough are cases in point. The Abbot of St. Edmunds, as early as 1235, professed complete ignorance of the location of his fifty-two fees.[2] His declaration may have been designed to throw dust in the eyes of the royal officials; but the fact that from 1228 onwards he consistently compounded for his service, suggests that it had at least some foundation. Evidently he was no longer able to exact corporal service from his tenants. The Abbot of Peterborough, whose original *servicium* of sixty was reduced in the thirteenth century to five, began during the Barons' Wars to experience difficulty in inducing his tenants to serve;[3] and when in 1277 he called them together to notify them of the summons issued by Edward I for his Welsh war, many failed to appear. Those few who attended either in person or by attorney engaged in a lengthy controversy as to the customs of the barony in military matters, eventually admitting that they were bound by their tenure to serve on the abbot's behalf 'sumptubus tamen, equis et armis ipsius abbatis'. When, however, the day fixed for the muster arrived, they neither came nor sent, and the abbot was obliged to dispatch his steward and one of his monks to make fine with the king.[4] This dispute seems to mark the final collapse of the military organization of Peterborough. The abbot apparently made no further effort to exact service from his knights. In all the Edwardian armies

---

[1] *Supra*, pp. 131 seq.   [2] *Book of Fees*, i. 584.

[3] In 1264 the chronicle notes: 'Hoc anno post natale durante guerra mandavit rex servicium suum apud Oxenforde: sed facta summonitione per ballivos feodales prout moris est, tenentes militiam nichil facere voluerunt' (Sparke, *Historia Anglicana*, Scriptores Varii, Chron. Walteri de Whytleseye, p. 134).   [4] *Chron. Petroburgense*, pp. 24, 25.

we find him compounding by a fine at the current rate upon the five fees of his reduced *servicium*, although in 1311 he made a preliminary attempt to satisfy the king's demand for corporal service by hiring men and horses. On the estates of the Archbishop of York also, the military bond between lord and tenant seems to have been completely broken by the last quarter of the thirteenth century. True, the archbishop served on several occasions under Edward I and II,[1] but there is no indication that his contingent was furnished by his vassals. On the contrary, in 1282 there is direct evidence that its expenses were paid from the archbishop's own coffers.[2]

As to the position of the sub-tenants in relation to scutage, no definitive pronouncement is possible, since so little direct information is available. We have seen that under John and Henry III the mesne lords were to an increasing extent feeling the need of external aid in levying scutage from their subinfeudated lands, even when such scutage represented the commutation of the service of the entire holding. When it represented merely the perquisites of the lord from those of his fees for which no corporal service had been rendered in his contingent, it is probable that the difficulty of collection was still greater; especially since the Crown would not readily be induced to lend its support where its own interests were not involved. Under Edward I the whole problem was immensely complicated as a result of the attempt of the king to convert the scutage into a general tax payable irrespective of service or fine. Although throughout the Edwardian period writs *de scutagio habendo* continued to issue from the Chancery on behalf of tenants-in-chief who had responded to the royal summons, the Crown was itself simultaneously endeavouring to collect the scutage of the sub-tenants on the plea that their obligations were not covered by the proffers of their lords. In consequence, the position of the occupants of the lower rungs of the feudal ladder was, in the fourteenth century, an anomalous one. On the one hand they were subjected to pressure

---

[1] e.g. in 1277, 1282, 1310, and 1323.

[2] *Register of Archbishop William Wickwane*, 1279–85, p. 325, under heading 'Libera de anno tercio', 22 June 1282: 'To S. Receiver of York. Pay to Sir John de Eyvile 100 li "ad expensas suas pro servicio nostro faciendo in Wallia".'

by their immediate lords for payment of scutage in accordance with the Chancery writ: on the other, to distraint by the royal officials for payment of scutage into the royal coffers. As we have seen, the tenants-in-chief were able in large measure to frustrate the attempt of the Crown to collect from their dependants; but the Exchequer policy would appear in most cases to have rendered nugatory the grants of scutage made by the Chancery to the mesne lords. The burden of the frequent petition of the magnates in the parliaments of Edward II is that their ancient rights should be restored to them, and that they should be allowed to have their scutage 'selonc ce qil ount eu et use tot tenps sa en arere'.[1]

The only direct references discoverable to collection on the clerical fees at this period relate to the priory of Dunstable, the archbishopric of Canterbury, and the estates of the Bishops of Bath and Wells and of Winchester. The Prior of Dunstable held no land in chief by military tenure; but he appears in the thirteenth century to have held $1\frac{1}{2}$ fees in Polluxhill of Amaury de St. Amand. As noted above, the annals of the priory record in 1286 the payment to Amaury's executors of the scutage due from the prior, who in turn collected from his sub-tenants.[2] The Archbishop of Canterbury seems duly to have paid upon the lands which he held by mesne tenure at this date; for when in 1310 Henry de Percy distrained Archbishop Robert Kilwardby for arrears of homage and fealty due from $3\frac{1}{2}$ fees held of him by knight-service, he acknowledged that he was seised of scutage for several occasions.[3] From the register of Bishop John de Drokenesford of Bath we learn that in 1315, following upon the issue of a writ *de scutagio habendo* for the army of 34 Edward I, Thomas Alloway, bailiff of the liberty of Wells, was granted letters of attorney to collect for the bishop's use the scutage of his fees in Somerset.[4] Five years later we find auditors appointed to hear the account of John de Barton, bailiff of Wells and of the episcopal franchises and receiver of the bishop's scutage.[5] Unfortunately there is nothing to show

[1] See particularly the petition of 1318. Cole, *Documents illustrative of English History in the Thirteenth and Fourteenth Centuries*, p. 7.

[2] *Annales Monastici*, R.S., iii, Annals of Dunstable, p. 325.

[3] *Year Books* published by the Selden Society, iii. 26 seq.

[4] *Register of Bishop John de Drokenesford*, p. 89.   [5] Ibid., p. 192.

whether the receiver had, in actual fact, any scutage to account for! In the case of Winchester, on the other hand, the pipe rolls afford specific evidence that a real, and in some measure a successful attempt was made to collect the scutage due from the episcopal estates for the second Welsh expedition of Edward I, during which the bishopric was in hand. The attempt was, however, belated and partial, for the account does not appear until 1297, and includes the receipts from some 26 fees only.[1] On the whole it seems probable that the majority of the under-tenants whether on lay or on ecclesiastical fiefs, while suffering the occasional inconvenience of distraint, were able to profit by the controversy between the Crown and its immediate vassals to evade payment of scutage either to the one authority or to the other.

[1] Ecclesiastical Commission Various, No. 159315, under *Marchaucia*.

CHAPTER V

THE ECCLESIASTICAL TENANTS-IN-CHIEF BY KNIGHT-SERVICE AND THE PROBLEM OF BARONY

'A fee which men nowadays call barony—as large a fief as that which belongeth to him who is called a baron of the king's realm' (*Thomas Saga Erkibyskups*, ed. Magnusson, R.S., i. 50).

'Nominavit idem quoque dominus Rex [Henricus] et memoravit omnes Anglie, quarum ei occurrit memoria, Baronias, invenitque ducentas et quinquaginta (Matthew Paris, *Chron. Majora*, v. 617).

No study of the ecclesiastical tenures-in-chief would be complete without some reference to the question of baronial status and tenure. What constituted an ecclesiastic a baron of the realm, and his fief a *baronia*? What relation, if any, existed between barony and *servicium militare*? Although no definitive resolution of the problem can be hoped for, it may be of some service to marshal here such evidence as is at present available, and to indicate possible lines for further investigation.

The initial difficulty in any approach to the question consists in the extremely fluid character of the terms *baro* and *baronia* throughout the medieval period. Round[1] distinguishes six different uses of the word *baro*, viz. to denote (i) a man, as distinct from a woman (the *baro et feme* of medieval legal French); (ii) a vassal (a man in the feudal sense); (iii) a vassal of a palatinate (e.g. the *barones* of the earldom of Chester); (iv) a royal vassal or tenant-in-chief (*baro regis*); (v) a royal vassal not otherwise distinguished (e.g. as earl, bishop, or abbot); (vi) a member of the upper stratum of this latter class, differentiated alike from the simple *miles* and the *baro minor*. No one of these uses ever wholly excluded the rest, but it is nevertheless true that in the thirteenth and fourteenth centuries the application of the term *baro* was tending to be confined to the members of the more important class of tenants-in-chief not distinguished by any other title.

Baronial status, whether of the tenant or the tenement, entailed certain privileges and obligations, as well as certain

---

[1] J. H. Round, *Peerage and Pedigree*, ii. 338–342.

legal consequences, which played their part in the delimitation of this narrow class of *barones majores*.

In the first place, the 'barony' was marked off from fiefs of lower status by certain peculiarities of organization, among which its essential unity was the most conspicuous feature. It was a unit as regarded its internal economy and a unit as re-garded its external relationships. Thus every lay barony had its *caput* or head—usually some castle or manor which gave its name to the entire estate. This *caput* was in law impartible and inalienable. It might not, Bracton tells us, be partitioned among coheirs or assigned to a widow in dower.[1] It symbolized the unity of the fief. The lands of the barony were themselves liable to subdivision, but however much they were partitioned the barony did not lose its identity, but continued to be regarded in theory as a single whole.[2] In the same way it retained its separate identity if it passed into the hands of the lord of another fee,[3] or even if it escheated to the Crown.[4] Hence the distinction that was observed between lands held of the king 'ut de corona', and those held 'ut de escaeta', 'ut de baronia', or 'ut de honore'.

As regards administration the same emphasis upon unity is apparent. A barony, like an honour, was administered as a single unit by a baronial bailiff and reeve, or by other baronial officers.[5] This method of organization was followed even where several baronies were concentrated in the hands of a single individual,[6] although the lord's household and council

---

[1] Bracton, *De legibus et consuetudinibus Anglie*, R.S., ii. 39.

[2] In case of division the coheirs were said to hold a 'moiety' or 'a third part' (as the case might be) of the barony concerned; e.g. in 14 Edw. I we find Robert fitz Walter paying £50 as relief 'pro medietate Baronie de Launvelley' (Madox, *Baronia Anglica*, pp. 44 seq.).

[3] In the thirteenth century the honours of Clare, Gloucester, St. Hilary, and a moiety of the Giffard honour were vested in Gilbert, Earl of Gloucester; while Earl Warrenne held, in addition to his own honour, that of l'Aigle (Madox, p. 33).

[4] Viz. the honours of Wallingford, Nottingham, Boulogne, Newcastle, which are detailed in Magna Carta (1215), c. 43.

[5] Sir H. C. Maxwell Lyte, *Documents and Extracts Illustrating the History of the Honour of Dunster*, Introduction and *passim*.

[6] For this information I am indebted to Miss C. A. Musgrave, who has made a special study of the organization of the Clare honours in the four-teenth century.

might superimpose an ultimate unity of administration upon the separate entities. Even on the judicial side the idea of unity might find expression (as in the case of the great lay fief of Dunster) in a court, dispensing justice to all the immediate free tenants of the fief. The principle of honorial jurisdiction Maitland held to have been clearly recognized; and that it was not generally applied he believed to be due to the peculiar position occupied by the Crown and by royal justice in England.[1]

The unity which was thus apparent in the internal economy of the barony was reflected in its external relationships. It seems clear that it was regarded by the Crown as constituting, in some respects at least, an administrative unit, and the baron as fulfilling some of the functions of an administrative official, although the degree of local autonomy enjoyed would vary according to the nature and extent of the baronial franchise. For many purposes both administrative and fiscal, the barony was treated by the Crown as lying within that county in which its *caput* was situated, and the baron answered for his tenement as a whole. Especially was this the case in the collection of feudal levies such as scutages and aids, when full payment was habitually made in a single county.[2] Moreover, the baron claimed the privilege of dealing directly with the Crown in financial, military, and judicial matters. He collected and paid his dues into the Exchequer by the hand of his steward or bailiffs, instead of through the medium of the sheriff; he was entitled to be summoned by individual instead of by general writ to perform the *servicium debitum* of his fief in the king's army, or to do suit at the king's court, and he led his retainers in person under his own banner in the feudal host.[3]

Apart from these peculiarities of organization, the barony was distinguished from lesser fees in a variety of other ways. The first and most conspicuous difference was in the amount of relief paid. This distinction was already recognized in the days of Glanvill, who wrote that, while the knight's fee paid

---

[1] Pollock and Maitland, i. 385; Maitland, *Select Pleas in Manorial Courts*, Introduction; Maxwell Lyte, *Honour of Dunster*.

[2] e.g. the Courtenays, lords of the Honour of Okehampton, habitually paid their dues in Devon, although the honour extended into several of the neighbouring counties; the de Mohuns paid in Somerset, &c.

[3] Pollock and Maitland, i. 280-1.

100 shillings, the amount of relief due from the holder of a barony was dependent upon the will of the king.[1] Early in the next century Magna Carta provided that the baronial relief should henceforward be fixed at £100;[2] an amount subsequently reduced to 100 marks.[3] Nor did the difference consist solely in the sum paid. The method of securing payment was different from that employed in the case of ordinary knights' fees. When a baron died, his heir, even if of full age, could not enter into immediate possession of his tenement, but the lands were seised into the king's hand, until the heir had given security for the payment of his relief.[4] A further indication of the peculiar status of the tenant *per baroniam* was afforded in the infliction of financial penalties. The baron who incurred an amercement was assessed, not by the sheriff or the justices on circuit, but by the king in council, and at a rate proportionate to his rank. To be amerced *ut baro* meant being mulcted to the extent of four or five times the amount exacted from an offender whose tenure was not baronial.[5] Finally the baron was distinguished by his exemption from service upon juries of whatever nature,[6] and by his liability to attend the king's councils and parliaments if called upon to do so.[7]

In 1285 the Statute of Westminster II established a further line of demarcation between the barony and fiefs of lower rank. In regulating the fees to be accepted by the marshal and chamberlains it provided that the former, whenever homage was performed by, or, alternatively, knighthood bestowed upon, a tenant-in-chief holding an entire barony (*baronia integra*), should be entitled to receive from him a palfrey, or its value in money; while the latter should receive a 'reasonable' fine.[8]

Of the characteristics of the lay barony not all were common to its ecclesiastical counterpart. As far as organization was concerned, conditions appear to have been broadly similar;

---

[1] Glanvill, ix. 4; *Dialogus de Scaccario*, ii. 24.

[2] Magna Carta (1215), c. 2.

[3] The change is sanctioned by Edward I's Confirmation of the Charters in 1297.   [4] Glanvill, ix. 6.

[5] Madox, *Baronia Anglica*, pp. 102 seq.; L. W. Vernon Harcourt, 'The amercement of Barons by their Peers', *E.H.R.* xxii. 732 seq.; Magna Carta (1215), c. 21.   [6] Pike, *House of Lords*, p. 95.

[7] Ibid., p. 94.   [8] *Statutes of the Realm*, i. 92, Stat. 13 Edw. I, c. 42.

although this is a point upon which it will be possible to pronounce with greater confidence when the study of local administrative history has made further progress. The baronies of bishops and abbots were units in the same sense as were the lay honours. Like them they were administered by stewards and bailiffs, who collected and responded for their debts directly at the Exchequer;[1] like them they were habitually treated by the Crown, for both administrative and fiscal purposes, as lying within that county in which their *caput* was situated;[2] like them they entitled their lords to a special summons to perform their service in the host or their suit at the king's court.[3] The judicial unity which found expression in the case of the lay fees in such institutions as the court of the honour of Dunster, was typified among the clerical estates by the Ramsey court of Broughton.

One distinctive feature of the administration of the great monastic estates was the separation of the lands of the abbot from those of the convent—a practice which was generally adopted in England shortly after the Norman Conquest.[4] We learn from Jocelin de Brakelond that the division at St. Edmunds was effected by Abbot Robert (1107–1112), and confirmed by Henry I.[5] The portion assigned to the abbot constituted his barony, and upon it rested the entire burden of military and other services.[6] At Ramsey a similar arrangement prevailed; certain manors being set apart for the maintenance of the convent, while the remainder were allocated 'ad baroniam Abbatis'.[7] At St. Albans also the obedientaries of the house

---

[1] *Supra*, p. 108.

[2] Thus Peterborough responds in the Pipe Roll in Northampton, Ramsey in Huntingdon, Glastonbury in Somerset, &c. Sometimes they seem to respond in that county in which the bulk of their land is situated, e.g. Westminster responds in Worcester. [3] *Supra*, Chapter III.

[4] Rose Graham, 'Finance of Malton Priory', *Royal Historical Soc. Transactions*, xviii. 135 seq.

[5] *Chron. Jocelini de Brakelond*, pp. 6, 59; *Monasticon*, iii. 153: 'res et redditus abbatis et conventus, quos Abbas Robertus bone memorie requisito consilio distinxit et ab invicem separavit.'

[6] Ibid., p. 59. The abbot's share is referred to as 'baronia que pertinet ad abbatem'.

[7] *Ramsey Cartulary*, i. 267 seq. List of the abbey's manors and their distribution. Against those allocated to the abbot is the note 'pertinet ad baroniam abbatis'.

had their own lands, according to the normal plan; but in addition we find several figuring among the military tenants of the abbot's barony. The almoner, for instance, held a fraction of a fee in Tyttenhanger, while the kitchener held on similar terms in Burston and Garston.[1]

In the same way the barony of a bishop was sharply distinguished from the lands of his chapter. In one case—that of the bishopric of Coventry and Lichfield—the estates of the monastic chapter themselves ranked as a barony. The priory of Coventry, as we have seen elsewhere, enjoyed the status of an independent abbacy, until Bishop Robert de Limesey moved thither the see of Chester in the reign of William II.[2] Henceforth the bishops of the diocese, whether resident at Lichfield or at Coventry, were considered the titular abbots of the monastery, its working head having simply the title of prior, as was the case with all the English Benedictine monasteries attached to cathedral churches. Their aim now became to consolidate their position by incorporating with their own estates the demesne and barony of the priory. Under Henry II the ambition seemed likely to be realized, for Henry granted the house and all its appurtenances to Bishop Hugh de Nonant, and his grant was confirmed by his successor Richard. The transaction was hotly resented by the community, but pressure was brought to bear upon Prior Moyses, who was eventually compelled to make a formal surrender at Reading in the presence of the metropolitan and of the Bishops of London and Rochester. When, however, the bishop later attempted to hold a synod within the precincts of the priory, he encountered strong resistance. A brawl ensued in the course of which the bishop himself had his head broken by a monk wielding one of the processional crosses! So serious an affront to the episcopal dignity was felt to merit condign punishment, and, with the support of William Longchamp, Bishop of Ely, who at the time was both papal legate and virtual ruler of the kingdom, Bishop Hugh effected the expulsion of the monks and their replacement by secular canons.

---

[1] *Supra*, table, p. 125. Cf. Abingdon, where the same principle of division is observed. Kirk, *Accounts of the Obedientaries of Abingdon Abbey*, p. xlvi; *Historia de Abingdon*, ii. 321–3. Cf. *Chron. Eveshamensis*, pp. 208–17.

[2] Freeman, *Norman Conquest*, iv. 419 seq.

The intrepid prior thereupon brought an action in the king's court against the bishop and the canons for wrongful disseisin; and eventually, through the intervention of Innocent III, whose attitude towards the monks was more sympathetic than that of his predecessor Celestine, he won the case. The restoration of the barony was completed in 1198 by Archbishop Hubert Walter, and thenceforward the prior's baronial status was unchallenged.[1]

Not only were the peculiarities of organization, whether internal or external, common to both lay and clerical baronies: the ecclesiastics shared the liability of their temporal peers to a special rate of amercement,[2] and to attendance by special summons at councils and parliaments.[3] The exemption from all kinds of jury service was also a common privilege; while under the provisions of the Statute of Westminster II, the clerical no less than the lay tenants *per baroniam* had their fixed scale of payment to the marshal and chamberlains on the occasion of their performance of homage or fealty.[4] Here, however, the parallel ends. Since the monastic and episcopal estates were the property of corporations and not of individuals, they escaped many of the burdens which were incidental to baronial tenure in the case of laymen. Questions of partition or of escheat, for instance, could not in the nature of things arise in connexion with the fees of the Church; while land held by the 'dead hand' offered few opportunities for the exaction of the regular feudal 'incidents'. True, the clerical no less than the lay tenants acknowledged the obligation to render financial assistance to their lord in times of special need, and we find them regularly contributing to the various aids on knights' fees which were levied between the reign of Henry II and that of Richard II.[5] Further, the claim of the Crown to the custody of

---

[1] *Victoria County History, Warwick*, ii. 52 seq.; Dugdale, *Monasticon Anglicanum*, iii. 177; *Rotuli Curiae Regis* (Rec. Comm.), i. 3, 66. Cf. the case of Glastonbury and the Bishop of Bath and Wells, *supra*, p. 61.

[2] *Infra*, p. 168, n. 3.　　　　　　　　[3] *Infra*, pp. 169 seq.

[4] *Statutes of the Realm*, i. 92, Stat. 13 Edw. I, c. 42.

[5] viz. for the aid to marry of 1166, the aid to ransom of 1193–4, the gracious aid of 1217, the aids to marry of 1235 and 1245, the aid to knight of 1253, the aid to marry of 1302, and the aid to knight of 1346, see *Red Book of the Exchequer*; *Book of Fees*; and *Inquisitions and Assessments relating to Feudal Aids, passim*.

vacant bishoprics and abbacies may be said to afford some parallel to the rights of wardship which it exercised in the case of lay tenants. That it was no less profitable to the lord paramount and no less unpopular with the tenant is certain. In fact the complications and inconveniences arising from its enforcement were, as Jocelin de Brakelond makes clear, largely responsible for the separation on the great monastic estates of the lands of the convent from those of the abbot. In case of a vacancy the former then remained under the control of the obedientiaries, who supplied therefrom the needs of the community, while the barony was administered in the interests of the Crown by the royal *custodes*.[1] The incident which in the case of the lay tenants served most clearly to distinguish between 'barony' and fees of a lower status, was not, however, exigible from the ecclesiastics. No relief could be claimed from a churchman. William Rufus, acting probably under the inspiration of the notorious Ranulph Flambard, made an attempt to remedy this deficiency by extorting contributions from the sub-tenants instead of from the lord of the fee. As the writ discovered by Dr. Round clearly shows, the king in 1095, on the death of Bishop Wulfstan of Worcester, arbitrarily assessed upon his knights the sum of £250 as a 'relevamen'.[2] His success was, however, purely temporary. Although the principle of relief on 'mutatio domini' was recognized on the Continent,[3] Rufus failed to establish it in this country. Throughout the Middle Ages the fiefs of the Church normally escaped payment of relief, and with it of most of the other feudal incidents.

Of the characteristics of barony above enumerated, those operated most directly to define the limits of the baronial class which involved financial or other burdens the tenant was unwilling to shoulder, or, alternatively, privileges he was eager to enjoy. In the case of the laity the most powerful agent in differentiating the baron from the knight was the special baronial relief.[4] It was to the obvious interest of the minor

[1] *Chron. Jocelini de Brakelond*, pp. 6, 59. Cf. R. H. Snape, *English Monastic Finance in the later Middle Ages.*

[2] Round, *Feudal England*, pp. 308 seq.

[3] Ibid., loc. cit., p. 310, n. 278.

[4] Round, 'Barons and Knights in the Great Charter', *Magna Carta Commemoration Essays*, pp. 46–77.

tenant-in-chief owing a service of ten knights or less, to assimilate his position as far as possible to that of the tenant 'ut de honore', whose holding was reckoned as a mere complex of knights' fees, chargeable at the 100*s.* rate authorized by Magna Carta. In 1306–7, for instance, William de Braose claimed before the barons of the Exchequer that he held the land of Gower in Wales of the feoffment of King John, by the service of one knight only, and not by barony. After scrutiny of his charters his plea was accepted, and he escaped on payment of a relief of £25 only.[1] He made a similar attempt to repudiate baronial status in respect of his lordship of Bramber in Sussex, but was here unsuccessful;[2] as also was Robert de Chandos in 1301 in regard to his lands in Herefordshire.[3]

Just as the relief was instrumental in drawing a distinction between the *baro* and the *miles*, so the individual summons to councils and parliaments was the most important factor in the delimitation of the class of *barones majores*. If potentially the *Magnum Concilium* of the post-Norman period comprised all tenants-in-chief, there can be little doubt that in practice it early came to include only those of the king's vassals whose presence he chose from time to time to invite by special summons. In the issue of such writs the Crown in the thirteenth century exercised a wide discretion; social, political, personal, or even geographical considerations combining with tenurial to determine the composition of any given assembly. Thus, although the distinction between the greater and lesser barons had been admitted as early as Henry II's day,[4] and was specifically recognized in the famous fourteenth clause of the Charter of 1215,[5] no hard and fast line of demarcation had as yet been drawn. Under Edward II, however, with the rise to power of the Lancastrian faction, a new conception of the parliamentary summons began to gain currency. In the course of the fourteenth century, the Crown, under pressure from the baronial party, gradually lost its original option in the issue of writs. With the

---

[1] Madox, *Exchequer*, pp. 372–4.
[2] Ibid., loc. cit. The baronial amercement also played its part. Compare the cases of Hugh de Neville (Exch. L.T.R. Mem. Roll, No. 94, Rec. Trin., m. 4 d); and Thomas de Furnival (Madox, *Exchequer*, pp. 371–2).
[3] Madox, *Baronia Anglica*, p. 127.   [4] *Dialogus de Scaccario*, ii. 24.
[5] McKechnie, *Magna Carta*, pp. 291–301.

triumph of the doctrine of a closed and limited 'peerage' there emerged from the nebulous mass of greater tenants-in-chief potentially liable to a summons a closely compacted group of magnates who, as the hereditary counsellors of the Crown, had acquired a prescriptive right to be summoned as of course to councils and parliaments.[1]

In this development the lesser baronage acquiesced with philosophy, since, so far from depriving them of a valued privilege, it relieved them from an unwelcome liability. There were, however, occasions when the interest of the tenant might dictate insistence upon his baronial status. Thus, for example, Ralph de Everdon, knight, claimed before the Court of Common Pleas in 1375 release from the obligation to jury-service, on the ground that he held as a baron. On his offering proof that he held a part of a barony his plea was accepted and he was discharged.[2]

In the case of the clergy the special fees and amercements played their part in the definition of a class of ecclesiastical *barones*. In 1315, for instance, the Abbot of Crowland, amerced *ut baro* on two separate counts in the Court of Common Pleas, denied his liability on the ground that he was not a baron and held nothing by barony. In spite of the fact that his predecessor had been similarly amerced in 1282, the abbot's contention was held, after inquiry, to be proved, and it was ordered that he should be reassessed 'secundum formam in Magna Carta contentam'.[3] The Priors of Durham[4] and Dunstable,[5] and the Abbots of Shrewsbury,[6] Leicester,[7] and St. James of Northampton[8] were all involved, during the fourteenth century, in disputes regarding the appropriate fees to be exacted from them under the terms of the Statute of Westminster II; alleging, as against the officials concerned, that their tenure was not baronial.

---

[1] T. F. Tout, *Chapters in Medieval Administrative History*, note on 'The Meaning of Peer', iii. 138–9, n. 2.

[2] O. Pike, *House of Lords*, p. 95. Compare the case of John de Wolverton (*Rot. Parl.* ii. 19 b).

[3] Ancient Petitions, 2023 a and b, 4140; Exch. K.R. Mem. Roll, No. 92, Rec. Hil., m. 23; No. 94, Rec. Easter, m. 14.   [4] *Rot. Parl.* i. 166.

[5] *Annales Monastici*, R.S., Annales de Dunstaplia, p. 412.

[6] Cole, *Documents illustrative of English History*, p. 14.

[7] Ancient Petitions, 171/8519.   [8] Ancient Petitions, E. 918/329.

Far more important as a delimiting factor, however, was the parliamentary summons. There seems little reason to doubt that in the early Norman period all ecclesiastical persons holding in chief, whether seculars or religious, were considered liable to suit of court. That even so highly privileged a prelate as the Abbot of Battle was expected to attend the royal courts and councils is clear from the charter of the Conqueror, granting to the abbot and two attendant monks a daily *liberatio* of bread, wine, and fish on the occasion of each summons, and for as long as their presence was required.[1] The succeeding century, however, wrought many changes from the standpoint of the Crown and of its ecclesiastical tenants alike. The steady triumph, especially in the favourable conditions created by the weak rule of Stephen, of the Hildebrandine conception of the relation between *regnum* and *sacerdotium* encouraged the clergy to evade or repudiate the secular obligations to which, as members of the feudal hierarchy, they were properly liable. The simultaneous extension of tenure in free alms, and the reservation, under the terms of the Charter of Oxford, of all land so held to the exclusive jurisdiction of the Courts Christian,[2] represented a further substantial advance in the direction of liberty and autonomy. Henry II, succeeding to the throne when the power of the Church was at its height, set himself to check its growing independence, and to restore the balance between the secular and spiritual authorities which had existed under his Norman predecessors. In the Constitutions of Clarendon, which purported to be a simple restatement of the customs of his grandfather's day, he included a definition of the obligations of his clerical tenants with regard to suit of court. The famous eleventh clause laid down that all ecclesiastical tenants-in-chief were to be regarded as holding 'sicut baroniam', and were bound to discharge all the obligations incidental to their tenure, including participation with the other barons in the judgements of the king's court, unless or until a question of life and limb was involved.[3]

In this particular at least, the attempt of Henry to reimpose upon the Church the limitations she had acknowledged under

---

[1] *V.C.H., Sussex*, ii. 52.
[2] Stubbs, *Select Charters* (1905), p. 120.   [3] Ibid., p. 139.

the Conqueror and his sons, was successful. The clause received the express recognition of both Becket and the Papacy;[1] and the succeeding century was to see the victory of the Crown carried still further. Tenurial considerations play a steadily diminishing part in determining the composition of the clerical element in the councils and parliaments of John, Henry III, and Edward I. The later Norman and early Angevin period had seen the rapid growth of monasticism, the introduction of new orders, the foundation of new houses by king and baronage alike, and the enrichment by pious benefactors of the older religious communities. As a result, tenure ceased to be a safe criterion of the political or social importance of a religious foundation. Many houses whose original territorial endowments were insignificant, or were held of mesne lords only, attained to a wealth and a social influence which made their 'counsel' indispensable to the Crown. The profits derived from wool-growing, for instance, by the Cistercians, Gilbertines, and Premonstratensians, aroused the cupidity of a needy monarchy, while politic considerations made it desirable that the king should establish a hold upon the English representatives of such highly-centralized orders as the Cluniacs, or the Knights Templars and Hospitallers. Hence we find that the cast of the net of the royal summons tends continually to widen. Little or no detailed information is available regarding the composition of the assemblies of the reigns of John and Henry III, and no satisfactory conclusions can be based upon the vague phraseology of contemporary records and chronicles. The extant enrolment of a writ addressed in 1204 to the Bishop of Salisbury suggests, however, that the king in that year summoned, through the bishops, all heads of religious houses to attend a council at London.[2] In 1210 he is said to have called together, for purposes of extortion, 'omnes Anglie prelati',[3] including abbots, priors, and even abbesses. Little can be safely postulated of the assemblies of Henry III's reign with regard to which we find employed such phrases as 'omnes archiepiscopi, episcopi,

---

[1] This is indicated by the insertion of the marginal note: 'Hoc toleravit.' See the copy of the Constitutions preserved among Becket's personal correspondence (*Materials for the History of Thomas Becket*, R.S., Letters, v. 73).　　　　　　　　　　　　　　　　　[2] *Rot. Lit. Claus.* i. 33.

[3] Matthew Paris, *Chron. Majora*, ii. 530–1.

abbates et priores', or 'universi Anglie prelati';[1] but by 1265, the year for which the first full official record has survived, the 'defeudalization' of the summons is seen to be complete as far as the clergy are concerned. To that famous assembly there were summoned—besides the bishops, and the Deans of York, Exeter, Wells, Salisbury, and Lincoln—the cathedral Priors of Durham, Carlisle, Ely, Norwich, Canterbury, Coventry, and Winchester; the heads of the Gilbertines, the Hospitallers, and the Templars; and sixty-five abbots and twenty-eight priors of every order, and of every degree of importance.[2] True, the Parliament of 1265 was summoned purely as a party expedient, and consisted only of the acknowledged partisans of de Montfort, so that it lies properly outside the main stream of parliamentary history. Nevertheless, we find that Edward I carried on the Montfortian tradition, at least to the extent of allowing considerations of policy rather than feudal principle to govern the issue of writs to the clergy. The porportionately heavy representation in his parliaments of the Cistercians and Premonstratensians, and of Welsh and Marcher houses, cannot be dismissed as without significance in this connexion.[3] There is, moreover, evidence that at this date the Crown was disregarding in other directions the limits imposed upon it by tenurial considerations. Its claim to the custody of vacant abbacies not of royal foundation is a case in point, and occasioned a protest from the baronage in 1258.[4] The elaboration of the machinery of the assize *utrum*, entailing the gradual loss by the Courts Christian of their competence in cases relating to frankalmoign tenure; and the subjection of land so held to an ever-increasing variety of secular, if not of strictly feudal burdens,[5] affords a further illustration of the success of the later Angevins in curtailing the privileges enjoyed by the Church in the preceding century.

---

[1] *Lords' Report on the Dignity of a Peer*, i. 76–110, 124–66.

[2] Ibid., pp. 142 seq.; iii. 32–6; Selden, *Titles of Honour*, pp. 598–9.

[3] Ibid. iii. 36–171. In 22, 23, and 24 Edw. I the religious summoned are listed under the headings: 'Exempti', 'Premonstracenses', and 'Cistercienses', pp. 60–76.

[4] Petition of the Barons, c. 11; Stubbs, *Select Charters*, p. 384.

[5] Kimball, 'Tenure in Frankalmoign and Secular Services', *E.H.R.* xliii. 341–53.

With the death of Edward I, however, a reaction begins to be apparent. The earliest indication, as far as Parliament is concerned, is the gradual disappearance from the lists of recipients of individual writs, first of the majority of the Welsh and Marcher abbots,[1] and then of the Premonstratensians and Cistercians, of whom after 1322 only John's foundation of Beaulieu continued to be summoned.[2] The first specific evidence of a movement for release on the part of the clergy themselves occurs in 1319. The Abbot of the Augustinian house of St. James of Northampton, summoned to the Parliament held at York in that year, advanced a claim to exemption on the ground that he held nothing in chief or by barony, but only in free, pure, and perpetual alms.[3] Twelve years later the name of the Prior of Bridlington is struck through on the roll, with the explanatory note 'nihil tenet de Rege'.[4]

These two cases afford the clue to the clerical position. As against the practice of the Crown in summoning whom it would to its counsels, the clergy asserted the principle that attendance was a liability incidental to tenure. The clause of the Constitutions of Clarendon which had stressed the obligation of the ecclesiastical tenants-in-chief to suit of court was given an inverted meaning in order to release from an unwelcome burden those who did not so hold. Nor was that all. An attempt was further made to differentiate from barony the tenures-in-chief which were in frankalmoign and not by service, and to obtain for these latter the same exemption as was claimed for the subordinate tenures. The wheel had come full circle; and the clergy seized the opportunity offered by internal dissension to reassert as against the Crown privileges which had been in virtual abeyance for the past century. The view that the

---

[1] See the lists of religious summoned temp. Edward I (*Lords' Report*, loc. cit.).

[2] Many of the Cistercians and Premonstratensians ceased to be summoned after 1314; the remainder (with the exception of Beaulieu) drop out of the lists after 1322. The fact that both these dates have special significance in the administrative history of the reign suggests a possible connexion between the variations in the issue of summonses and the fluctuations of party strife. Close analysis of the lists of clergy summoned, particularly under Edward I–II, would probably yield interesting results.

[3] Selden, *Titles of Honour*, pp. 604–6; Cott. MSS. Tiberius, E. v, ff. 266 d seq.   [4] *Lords' Report*, iii. 367.

significance of free alms tenure was essentially spiritual—that land so granted was a gift to God, made for the benefit of the donor's soul, and hence properly unburdened by any secular obligations whatsoever, had never been abandoned by the Church, although in the thirteenth century it had found scant support from either the Crown or the lawyers. Now, when frankalmoign was already becoming, through the operation of the statutes of Mortmain and *Quia Emptores*, a stationary and decaying tenure, this conception began to gain a wider currency. In the legal sphere it triumphed to the extent that it was for the first time admitted as a legal axiom that the distinguishing feature of tenure in free alms was the absence of any service enforceable in a court of law.[1] Simultaneously, frankalmoign began to be alleged as a ground for exemption from every variety of secular exaction or demand, ranging from the obligation to attendance at Parliament, to the duty of providing for corrodies, or for the custody and maintenance of prisoners of war.[2]

In 1340–1 the definition of the clerical point of view was carried a stage beyond that reached in 1319. In March 1340 the prelates present in Parliament were constrained—contrary to the custom with regard to clerical taxation which had been established under Edward I—to join with the lay baronage in granting to the Crown the ninth sheaf, fleece, and lamb for themselves and their tenants, with the proviso that lands already included in the clerical tenth (granted in 1339) should be exempt from contribution.[3] Friction arose over the assessment of the levy. The intention of the Crown was to secure the taxation to either the tenth or the lay subsidy of all clerical lands whatsoever, and more especially of those acquired since the valuation of Pope Nicholas in 1292. The clergy, under the leadership and inspiration of Archbishop Stratford, who was engaged at the time in his famous quarrel with Edward III, strongly opposed the royal policy, contending that the ninth was properly exigible only from those of their number 'qui per baroniam

---

[1] Kimball, 'Tenure in Frankalmoign', *E.H.R.* xliii, loc. cit.

[2] The Ancient Petitions and the Memoranda and Plea Rolls of the Exchequer at this date abound with examples. Compare Kimball, loc. cit.

[3] D. Hughes, *Early Years of Edward III*, Chapter IX, *passim*; *Rot. Parl.* ii. 112.

tenent et ad parliamentum venire solent'.[1] At length in April
1341 the king conceded that the ninth should be paid by those
ecclesiastics only 'qui tiegnent du roi par baronie et deyvent
venir au parlement par semonse'; while the remainder who did
not so hold 'ne ne sont pas acoustume destre somons au parlement' were to contribute to the tenth.[2] The effects of this
surrender were far-reaching. In the months following, those
heads of religious houses who were not personally summoned
to Parliament made haste to obtain writs to the collectors of
the ninth superseding the levy in their case, while many abbots
and priors who had been summoned sought to establish their
right to exemption from attendance, and simultaneously from
contribution to the ninth. The Abbots of St. Augustine's,
Bristol,[3] of Beaulieu,[4] Oseney,[5] Thornton,[6] Bardney,[7] Colchester,[8] Crowland,[9] Waltham,[10] and St. Mary's York,[11] the
Priors of Sempringham[12] and Spalding,[13] all claimed release on
the ground that their tenure was not baronial. From this time
forward the names of the clerical recipients of individual writs
show little or no variation. In 1352 the Abbot of Leicester,[14]
and fifteen years later the Prior of Lewes,[15] secured exemption

---

[1] See Stratford's letters on the subject to the Chancellor (Hemingburgh, *Chronicon.* ii. 354) and to his suffragans (ibid. 373; cf. Wilkins, *Concilia*, ii. 359).   [2] *Rot. Parl.* ii. 129–30.

[3] Rymer, *Foedera*, p. 1158; *C.P.R.*, 1340–1343, p. 183.

[4] Ancient Petitions, 8017; Exch. K.R. Mem. Roll, No. 117, Brev. Bar. Trin., m. 13 d; *Lords' Report*, iv. 533–4; *C.P.R.*, 1340–1343, p. 243.

[5] Exch. K.R. Mem. Roll, No. 118, Brev. Bar. Mich., m. 9 d; *Lords' Report*, iv. 534; *C.P.R.*, 1341–1343, p. 297.

[6] Exch. K.R. Mem. Roll, No. 117, Brev. Bar. Mich., m. 20; *Lords' Report*, iv. 529; Chanc. Misc. 67/1, No. 18.

[7] Exch. K.R. Mem. Roll, No. 118, Brev. Bar. Mich., m. 5 d; m. 23 d.

[8] Exch. K.R. Mem. Roll, No. 117, Brev. Bar. Trin., m. 10.

[9] Exch. K.R. Mem. Roll, No. 119, Brev. Bar. Mich., m. 16; *C.P.R.*, 1340–1343, p. 337; *C.C.R.*, 1341–1343, p. 270; *Lords' Report*, iv. 534.

[10] Exch. K.R. Mem. Roll, No. 118, Brev. Bar. Mich., m. 6, Com. Rec. Mich.

[11] Ancient Petitions, 13975.

[12] Exch. K.R. Mem. Roll, No. 117, Rec. Mich., m. 4; Brev. Bar. Mich., m. 20 d; *Lords' Report*, iv. 529; *C.P.R.*, 1340–1343, p. 190.

[13] Exch. K.R. Mem. Roll, No. 117, Brev. Bar. Mich., m. 24; No. 118, Brev. Bar. Mich., m. 29 d; *C.P.R.*, 1340–1343, p. 278; *C.C.R.*, 1341–1343, p. 217.

[14] *C.P.R.*, 1350–1354, p. 230; Selden, *Titles of Honour*, p. 734; Knighton, *Leycestrensis Chron.* (R.S.), ii. 126–7.

[15] *C.C.R.*, 1364–1368, p. 100; *Lords' Report*, iv. 638–9.

from further attendance at Parliament on grounds similar to those advanced in 1341. During the rest of the medieval period the average number of religious summoned was twenty-seven, including the Abbots of Abingdon, Bardney, Battle, St. Augustine's Canterbury, Cirencester, Colchester, Crowland, Evesham, Glastonbury, Gloucester, Malmesbury, Peterborough, Ramsey, Reading, St. Albans, St. Benet's Holme, St. Edmunds, Selby, Shrewsbury, Thorney, Waltham, Westminster, Hyde (Winchester), Winchcombe, and St. Mary's York, and the Priors of Coventry and St. John of Jerusalem. To these the early Tudor period saw the addition of the Abbots of Tavistock and Tewkesbury. Thus, as in the parallel case of the lay magnates, there had, by the end of the fourteenth century, emerged from the large and indeterminate body of clergy potentially liable to a summons a narrow group of 'parliamentary' abbots and priors to whom a summons was issued as of course. In 1388, during the deliberations in the 'Merciless' Parliament upon the fate of the adherents of Richard II, the claims of this clerical element were defined by Archbishop Courtenay in a familiar passage. 'Of right and by custom of the realm of England', he declared, 'it belongeth to the Archbishop of Canterbury for the time being, as well as others his suffragans, brethren and fellow-bishops, abbots and other prelates whatsoever, *holding of the lord the king by barony*, to be present in person and in all the king's parliaments whatsoever as peers of the realm aforesaid.'[1]

Although, however, the tenurial basis of the summons of the clergy to Parliament was in the fourteenth century accepted doctrine, and remains, at the present day, a fundamental article of the creed of our constitutional historians,[2] investigation proves that the selection of the narrow ecclesiastical 'peerage' of the later Middle Ages was not in fact effected on any consistent principle. On the one hand, it is evident that by no means all the prelates holding in chief, whether by service or in alms, were summoned to Parliament; on the other, analysis

---

[1] *Rot. Parl.* iii. 236–7. The prelates, of course, were subsequently deprived of the status of 'peers' which they had claimed in 1388. Tout, *Chapters*, iii, loc. cit.; Pike, *House of Lords*, pp. 163 seq.

[2] See, in particular, Pike, *House of Lords*, Chapter IX, pp. 151–167.

clearly establishes that of those who were so summoned not all were tenants-*in-capite* in the one sense or the other, while only fifteen of the twenty-one bishops and a bare half of the religious who attended held *in capite per servicium militare*.[1]

The Crown did not submit without resistance to the restriction of its freedom in the issue of writs, but continued to assert its right to override in the general interest the limitations imposed upon it by the tenurial principle. It is significant that the Abbot of St. James of Northampton dared not refuse to obey the summons issued to him in 1319, lest he should be held contumacious 'eo quod omnes de regno de quocumque vel qualitercumque teneant veniant ad citationem domini regis'.[2] Even the *Modus tenendi Parliamentum* reserves to the king the right to summon the *minores cleri* if their presence is required 'aliunde quam pro tenuris suis', or is considered useful or necessary for the transaction of the business in hand.[3] That a discretion in the granting or withholding of exemptions was both claimed and exercised is certain. In each case the plea advanced by the petitioner was subjected to careful scrutiny, and was checked not merely by the muniments of the house, but by the Chancery records and the rolls, memoranda, and books of fees of the Exchequer.[4] A mere unsupported plea of non-baronial tenure was not accepted as an adequate ground for release; the petitioner had further to show that he had not previously been in regular receipt of a writ of summons. Of the eleven religious who petitioned for exemption in 1341, no less than five—the Abbots of Bardney, Colchester, Crowland, Waltham, and St. Mary's York—had their plea rejected; and that despite the fact that Waltham and Crowland alone could be claimed as of royal foundation, and that all held their lands in frankalmoign.[5] The Abbot of Crowland, indeed, had proved

---

[1] Compare the list given on p. 175 with those on pp. 4–5. The Welsh bishops and the Bishops of Rochester and Carlisle rendered no secular service to the Crown, but do not appear at any time to have denied their liability to attendance.

[2] Selden, *Titles of Honour*, p. 605.   [3] Stubbs, *Select Charters*, p. 503.

[4] This clearly appears from the wording of the charters of exemption, &c.

[5] The abbey of Bardney was of pre-Conquest origin, but was re-endowed by the family of de Gaunt, and held all its lands by royal confirmation in frankalmoign (*Monasticon*, i. 622 seq.). The abbey of St. John's, Colchester, was founded *c.* 1096 by Eudo Dapifer and held all its land in free, pure, and

to the satisfaction of the Exchequer as recently as 1322 that he was not a baron and held nothing by barony.[1] All five, however, had regularly attended the parliaments of the Edwardian period.

Even those of the clergy whose suit was successful did not gain their point without difficulty or unconditionally. Brother Henry de Blithesworth, the proctor appointed by the Abbot of St. James of Northampton in 1319, was informed, on prosecuting discreet inquiries in the Chancery as to the conditions in which the summons had issued—'utrum per simplex breve vel per registrum'—that the name of his house had been enrolled 'inter citandos ad parliamentum', and that the abbots would therefore be liable to be summoned to all future parliaments. On the plea that they held only in frankalmoign he besought William de Ayrmynne, then Custos Rotulorum, to delete the name of the house from the register; but Ayrmynne replied that he neither could nor would do anything of the kind. In despair at this 'hard and unjust' retort Brother Henry framed a petition to Thomas of Lancaster, patron of the house, and still the most influential man in England, begging for his assistance in the matter; but afterwards, realizing that such an appeal would merely excite the anger of the Chancery officials against him and increase their hostility to his demands, he decided instead to address his plea to the Chancellor in person. This time he was successful. Since the abbot held nothing in chief or by barony, and had never before been summoned to Parliament, Bishop John de Hotham agreed to delete his name from the rolls of the Chancery. The deed was duly performed in the presence of numerous witnesses, and a formal record of it was made for the safeguarding of the abbot's interests in future.[2] The grounds upon which the remainder of the religious

perpetual alms (*Monasticon*, iv. 601 seq.). Waltham, originally endowed by Harold Godwineson as a college of secular canons, was refounded by Henry II to hold 'quietus a me et ab omnibus heredibus meis' (*Monasticon*, iv (i), pp. 56 seq.). St. Mary's, York, claimed to have been founded by 'Estevene nadgiers Ducs de Bretaigne et Count del Rychemond' (Ancient Petitions, 13975); Crowland's early history is wrapped in obscurity, but a monastery was in existence there in 1051, and a charter of Stephen (1142) survives, confirming the abbey in its lands and possessions (*V.C.H. Lincoln*, ii. 105 seq.).   [1] *Supra*, p. 168.

[2] Selden, *Titles of Honour*, pp. 604–6. In point of fact, the abbot had been summoned to the Parliament of 1265 (*Lords' Report*, iii. 32–6).

obtained exemption are all broadly similar. The Abbot of St. Augustine's, Bristol (Augustinian), alleged in 1341 not merely that he held nothing in chief or by barony, and that his house was not of royal foundation, but that, until 1336, when certain enemies of the community had maliciously procured the issue to him of a writ of summons, the abbots of his house had never attended parliaments or councils.[1] The Abbot of Beaulieu (John's Cistercian foundation) pleaded tenure in free alms, adding that none of his predecessors had been summoned before the time of Edward II, and that no other members of his order were accustomed to attend.[2] The Abbot of Oseney (Augustinian) contended that he held in frankalmoign of the foundation of Robert de Olleio, and not of the king or his progenitors; and that the abbots of his house had never been summoned to Parliament before 1319, since when they had attended only at intervals.[3] The Abbot of Thornton (Augustinian) similarly re-enforced the plea of frankalmoign tenure by that of exemption from attendance until 1312.[4] The Prior of Sempringham, head of the English order of that name, claimed release on the ground of non-baronial tenure, and of non-attendance at Parliament prior to 1309;[5] while the Prior of Spalding (Benedictine) urged that the priory was of the foundation of the earls of Lincoln, and that its lands were held of the honour of Bolingbroke and not in chief 'ut de corona', adding that the priors had not been summoned to Parliament before 1309, and had since attended only intermittently and 'voluntarie'—not of right.[6] The Abbot

---

[1] *Foedera*, p. 1158; *C.P.R.*, 1340–1343, p. 183. The abbot had been summoned on several occasions under Edward I, but was listed in 6 Edw. III among those who 'non solebat scribi in aliis parliamentis' (*Lords' Report*, iv. 408).

[2] Ancient Petitions, 8017; *C.P.R.*, 1340–1343, p. 243. The abbot had, in reality, been regularly summoned under Edward I (*Lords' Report*, iii. 36–171, *passim*).

[3] *C.C.R.*, 1341–1343, p. 297. Again, the claim advanced is unhistorical. The abbot had been occasionally summoned under Edward I.

[4] *Lords' Report*, iv. 529. The abbot seems to have been summoned twice under Edward I.

[5] Ibid. iv. 529; *C.P.R.*, 1340–1343, p. 190. Here, again, the claim was entirely unhistorical. The order had been regularly represented in Parliament down to 1322, although both the prior and the master were listed in 6 Edw. III as unaccustomed to be summoned (*Lords' Report*, iv. 408).

[6] *C.P.R.*, 1340–1343, p. 278; *C.C.R.*, 1341–1343, p. 217. The prior had

of Leicester's plea in 1352 followed very similar lines, adding
to the statement that the house was of the advowson of the
earls of Leicester and not of the king the somewhat naïve
assertion that none of the abbots had been summoned to Parliament before 1265,[1] when 'all the abbots and priors of the kingdom' attended. Finally, the Prior of the Cluniac house of Lewes
declared in 1365 that his predecessors had received no summons
of earlier date than 4 Edward II, and that their subsequent
occasional attendances had been 'voluntarie non de jure'.[2]

In acceding, therefore, in these cases, to the demand of the
clergy for release from the obligation to attendance at Parliament, the Crown did not commit itself without reservation to
the doctrine of the tenurial basis of the summons, and it was
careful to safeguard its position still further by making the
exemption in certain instances conditional. Thus, the Abbot of
Beaulieu and his successors were granted release only 'nisi
eorum presencia ob aliam causam nobis vel heredibus nostris
necessaria fuerit vel opportuna';[3] while in 1349 the Abbots of
Oseney and Thornton were summoned to parliament 'quibus-
cumque cartis seu litteris nostris patentibus in contrarium prius
factis non obstantibus'.[4]

The final outcome, therefore, of the conflict between the
royal and the clerical points of view, was the evolution of an
artificial parliamentary baronage, or—to adapt the phraseology
of the peerage historians—a class of ecclesiastical 'barons by
writ', by no means necessarily coincident with the class of
ecclesiastical 'barons by tenure'. The bearing of this development upon our immediate problem, though indirect, is none
the less important. By stimulating a desire on the part of the
clergy to repudiate baronial status, it tended to the closer
definition of tenure *per baroniam*, and gave new significance to
the inherent antithesis between barony and frankalmoign.

attended de Montfort's Parliament, but his name does not reappear until
the beginning of the reign of Edward II.

[1] *C.P.R.*, 1350–1354, p. 230; Selden, *Titles of Honour*, p. 374. There is
no record of the abbots' attendance at Parliament between 27 Edw. I and
12 Edw. II.

[2] *C.C.R.*, 1364–1368, p. 100. The priors had been consistently summoned
since the beginning of Edward II's reign.

[3] *C.P.R.*, 1340–1343, p. 243; *Lords' Report*, iv. 579.

[4] *Lords' Report*, iv. 579.

As with the laity, there were rare occasions upon which the interest of the tenant required not the denial but the assertion of baronial status. The cases of the Abbot of Glastonbury[1] and the Prior of Coventry,[2] already cited in another connexion, illustrate this aspect of the question. In both instances the tenurial plea was legitimately and successfully urged as a defence against the threat of absorption into the barony of the bishop of the diocese.

Having examined certain of the more important factors operating in the thirteenth and fourteenth centuries to define and limit the application of the terms *baro* and *baronia*, among both clergy and laity, it remains for us to determine on what principle, if any, the differentiation between barony and the other tenures-*in-capite* was effected. Why did some estates continue to be regarded as baronies and to be burdened with special duties, while others escaped? Was it merely a matter of chance or convention, or had the distinction some logical basis?

The dogmatic pronouncements of such late medieval writers as the author of the *Modus tenendi Parliamentum*, who deduced from the respective rates of relief for the knight's fee and the barony that the latter was an estate containing $13\frac{1}{3}$ of the former and having a fixed value of 400 marks,[3] do not demand serious consideration. Modern investigators of the problem fall into two main groups. Of these, the first, which includes a long succession of writers from Selden and Madox to Maitland, Stubbs, Round, and G. B. Adams, leans to the view that the distinction between the *baro* and the ordinary tenant-*in-capite* was purely arbitrary—a matter of custom and convention and not of principle. As Madox put it, barony was but 'knight-service embaronied, that is, knight-service enlarged and erected into a barony, or, if you please, made a barony at its first creation'.[4] To Maitland a barony is merely an aggregate of knights' fees held of the king by one of his more important tenants-in-chief—'a mass of lands which from old have been held by a single title';[5] and Adams follows him in defining tenure

---

[1] *Supra*, p. 61.
[2] *Supra*, pp. 164 seq.   [3] Stubbs, *Select Charters*, pp. 503-4.
[4] Madox, *Baronia Anglica*, p. 241.
[5] Pollock and Maitland, *History of English Law*, i. 279, 282.

per baroniam as 'nothing more than the tenure of a group of fees as a unit, a unit tenure'.[1] To these authorities the special relief and other legal consequences of barony have scarcely more than an accidental significance.

The second group takes the opposing view that the legal consequences of baronial tenure which Maitland dismisses as 'subordinate' were in fact sufficiently significant to justify the conclusion that the distinction between the *baro* and the rank and file of the tenants-in-chief was real and not conventional. Among the earlier authorities Madox seems originally to have inclined to this opinion, but to have been at a total loss to decide in what the difference consisted. His followers have been few, and it was only as recently as 1920 that an attempt to provide a solution to the problem was made by Dr. Rachel Reid. In a closely reasoned article in the *English Historical Review*,[2] she advances the suggestion that the clue to the meaning of barony is to be found in Bracton's familiar description of barons as 'potentes sub rege'. This phrase, she maintains, can only be interpreted as implying the possession of concrete powers; in effect, of some kind of administrative office under the Crown. That such was the connotation of the term 'baron' in contemporary Normandy she makes clear. The Norman *baro* was distinguished from men of lesser status by the possession of justiciary rights—of those 'pleas of the sword' which constitute what in feudal parlance is known as 'la haute justice'. But the word *baro* was introduced into England from Normandy after the Conquest, and it is therefore reasonable to suppose that the Norman clerks found in existence in this country an institution sufficiently resembling their own 'barony' to be identifiable with it. Such, indeed, was the institution of thanage. Though differing in many respects from the Norman baron, the English king's thegn had one thing in common with him, viz. the possession of public rights of justice. In the ancient English 'customs' of 'sac and soc, toll and team, and infangthef', we may see, according to Miss Reid, the counterpart of the Norman 'pleas of the sword', and hence the explanation of the fact that the word *baron* is first met with in England as an alternative

---

[1] G. B. Adams, *Councils and Courts in the Anglo-Norman Period*, pp. 176–8.
[2] 'Barony and Thanage', *E.H.R.* xxxv. 161 seq.

rendering of the word *thegn*. Thus the baron of medieval England derived on the one hand from the Anglo-Saxon *cynges thegn*, on the other from the Norman *baro*, and, as with both these officials, the feature which specially distinguished him was the possession of a 'liberty', or of rights of public justice, together with a court (*curia baronis*) in which to exercise those rights. To sum up, Miss Reid maintains the theory that baronial status did not depend upon the size or value of the holding, nor even upon the nature of the tenure or of the service rendered, but solely upon the possession of a franchise, which might vary considerably in extent, but which constituted the possessor in some sort an administrative officer under the Crown. To say of a man that he is a baron, or that he holds by barony is, from her point of view, simply to say that he has the right to hold a *curia baronis*. As for the *barones majores* of Magna Carta, she suggests that we may see in the individuals so designated the holders of franchises sufficiently extensive to constitute them 'castellaries' on the continental model.

Dr. Reid's theory, satisfying as it is to the modern mind with its craving for precision and definition, seems to credit our medieval ancestors with a greater capacity for drawing and enforcing logical distinctions than can safely be ascribed to them. Certainly the records afford no evidence that in the thirteenth and fourteenth centuries barony had the meaning she assigns to it. About the very time that Bracton was framing that description of barons as 'potentes sub rege' which Miss Reid makes the text of her argument, disputes as to the nature of tenure were becoming, as we have been, increasingly frequent. It is to the issues on which such cases were decided that we must look for an indication of the significance of barony in contemporary law and theory. What were the tests applied to determine the status of tenant or tenement? If the possession of justiciary rights was indeed the essence of barony, the exercise of such rights would afford a natural criterion of baronial tenure. Yet, although the *quo warranto* proceedings of the thirteenth century, and particularly those of 1274,[1] supplied the Crown with a compendium of information

[1] H. M. Cam, *The Hundred and the Hundred Rolls.*

concerning the liberties claimed and exercised by clergy and laity alike, we find no instance of the reference of a case of disputed tenure to the arbitrament of the Hundred Rolls. Analysis of the available material proves, on the contrary, that unless the tenant could produce a charter of feoffment, the issue was invariably decided on the evidence of the records of the Exchequer, the treasurer and barons being required to certify the Crown of any relevant information yielded by a scrutiny of the rolls and memoranda in their custody, or of Domesday Book and the various books of fees.[1] As a last resort, or in the case of conflicting evidence, recourse might be had to the method of the sworn inquest.[2] Round showed that there are grounds for supposing that in the thirteenth and fourteenth centuries the tenant-in-chief *ut de corona* who owed the service of a single knight or less was acknowledged to rank as a simple *miles*, and to be liable for relief at the 100 shillings rate;[3] but of those whose obligations were heavier all that can safely be said is that they were assumed to be barons unless or until they succeeded in repudiating baronial status. Normally the formal entry of a fief in a record as a 'barony' or 'honour', or even its inclusion without specific title among the *carte* returned in the great inquest of 1166, was regarded as conclusive. Evidence of the consistent amercement *ut baro* of the tenant of the fee, or, in the case of a lay fief, of his regular assessment for the special relief, was also accepted as *prima facie* proof that the tenure was baronial.[4] There is, in fact, no suggestion in the

---

[1] The order to the treasurer and barons runs as follows: 'Volentes certis de causis certiorari si . . . x . . . teneat aliqua terras seu tenementa per baroniam . . . vobis mandamus quod scrutatis libris nostris de Domesday et feodorum necnon rotulis et memorandis scaccarii nostri . . . de eo quod inveneritis nos . . . mittatis.' See especially Exch. K.R. Mem. Rolls, Nos. 117 and 118 for the procedure employed in the case of the disputed ecclesiastical tenures (1340–1) (*supra*, p. 174). Corroborative evidence on the lay side is afforded by the de Braose (Madox, *Exchequer*, pp. 372–4), Furnival (ibid., pp. 370–2), de Chandos (Madox, *Baronia Anglica*, p. 127), and de la Mare (*Lords' Report*, i. 225–6) cases, in all of which recourse was had to the records of the Exchequer and the books of fees as a means of establishing the nature of the tenure.

[2] In the Crowland case, for instance (*infra*, p. 186), and the Furnival case (Madox, *Exchequer*, pp. 370–2).

[3] 'Barons and Knights in the Great Charter' in *Magna Carta Commemoration Essays*, p. 75, and *passim*.   [4] Round, loc. cit.

records that to the official mind of the thirteenth or fourteenth century barony had any but a purely conventional significance.

The tests applied in the case of the clergy were precisely similar to those employed where lay tenures were concerned, but here the issue was complicated by the conflicting tendencies described above.[1] On the one hand, the Crown and its representatives were disposed to enlarge the class of clerical *barones* as defined in the Constitutions of Clarendon by using the term in a social rather than a tenurial sense, and treating 'baron' as a synonym for 'prelate'; on the other, the clergy inclined to reduce it by antithesizing barony and frankalmoign. The former tendency is aptly illustrated by the case of the Abbot of Crowland. When the treasurer and barons of the Exchequer inquired of the justices of common pleas their reasons for including the abbot's name in the list of those to be amerced *ut barones*, they received the significant reply: 'quod aliam evidenciam non habuerunt nisi quod idem abbas putabatur baro'.[2] Evidently it was the practice, where amercements, fees, and other liabilities were concerned, to assume the baronial rank of any prelate, or of any of the greater and more ancient ecclesiastical fiefs, unless or until it was challenged and disproved. The status of clergy who, through ignorance or indolence failed to combat the royal policy, was therefore liable to suffer gradual transformation. In most cases, however, the burdens to which tenure *per baroniam* was subject supplied an incentive to resistance; and the antithesis between barony and frankalmoign implicit in the conception of free alms tenure which gained currency in Stephen's reign afforded a pretext for carrying the war into the enemy's country. Though obscured as a result of the transference from the ecclesiastical to the royal courts of jurisdiction over land held in alms, and of the general tendency of the Crown in the thirteenth century to disregard the tenurial principle in its dealings with the clergy, it had not been forgotten. Upon it turned the case of the Bishop of Rochester in his long dispute with Boniface, Archbishop of Canterbury (1253–9), regarding the feudal obligations of his see. As against the archbishop's claim to collect and respond

---

[1] *Supra*, pp. 169 seq.
[2] Exch. K.R. Mem. Roll, No. 94, Rec. Easter, m. 114.

for the aid due from the Rochester fees, the bishop alleged that he acknowledged no overlord but the king. Confronted with a charter of John granting to Stephen Langton the patronage of the church and bishopric of Rochester, he shifted his ground, declaring that all the lands of the see were and always had been held in frankalmoign 'absque omni genere auxilii vel servicii secularis', and that the king could not transfer to the archbishop more than he and his predecessors had themselves been seised of. He contended that he and his brother of Carlisle were distinguished as being the only bishops who did not hold *per baroniam*, basing his argument upon the fact that barony implied *servicia militaria*, and that no such services had ever been rendered by them. To prove his contention he boldly put himself, by the advice of 'a faithful friend' whom he was fortunate in having at the Exchequer, upon the record of the Exchequer rolls, 'quibus creditur in omnibus illis que feoda continguntur sicut sancto evangelio'. His confidence was not misplaced, for the barons, instructed to make search 'a tempore primi conquestoris usque ad tempus huius regis', reported that the rolls and books of fees yielded no evidence of the performance at any time by the bishops of Rochester of temporal service to the king. Eventually peace was made between the parties in 1259 on the basis of a compromise which left the main points at issue undetermined.[1] In point of fact the bishop's plea was unhistorical. There is, as we have seen, proof that in the twelfth century his predecessors had recognized and performed service on some fourteen fees to the Archbishop of Canterbury, to whom, since the days of Lanfranc, they had stood in a dependent relationship.[2] Its interest from the standpoint of the present discussion lies, however, in the fact that it hinged upon the differentiation between baronial and eleemosinary tenure, and that the implied identification of barony with knight-service was apparently acquiesced in by the Crown and its officials. Scarcely less significant is the fact that among the privileges expressly claimed by the bishop in the course of his defence were those 'libertates Anglicane que sake et sokna vocantur' which Miss Reid regards as the essence of tenure *per baroniam*.[3]

---

[1] *Registrum Roffense*, ed. Thorpe, pp. 70 seq.
[2] *Supra*, p. 7.   [3] *Registrum Roffense*, p. 79.

The pleading in the case of the Abbot of Crowland, half a century later, is closely parallel. The abbot, amerced *ut baro* in 1315 at the instance of William de Bereford and his colleagues, denied his liability on the ground that he was not a baron and held nothing by barony. The treasurer and barons of the Exchequer found on investigation that in 1282 a former abbot of the house had been similarly amerced by the justices itinerant in Lincolnshire, and consequently his plea was rejected. Undeterred, the abbot again made suit to the king, declaring his readiness to prove 'par livere des feez del Domesday del Esekere ou les feez nouns de countes et de barouns sunt registres' that he held not by barony but in frankalmoign 'de la foundacioun des progenitors nostre seinour le roy'. Accordingly, a further search was ordered, the treasurer and barons being instructed that if, after examination of the books of fees, the rolls and memoranda of the Exchequer, and all other relevant documents, they found that the abbot held nothing by barony, and had rendered no service in the armies of the king or his progenitors, they were to relax their demands upon him forthwith. Scrutiny of the Exchequer records and of the marshal's rolls proving inconclusive, recourse was finally had to the method of the sworn inquest. The jury returned a verdict in the abbot's favour. It found that he held nothing of the king *per baroniam* and owed no service in the royal host, and hence that he was not liable to be amerced 'ut baro'.[1] Here the dissociation of barony from frankalmoign, and its association with *servicium militare* is even clearer than in the Rochester case; while once more we find the petitioner in enjoyment of precisely those justiciary rights which Miss Reid regards as the true constituents of barony.[2]

What then is to be our conclusion regarding the ecclesiastical *barones*? We can discern in the medieval period two opposing concepts. The first, sanctioned by the Constitutions of Clarendon, and representing presumably the Norman tradition, regards as barons all who hold in chief. Possibly we may see in the use of the phrase *sicut baroniam* in place of the more usual

---

[1] Exch. K.R. Mem. Roll, No. 92, Rec. Hil., m. 23; Rec. Easter, m. 114; Ancient Petitions, 2023 a and b, 4140; Madox, *Exchequer*, pp. 368–70.

[2] *Monasticon*, ii. 120.

per baroniam a concession to the difference between the tenures by service and the tenures in alms, but discharge of the liabilities incidental to baronial status was required of all tenants-*in-capite* without exception. The second (representing the Hilde-brandine principles which became current in the first half of the twelfth century) antithesized barony and frankalmoign, thereby limiting the application of the former term, by implication, to tenants-*in-capite per servicium militare*—that is, in effect, to those of the clergy, secular and religious, upon whom military obligations had been imposed by the Conqueror in 1070. Temporarily discredited through the efforts of Henry II, this latter interpretation gained renewed credence in the course of the later thirteenth century. Its currency in the Edwardian period is attested, in general, by the regular reference of all cases of disputed tenure to the arbitrament of the Exchequer records and the books of fees, and, in particular, by the examples given above.[1] To argue from these premises the existence in the later Middle Ages of a clearly defined body of ecclesiastical tenants *per baroniam* would, however, be false logic. In actual fact, as we have seen, the Crown and its officials treated as of baronial rank all the more important ecclesiastical persons and properties, without regard to the conditions of their tenure. Only where this policy challenged successful resistance did theory directly influence practice. Consequently, baronial status among the clergy was in reality as much a matter of convention as among the laity.

Summing up the impressions left by a study of English feudalism—not as the figment of the imagination of the medieval lawyer, but as the living institution revealed in process of growth and of decay by the records—we find little reason to doubt that in origin the significance of barony was tenurial. To hold as a baron was to hold of the king in chief by knight-service, or, by analogy, by some other honourable tenure such as cornage or serjeanty in the case of the laity, or frankalmoign in that of the clergy. If possession of a liberty was a normal concomitant of baronial status, the association would appear to have been rather accidental than essential. There is no evidence to prove that, as Miss Reid would have us believe,

[1] *Supra*, pp. 182 seq.

it was the liberty that made the baron. In proportion as the tenurial bond weakened, however, increasing importance came to be attached to the incidental burdens of barony. Here, in the profits accruing to the king from lands held *per baroniam*, is to be found the explanation of the emphasis laid by the lawyers upon the unity and integrity of the *baronia*, and upon the survival of its identity in spite of changes of ownership or partition among coheirs. The stressing of the liabilities of baronial rank had the effect of throwing into strong relief the conflicting interests of Crown and tenant. While it was the natural aim of the former to derive from its feudal prerogatives the maximum of advantage, the object of the latter was to escape with the minimum of obligation. The limited baronial class of the later Middle Ages was, I would suggest, the product, not of consistent reference to some norm of barony such as Miss Reid envisages, but of this clash of interest, the decisions arrived at in individual cases determining, in practice, where the line of demarcation should be drawn.

INDEX

s.d. = *servicium debitum.* A. = Augustinian. B. = Benedictine.
C. = Cistercian. Cl. = Cluniac.

PRINTED IN GREAT BRITAIN AT THE UNIVERSITY PRESS, OXFORD
BY JOHN JOHNSON, PRINTER TO THE UNIVERSITY